To Joan

H Schmidt M D

GOD

GENE

NUMEN

SUMMUM

BONUM

GOD IS THE GENE OF THE SPIRIT OF SUPREME GOODNESS

DR. H.R. SCHMIDT

Printed in the United States of America
by Mennonite Press, Inc., Newton, Kansas 67114.

Library of Congress Catalog No. 98-90051

ISBN 0-966-2238-0-2

ACKNOWLEDGEMENTS

Credit for this book goes to my daughter, Susan Schmidt Rhoades, who dared to withstand the controversy of this dissertation to do all the typing and word processing. Her courage and intellect helped her to realize that it is not evil to match parameters in the field of science with opposing parameters in the field of traditional religion, and to subject each opposing parameter to the process of reasoning in order to make a diagnosis of who we are and who God is.

Similar credit goes to my grandson, David Ensz, a commercial artist of Pasadena, California, who has done the art work for this book.

HRS

TABLE OF CONTENTS

INTRODUCTION

God is the Gene of *Numen Summum Bonum*

HERBERT R. SCHMIDT

To introduce this book is to introduce myself. I was born on a Kansas wheat farm, where I lived well although our family always lived in near poverty.

When I was about five years old, I was told by Papa, who was sitting in a chair, to kneel on the floor in front of him, fold my hands on his knees, and pray my bedtime prayer: "Lieber Heiland, mach mich fromm, doss ich in den Himmel komm." (Dear Saviour, make me pious so that I go to heaven.) But even at five, I was never convinced that there was a place called heaven.

That little prayer had migrated with my Mennonite ancestors from the Netherlands to Germany to Russia to the United States over a period of 200 years. In a Chaco family, that same brief prayer migrated from the Netherlands to Germany, Russia, China and Paraguay, and then to the United States. The two prayers met here in Kansas as part of the same tradition, i.e., that the only purpose of human life was to reach heaven above, somewhere out yonder, where Christ ruled forever.

Today science gives me the real meaning to this short prayer: Jesus resides in my soul, and there he motivates me to live this life so as to create heaven right here in my home at this moment if I choose to do so.

I finished eight grades in six years, becoming the first graduate in our one-room school, and received my elementary-school diploma at the McPherson Opera House, McPherson, Kansas. (Eighty years later, this opera house was being rehabilitated.)

The next important event in my life was baptism so that I could join the church. I was baptized upon confession of all my sins. I could not remember anything I had done willfully that was so bad it needed a special procedure, but I relented and made a confession because everybody else did. That was tradition. I felt good about the process because it pleased my mother, who had sewn me a colorful new shirt of pure silk for the occasion. The feel of pure silk on the skin of my arm seemed almost divine.

The next two years were an academic disaster. To keep with tradition, I was forced to spend two years attending a little Bible school called the Goessel Preparatory School. My tall, slender black mare named Katie, who had helped pull my plow all summer, now pulled my sulky 10 miles to and from this school through mud, rain and snow for these two years.

The schoolteachers were two of the preachers in our church, and their textbooks were the Bible, hymnbooks and Mennonite church-history books. I failed to see that memorizing so much from the holy books would advance my education because if I needed biblical information, I could read our family Bible. The lack of opportunity to learn mathematics and science in that school disenchanted me to the point that I flunked everything.

The following summer a friend and I operated a large wheat-bundle threshing rig. One hot Sunday after church we hand-cranked the Model T Ford to drive to Bethel Academy and College at Newton to seek some advice. As a result, after graduation from Bethel College, I attended the Kansas University Medical School.

My interest in the concept of human evolution came to life at KU in 1927 when Dr. Ray Brewster, head of the Chemistry Department, taught me about organic substances such as deoxyribonucleic acid (DNA). (Dr. Brewster and I also sang in the Baptist choir on the Hill.) "Nuts" Nelson taught the toughest course, Biochemistry. He showed us how organic chemistry applies to the human body. In spite of my fear of Dr. Nelson then, I can now say that he was completely ignorant of the biogenetic evolutionary process. Dr. Johnson taught Comparative Anatomy, which led him to disbelief in the biblical God; however, he accepted a supreme being of creation—God as the first cause.

Dr. Tracy, head of Gross and Microscopic Anatomy, taught intracellular microscopic activity, which is basic in understanding molecular genetic evolution today. He was a tall, patient, humble, pipe-smoking giant. When his secretary ushered me into his book-laden office for my two-hour oral examination, necessary to pass one and a half years of anatomy, he had a tobacco-filled pipe in his left hand, a burning match in his right hand, and a large German Shepherd at his side. They looked me over.

"You are a Mennonite," he said. (He already knew what my grade would be.) He asked what in the Mennonite culture could have produced such varied persons as Joe Goering and Dave Pankratz, on whom he had recently conferred doctoral degrees. Joe was a quiet, serious-minded, studious, agonizing, very intelligent anatomy student. He became an anatomy professor at New York University, but apparently the agony of equating evolution with traditional Christology drove him out of the science community into oblivion. Dave was a charismatic 440 track star at Bethel College who refused to let traditional religious beliefs stop him from learning more about science. He served for many years as dean and chief executive officer of the Mississippi University School of Medicine. I think Dr. Tracy and I concluded that the margin between traditional Christology and scientific knowledge is paper-thin, but meditation could lead Joe and Dave apart to eternity.

Also at KU Medical School was Dr. Harry Wahl, dean (CEO) and head of the Pathology Department. He was a flat-faced little "Dutchman" with tremendous energy, intellect, ability and motivation. (He helped four Schmidt brothers to medicine.) At that time Dr. Wahl stated that cancer cures will not come until we learn what controls life. Dr. Wahl, I am happy to report there is now at least one cancer that has a genetic cure—one of probably 1000 cancers that need a genetic cure. (This genetic cancer cure will be related later.)

After I graduated from medical school, I practiced medicine and surgery for 50 years. In 1990, my wife of 60 years, a retired college professor, became bedfast due to a number of strokes. Upon her desire, I placed a hospital bed in the center of our long living room, where to the best of my ability I gave her complete care for two and a half years.

She prayed to go to heaven and I encouraged her in this prayer. However, I meanwhile began to research the concept of heaven with Christ as gatekeeper of many mansions waiting for her. I am not a preacher or theologian or molecular biologist or archeologist or historian or writer, and am really not a specialist but a dabbler in many things, as my professor wife often reminded me. But as a participant in the pleasures of mathematics I had to have a reason for everything. Thus after consulting more than 100 books and publications on science and religion I want to present some concessions that science and religion have to make to resolve their controversy and become compatible.

Christian and Muslim faiths accept the Bible and the Koran as documentations of the traditional incarnation about 2000 years ago of the God-Christ spirit, the spirit that was with us forever and will remain in our soul forever. These religious books have very successfully recorded the incarnation of the genetically induced God-spirit in human lives in ancient times. Since there was then no knowledge of evolutionary creation processes, the worldview of the writers could not have been presented otherwise.

Today science tells us how God created everything by way of the genetic process. Therefore religion has to concede the truth that the gene of the DNA molecule is the only being of God-Christ, who is the first cause of all creation on Earth and who controls our existence and our destiny. Science has to concede that in Nature are incomprehensibles that we have to turn over to God to keep in trust because our mind cannot deal with them.

I will present tenets and premises that lead to a resolution of the science and religion controversy through reasoning and meditation.

PREFACE
AN OVERVIEW OF THIS BOOK

The sciences and the three monotheistic religions of the Jews, Christians and Muslims have never fully accepted the existence of each other.

The teleology of the creation story as narrated in the Bible and the Koran completely ignores the facts of science. The Bible and the Koran say nothing about the evolution of the geology of our planet Earth that has taken place for billions of years and is going on today. The Bible and the Koran say nothing to recognize the evolution of organisms over the last 3.5 billion years by deoxyribonucleic acid (DNA) molecules and the gene. These religions say nothing about the evolutionary process by the gene of the social culture in our animal body that raises the level in our genome today of the *numen summum bonum* (spirit of supreme goodness) of our psyche—our soul, mind and intelligence.

In this book, the *numen summum bonum*, as the essence of the divine that we must worship, will be referred to by the letters NSB, meaning the spirit of supreme goodness that is our God within us.

The narratives of the Bible and the Koran ignored the facts of science because ancient writers were ignorant of the truth and reality of NSB (God) and humanism that science shows us today. The prophets who wrote the Bible and Koran narratives did not know about the gene and its evolutionary creation process of the soul that had happened. They had to resort to their only option of telling about God and human existence "in his image" in the format of incarnation, eschatology, teleology, creation *ex nihilo* and apocalypse. Ignorance and bigotry was so pervasive that as late as the 17th century the religious community threatened to excommunicate Galileo because he taught that the earth was round. It took religion almost 400 years before it made a posthumous apology to Galileo acknowledging that the church had lied to science and to Galileo.

The commonality of the urge to be good that the gene has been putting in our animal bodies for more than a million years did not surface until cuneiform and alphabet writing became available about 6000 years ago. At that point in time, narratives about the existence of God, who was called by different names, appeared all over the world. Worshiped in Egypt was Osiris, whose statue has appeared at the entrance of the Nile tombs of the Pharaohs. Zeus of the Aegeans was thought to live on Mount Olympus. These ruling gods were thought to have resurrected from the dead; resurrection was a common concept.

The Sun God of Babylon handed law tablets to King Hammurabi 1000 years before Moses accepted the Ten Commandments from God on Mount Sinai. That event of Hammurabi is carved in a stone shaft that is today in a museum. Then there was Sargon of Assyria and, finally, the God Yahweh of the Hebrews and the Christ of the New Testament and the Allah of Islam.

The culture-genetic evolution of the God-Christ-Jesus spirit of NSB in the soul of every human being that has ever been born may have started with Australopithecus three million years ago. We are still discovering and learning. With its present knowledge, science traces the steps through fossil findings somewhat adequately from Australopithecus to Homo Habilis to Homo Erectus to Homo Cro-Magnon (anatomically modern Homo Sapiens). These steps are well illustrated in scientific literature. In science, the process of the creation evolution comes in three phases:

1. The first phase is inorganic, with findings that establish the creation of galaxies, stars, planets, satellites and the atmosphere with its debris. The process has no beginning and no ending.

2. The second phase is the genetic evolution of organic matter including the human body. Archaeology presents findings to prove the validity of this process, which started 3.5 billion years ago (more details later).

3. The third phase of the organic evolutionary creation process is the evolving of culture. The gene infused the psyche—soul, mind and intelligence—into the animal bodies of our ancestors. This we will discuss in more detail through the Ice Age, fossil-remains age, Stone Age and art age.

The teleological teaching of the Bible and the Koran gives no room for evolutionary creation in any of the three phases of which

Christ is the first cause according to New Testament writers John and Paul. The Bible story of creation *ex nihilo* (out of nothing) belies proof that the universe has no beginning. The biblical story of resurrection from the dead was featured at Easter 1996 in *Time, Newsweek, US News and World Report*, which indicated physical resurrection is scientifically untrue. However, science can accept the Bible Christ of the first cause of all creation.

Science and religion have to make concessions to become compatible enough to speak to each other. Scientists must concede that nature has some incomprehensibles that science can never delineate with a formula. Some of the incomprehensibles are time and space and how a DNA molecule could evolve from a purely inorganic universe. The most relevant incomprehensible is the powers the gene demonstrates. The Germans call it *Lebenkraft*. The Apostle Paul in his more realistic mood called it the power that holds everything in place.

Science concedes that these incomprehensibles are parameters that belong to God-Christ, who is the only source that can handle them. The religions have to concede that the Christ of the first cause of all creation was never resurrected and never lived in heaven. His spirit lives in the human soul only and nowhere else.

Who is God? In our culture, God has the connotations of immortality, omnipotence, omniscience, beneficence and divinity. The first connotations fit the DNA molecule of evolution, or God-Christ, first cause of all creation. The divine God-DNA, a spirit who can be hosted only by the human soul, is presented to us as the Jesus-spirit. The DNA molecule is the truth of immortality, omnipotence, beneficence and divinity. The details of such a true existence is what we are presenting.

Scientific knowledge relegates the Bible and the Koran to a narrative of metaphors written by a host of prophets in a prescientific culture, dramatizing the God-form on the stage of history by actors such as Moses and Mohammed and finally by the leaders of all religious activity.

Religion has further to accept the scientific fact that we are the progeny of our ancestors in the animal kingdom. Therefore we carry the evil-desires genes of our animal ancestors. Also, the devil, or Satan, and sin, i.e., evil, come from the action of our inherited animal genes. There is no Satan or hell. These animal genes that we will carry forever in our offspring are hindrances to human behavior.

Why is this concept of the Jesus-spirit-NSB in our soul important now when Christianity has served so well? Because:

1. It is the truth of what is real today, in contrast to the imagination of 2000 years ago.

2. We who expect heaven after death will miss the happiness of heaven on earth if we do not choose to create heaven here and now.

3. The time has come for us to take all the responsibility of determining who God is and who we are instead of putting all of the responsibility on an imaginary God.

4. The traditional God in heaven has never appeared to us to help us with our problems as the biblical narrative says he did for Abraham.

5. Most wars and killings could be avoided if we could rid ourselves of the bigotry in concepts of Yahweh, Christ and Allah, and get rid of the gods of deism.

6. We must recognize that our evil desires originate in our animal genes before we can correct them with the Jesus spirit.

In the most profound humility I write this interpretation of who God is and who we are. The end point of my story is that God-Christ is the first cause of all creation. The God-Christ gene of the holy is in our soul. It is working for the betterment of the genes of our animal ancestors and the genes of the psyche of the soul and intelligence, that God-Christ through the gene infused into every human body. It is entirely our responsibility to activate the genes for the good of God's *numen summum bonum*, or NSB.

While the traditions of the Bible and the Koran have wandered in the realm of imagination, science has presented us with facts that are the basis for all discussion in the book:

1. In a billion years God the Creator has gained importance; i.e., the understanding of the power of God has increased beyond belief.

2. Heaven and hell as actual *places* are nonexistent.

3. The Bible, the Koran, heaven, God, Christ, Allah and Satan are all metaphors for the spirit.

4. Jesus is the only biblical "deity" who is not a metaphor. The spirit of the life of Jesus leads all our meditations.

5. In science a physical resurrection is impossible.

6. Science relegates us to the progeny of our animal ancestors.

7. God bears all the secrets of creation that science cannot comprehend—they are the incomprehensible mysteries of a God without form.

This book is not well written because I am not a writer. I present facts to the best of my knowledge. I do not claim to inform the reader of any theophilosophical interpretations because none are important to this dissertation. This book rests on the process of reasoning. It lists scientific facts and religious interpretations available to my limited knowledge, setting parameters that enable a reasoning process for arrival at logical conclusions as to who God is and who we are.

A parameter is a constant whose values determine the operation or characteristcs of a system. The conclusion from such parameters is reached through continuous contemplative thought, meditation (prayer), planning and reason; in German this is *Nachdenken* (after thinking).

I draw support and inspiration in this effort from prehistoric ancestors of Avignon (details later), Socrates and Aristotle, the historical Jesus, Mormon Joseph Smith, Gandhi, Dr. Albert Schweitzer, and now Dr. Gordon Kaufman of Harvard, and Dr. Daryl Schmidt of Texas Christian University, whose recent seminar here was titled "Get Jesus out of the Bible" (i.e., look for the real Jesus). I will attempt to relate the details of all of the above.

I. PREHISTORIC CIRCUMSTANCES

Geology—Study of Planet Earth

Creation—Beginning of the Natural World

Ice Age—Glaciation Cycles Affect Culture

Stone Age—Stone Remains Monitor Culture

Prehistoric Humans—A Million Years of Culture

The Orient—Where Civilization Began

GEOLOGY—STUDY OF PLANET EARTH

Geology is the study of the inorganic creation process of the Earth planet.

Earth has a thin crust over red-hot molten magma. The crust is composed of unattached tectonic plates that are sections of the crust floating on the magma. These tectonic plates are probably hundreds of miles across, and they are from five miles thick in the deepest part of the ocean to 30 miles thick at the highest mountains. The tectonic plates are in constant motion and always have been. These plates carry all our continents and all our oceans.

In the history of findings about our earth, geologists have postulated that 500 million years ago there were two groups of continents. The tectonic plates with the northern-hemisphere continents, called Lourasia, carried North America, Europe, Siberia and China, all in juxtaposition. At the same time, southern-hemisphere plates carried Africa, South America, India, Australia and Antarctica, all in one juxtaposition called Gondwanaland.

In the next 200 million years, Lourasia and Gondwanaland collided and formed one grand mass of land called Pangaea. Such activity is important to know, to show that even the inorganic creation process has always been in creative motion. When India collided with Siberia, the force of that collision produced the world's most enormous mountain range, the Himalayas, and its highest peak, Mount Everest, the same mountain that my wife Mariam admired for three years while she was a student at Darjeeling in northern India.

Gradually the continents separated to take on their present-day configuration, according to the assumption that centrifugal force at the tectonic-plate level, traveling at the speed of 1000 miles an hour, separated and scattered all the continents into their present location, with the magnetism of gravity holding them together. This balance of centrifugal and centripetal forces is one of God's secret incomprehensible mysteries.

The tectonic-plate activity of earth's crust establishes that the inorganic creation process of God the first cause is still active and always has been active. This evolution process is a geologic fact; it took place over billions of years. We know that this process is involved in the ongoing creation of organic life and human culture because mountain-creating forces exposed plate edges (rock) containing most of the fossils of the organic creation process.

One interesting result of the separation of Pangaea into separated continents is the history of a marsupial, the opossum of Pangaea time. Through the DNA molecule, in Australia it evolved into the kangaroo while in North America it continued to replicate as an opossum.

Very significant here is that the ape and monkey were never native in North and South America. This fact demonstrates the dynamic correlation of organic and inorganic processes. The evolution of mammals into pre-hominids had not reached the ape stage in Pangaea when the separation of continents took place about 300 million years ago. After this separation a suitable climate developed in Africa to accelerate the evolution of mammals to apes to hominids to us as Homo Sapiens — but not in the Americas.

Today our traditional ego would rather keep us ignorant of this evolution over many millions of years that science shows to be a fact. We would rather set ourselves up as an imaginary special creation produced in the mode of the teleology (instant creation) of the Bible. Such a setup avoids our acceptance of the scientific fact that we humans have a common ancestry with the ape because acceptance embarrasses us. It is humiliating to our pride.

Carbon (oil) deposits of organic origin indicate that Alaska, Siberia and the African Sahara have seen enormous changes in position on Earth during the first three billion years. These areas grew enough organisms to form all the petroleum products and benzene compounds that now supply us. Early plants and animals once flourished in areas that are now under permafrost or have become desert.

The atmosphere of earth's crust is held in place by gravity. The inorganic creation process created a transfer of water from the sea into an ice build-up of mile-high glaciers at the two magnetic poles of the Ice Age. Cycles of freezing and thawing followed. During the freezing period of the cycle, heavy glaciers came down to cover North America as far as the northern border of Kansas, and they covered most of Europe.

This transfer of water to ice lowered the sea level so that early humans were able to cross from Asia to North America, and in Europe to make beautiful cave paintings in a French cave that is now far underwater (see "Stone Age").

Evidence of the movements of continents coincides with fossil findings related to the culture creation process of humans. The first two million years of that process took place in Africa because of its position on the earth. It had the favorable climate, and it was isolated from the rest of the world; therefore no early hominid fossils are found in the Americas, Europe, Australia or East Asia.

During the last million years of culture, hominids evolved into Homo Erectus, who was able to travel. With the aid of the Ice Age, he reached all the world. With the lowering of the sea level, Homo Erectus could populate all of the Far East and Australia.

CREATION—BEGINNING OF THE NATURAL WORLD

Creation in our Western Christian culture refers to a God who brought our world into existence.

In this culture, many people still feel that God created the world in six days. When they are confronted by scientists who say that scientific and archeological findings determine that such a creation is untenable, they may respond with a belief that maybe those days each represent 1000 years. More recently, theologians have offered some compromises. For instance, Reinhold Niebuhr, called the genius of religious mythology, said, "Christianity has promoted old religious myths and symbols without rationalizing them." Albert Schweitzer said religion must come with reason.

Creation myths all over the world have had many views of a person or a being that created the universe and mankind. Such creating beings may be animals, humans, deities or parts thereof. A rich variety of myths recounts the creation as a separate process of the constituent parts of the universe, such as sun, moon, stars, planets, animals and human beings. Many creation myths, according to the *Encyclopedia Americana,* tell that humans were created from the blood, sweat and spittle of the creator.

The Babylonian myth of creation during the time of Moses had the universe created by the gods, in contrast to Moses' insistence that there was only his God who did everything. In the Babylon story, one god split the body of another god; half of the god was the sky and the other half was the earth. Babylonian myth had a hint suggesting that creation might be an ongoing process (in contrast to Moses' concept of pure teleology) by calling the creation of the human being the creation of a primeval man. To create a primeval man meant that man was created since then. Researchers tell us the creation myths of Babylon and Moses had great influence upon each other. In this relationship Babylon had a more realistic concept of the creation process than Moses.

Iranian myths taught that there were two spirits, one good and one evil. The good spirit created all the parts of the universe. The India myth said that Indra was so drunk and so strong that he separated heaven from earth. The concept in India of heaven and earth reflects the influence of some Aryans who invaded the Indus Valley and brought with them the old Zoroaster concept that had little concern for the creation process. It taught the way to learn is through the soul of everyone alive. Japanese-Chinese mythical cosmology begins with one egg. The white part became heaven and the dark part became the earth. The Aztec creation myth had several gods who created everything. The monstrous earth god split into two parts, one part forming the earth, the other part forming the firmament. A Canaanite creation myth had even the heaven castrated.

The Old Testament creation story in Genesis is as follows: The first day, God made light, which he divided into day and night. The second day, he separated the vapors, sky above and water below. The third day, he gathered the water into oceans, leaving dry areas called earth, and let the earth burst forth with grass and trees with seeds inside. The fourth day, he made two lights, the sun and the moon, and also made stars. The fifth day, he let the waters teem with fish and the sky teem with birds. The sixth day, he let the earth bring forth every kind of animal and reptile. "Then God said, 'Let us make a man—someone like ourselves....'" (1: 26, *The Living Bible*). He blessed man and said, "'Multiply and fill the earth and subdue it....'" (1:28).

The scientific community, which includes all the major universities of the world, considers that the above creation story is completely untenable. The blessing to be fruitful, to "multiply and fill the earth and subdue it," has 3000 years later come to be a double curse upon humankind on earth, leading to overpopulation and planetary pollution. These curses have led the people of God into hell. Hell is not down below somewhere; it is right here wherever there is poverty and suffering and conflict, as in Sarajevo, Palestine, Rwanda, Haiti and Northern Ireland.

In the first 17 books of the Bible, after creation God was portrayed as an angry God full of vengeance, who ruled with fear and force. He exterminated all human beings who were considered enemies of his people, the children of Israel.

Following those years of horror, God is changed from one of horror and killings to a God of love and mercy as portrayed in Job, Psalms, Proverbs, Ecclesiastes and Songs of Solomon. In Proverbs 8 his creation process is reversed. "Miss" Wisdom (the legendary wisdom of King Solomon personified) speaks in verses from 8:22-31: "The Lord formed me in the beginning, before he created anything else. From ages past, I am. I existed before the earth began....I was there when he made the blueprint for the earth and oceans. I was always at his side like a little child....And how happy I was with what he created—his wide world and all his family of mankind!"

In the New Testament, John starts out very specifically, stating that Christ, one with God, created everything that is. Christ in his creation process gave life, and eternal life, to all humankind. Then Paul in his letter to the Colossians says in 1:15-17: "Christ is the exact likeness of the unseen God. He existed before God made anything at all, and, in fact, Christ himself is the Creator who made everything in heaven and earth, the things we can see and the things we can't; the spirit world with its kings and kingdoms, its rulers and authorities; all were made by Christ for his own use and glory. He was before all else began and it is his power that holds everything together."

Because the DNA molecule is God-Christ in action, science can demonstrate that Christ through the DNA molecule inserted soul into his creations, to develop human beings out of our ancestors in the animal kingdom. Solomon's "Miss" Wisdom and the New Testament Christ present a tenable creation process. It is only in recent times that we have become more knowledgeable about the specifics of how God-Christ the Creator came on so fast that the teleology of Moses got lost.

The procedure and length of time of the creation process started by Wisdom and Christ is becoming more and more specific day by day. There were three stages, beginning with inorganic creation in the form of solids, liquids and gases. These forms consist of all the inorganic elements listed in any chemistry textbook. In most cases, these elements exist in combinations with each other. In the creation process these combinations change in structure constantly, but none are ever destroyed into nothing. We learned long ago that in God's law, energy and matter never go to waste.

The massive collection of these inorganic substances in our creation process make up our planet Earth, our star the sun, and all the other stars

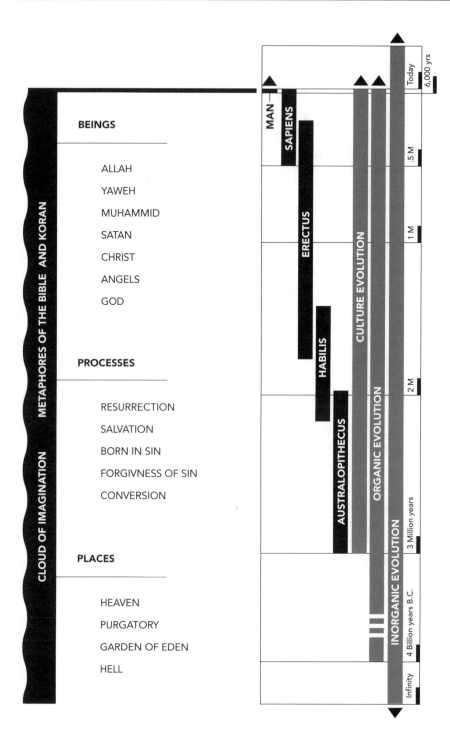

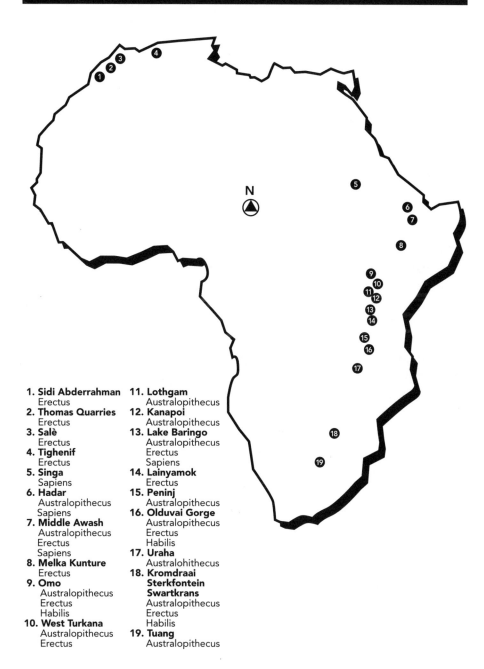

1. **Sidi Abderrahman**
   Erectus
2. **Thomas Quarries**
   Erectus
3. **Salè**
   Erectus
4. **Tighenif**
   Erectus
5. **Singa**
   Sapiens
6. **Hadar**
   Australopithecus
   Sapiens
7. **Middle Awash**
   Australopithecus
   Erectus
   Sapiens
8. **Melka Kunture**
   Erectus
9. **Omo**
   Australopithecus
   Erectus
   Habilis
10. **West Turkana**
    Australopithecus
    Erectus

11. **Lothgam**
    Australopithecus
12. **Kanapoi**
    Australopithecus
13. **Lake Baringo**
    Australopithecus
    Erectus
    Sapiens
14. **Lainyamok**
    Erectus
15. **Peninj**
    Australopithecus
16. **Olduvai Gorge**
    Australopithecus
    Erectus
    Habilis
17. **Uraha**
    Australohithecus
18. **Kromdraai**
    Sterkfontein
    Swartkrans
    Australopithecus
    Erectus
    Habilis
19. **Tuang**
    Australopithecus

FINDS IN AFRICA

and galaxies. Since under God's law no substance or energy is lost, we are led to believe that the inorganic has existed forever. Our sun is one of a million stars in a galaxy, and the number of galaxies is beyond comprehension. Our Earth, one of the nine known planets of our star, the sun, is the seed bed upon which the organic creation process can evolve.

Darwin's concept of evolution tells us something only about how God created us as human beings. How the first DNA molecule started is the subject of great research consideration. I agree with the theory of Thomas Aquinas of the 13th century that the first cause of this creation process is God.

How God did this we are very near to discovering. In April of 1993 at Scripps Research Institute in LaJolla, California (*Time*, October 11, 1993), a molecule appeared that seemed not to be alive and yet behaved astonishingly lifelike. This snippet of synthetic ribonucleic acid (RNA), one of the master molecules of all cell nuclei, proved unusually talented. Within an hour of its formation, it had commandeered the organic material in a thimble-sized test tube and had started to make copies of itself. Then the copies made copies. Before long, the copies began to evolve, developing the ability to perform new and unexpected tricks. The surprised and excited scientists who witnessed that event found themselves wondering: Is this how life started?

Never before, the *Times* report stated, have the creations of laboratories come so close to crossing the threshold that separates living from non-living, the quick from the dead. It is as if the most fundamental questions about who we are and how we got here are being translated into thread-like entities smaller than specks of dust. In the flurry of research now under way and the philosophical debate that is certain to follow, scientists find themselves confronting anew one of earth's most ancient mysteries. What exactly is life, and how did it get started?

The article goes on to say that the answers to these questions are changing so rapidly that they prompted a meeting of the world's creation scientists in 1993 in Barcelona, Spain. Origin-of-life researchers discussed how the first DNA molecule got started and how through RNA it produced the first protein molecule to form the first form of organic life—the first plant.

Research gives evidence that microbial activity left imprints between rocks. The Greenland DNA findings on the start of the organic creation process on Earth are clocked at 3.5 billion years old and are corroborated by the discovery of possible DNA on Mars. All this would indicate that the DNA molecule and the organic creation process started soon after the earth was formed. It is also quite conceivable that organic creation starts were repeatedly destroyed by meteor showers before one survived and developed for hundreds of millions of years until humankind appeared about two million or more years ago.

The stellar planet process has supported organic creation on our earth of plants and animals for about four billion years. During all these four billion years the organic process was very busy every day. It advanced the creation process from algae, as a starter, about 3.5 billion years ago, as shown in fossil remains in sedimentary rock. Almost a billion years later, oxygen-producing photosynthetic organisms appeared. The beginning of an oxygen-rich atmosphere made possible the creation of one-celled animal ancestors. The animal kingdom evolved from crustaceans to quadrupeds and finally to bipeds.

At this stage of the creation process about three million years ago, we assume that God-Christ with the DNA molecule created the third phenomenon of the creation process. This phenomenon, the introduction of the psyche gene into the genetic chain, has been actively creating man to become more perfect by developing the psyche's important contents of the soul, mind and intelligence. The evolution of the psyche is more active today than ever before.

During that evolution of the soul in the psyche for more than a million years, the Bible God and his goodness first appear. The goodness of God, or the Holy Spirit, had no place to reveal itself until humans were capable of worshiping God. As the Holy Spirit in our soul became more powerful, there came a time in the last million years when the Holy Spirit craved identification. This yearning started in prehistoric times.

In 1912 Wilhelm Schmidt, an anthropologist born in 1868 in Austria, wrote a 12-volume dissertation, *Ursprung der Gottesidee* (Origin of the Idea of a God). He was a professor in Vienna until Hitler drove him into Switzerland, where he continued his work. He studied pygmies in Africa, and he studied and researched the history of Neanderthal man. He researched beliefs of primitive people in Brazil, India, Tibet and Australia. Schmidt then made some conclusions.

He discovered that in all cases the beliefs of these people were very simple. They believed in a super-power that created everything, for which they expressed thanks. Schmidt prays for more respect for that simple concept of the power of the unknown by these simple people. They had no priests, no prophets, no severely structured ceremonies. He wrote about the unilinear step-by-step evolution of beliefs and customs from the primitive state and called this the "cultural, historical method" in which ethnology is regarded as a branch of cultural history.

His findings depicted the existence, growth and activity of primitive people as fully human types. The agony caused by religious bigotry expanded later when writing came into being.

ICE AGE—GLACIATION CYCLES AFFECT CULTURE

The Ice Age is another process on this planet that, by artifacts left in its path, verifies the culture creation of the psyche in animal bodies.

In the 3.5-billion-year creation process, glaciers advanced from the south and north poles toward the equator during a very cold cycle, followed by receding of these glaciers during a warming cycle. The cycles may have been a million years long or only 50,000 years. At times they covered one third of the earth's surface, and the build-up of ice produced a glacier thickness of one mile or more. Water vapor from the oceans that froze to form those glaciers lowered the sea level around the earth by as much as 300 feet. These cycles are called glaciations.

Glaciation cycles verify the credibility of the step-by-step process of the creation of the psyche in our animal bodies to form us as human beings. Scientific findings show there have been at least four glaciation cycles during the last half-million years. The early cycles of this period have buried bones of our ancestors by as much as 85 feet below the present surface of the earth. The bones tell us that the creation process of our soul was going on a minimum of 500,000 years ago.

Findings also tell us that during one of these freezing cycles, the sea level lowered enough and long enough to allow Homo Erectus and his offspring in the Orient to walk from Asia across the Bering Strait into North America on dry land as ancestors of Native American Indians. We can verify such an event by comparing characteristics of Native Americans and Chinese; they have sparse, fuzzy beards and similar facial features.

Also, the absence of sufficient warming periods during the last two million years of the estimated three million years of the culture creation process kept most of North America, Europe and Northern Asia covered with thick ice sheets. Thus flora and fauna flourished over what is now desert in Africa and the Middle East. Therefore this area is where all early fossil specimens of human evolution are found. For more than three million years we progressed from Australopithecus to Cro-Magnon to Homo Sapiens in the culture creation process.

Each glaciation cycle left remains of human bones and human stone tools and possessions in layers that present the sequence of the stages in our evolution as human beings. (These fossils and artifacts are discussed in "Stone Age.")

Evidence of the Ice Age as a very essential component of the culture creation process appeared in a nine-page feature about a Paleolithic cave near Avignon, France, in the February 13, 1995 issue of *Time*. The cave is called a virgin finding because no one has invaded it for probably 20,000 years. The reason is that the opening to the cave is deep below the level of the Mediterranean Sea on the eastern shore of France and was found by a scuba diver merely by coincidence. (See "Stone Age.") Cro-Magnon people made the drawings when the level of the sea was lower than the cave opening. Such low water levels took place during the buildup of water from the sea into glaciers during the glaciations of the Ice Age. The most recent glaciation cycle in the recent Pleistocene Ice Age occurred about 50,000 years ago. This cave art is important because it adds to the credibility of our story of how we humans evolved our psyche over so many millennia. The Ice Age gave us other happenings that verify the truth of the culture evolution process.

The history of the Ice Age leads to logical speculation about the enormity of the inorganic and organic creation processes that the God-gene of the first cause has given us. For instance, take the huge quantities of hydrocarbons that have been deposited under Alaska and Siberia that we are now extracting in the form of petroleum. Such deposits of hydrocarbons formed from organic carbon atoms mean that somewhere, sometime, on this planet a climate and favorable surrounding conditions produced flora and fauna of such quantity, piling layers high with organic carbon atoms, that after hundreds of thousands of years of such growth, the Ice Age cycle of glaciers came down and put cold pressure on this thick organic layer to form what we now extract as coal or petroleum crude oil. This creation process is so enormous that it is one of God's incomprehensible secrets until we learn more about such happenings.

David Howell, of the United States Geological Survey, said in a February 20, 1995, Associated Press report that 1500 feet below the continental shelf all over the world is a frozen layer of methane CH4, a gas hydrate that could produce twice as much energy on this planet as all the coal and crude oil combined that still exist to be found on earth. Since this hydrocarbon with its carbon atom can come only from an accumulation of the organic process, we have here two creation processes at work by God as first cause. The God-gene produced the organic component, and the inorganic process provided the climate change to stimulate growth and then proceeded to continue the Ice Age cycle of glaciers so that pressure created hydrocarbons. That presuppposes the migration of continents into climate changes.

It seems appropriate to conclude with a scientific prediction of future events that may be disastrous for the survival of the human species. These events that will destroy human civilization are based on our scientific knowledge of the geology and meteorology of Earth. Our planet has certain routine behaviors: it rotates on its axis to make day and night, and it orbits our star, the sun, every 365 days to make the seasons of the year. The earth has another routine that is less well known and less familiar. For four billion years, Earth has had cycles of glaciations. The Ice Ages of the earliest three billion years, protozoic, Paleozoic, and phanerozoic, are not well understood for lack of findings.

In the last 500,000 years was the Stone Age, in which the Early Stone Age had more than two glaciation cycles; the Middle Stone Age, two glaciation cycles; and the Late Stone Age, half of the last cycle in the warm stage of today. We can expect the glaciers to begin moving south again and in the next 10,000 years to grind Seattle, Chicago, New York City and points between into a pulp above the 40th parallel of our world globe.

The already overpopulated world will become so crowded with humans that lowered resistance to the virus, the killer of human bodies, will threaten the survival of the human species. Acquired immune-deficiency syndrome (AIDS), caused by the human immunodeficiency virus (HIV), is just a starter.

These are only two scenarios that could cause extinction of the human species along with the dinosaurs and the millions of other species that have already become extinct.

STONE AGE—STONE REMAINS MONITOR CULTURE

The common concept of the Stone Age in science literature covers the whole one million years in which Homo Erectus roamed over Europe, Africa and Asia, and began to fool with stones as tools. However, the Stone Age in present literature is the last half-million years of the culture creationary process brought about by genetic activity.

This 500,000 years of genetic enhancement of the psyche (soul, mind and intelligence) in our animal bodies was largely controlled by the last four or more glaciation cycles of the Ice Age. In the early, middle, and late periods of the Stone Age, the development of the human psyche can be traced by the expertise demonstrated as humans learned to improve stone tools to aid them in making a better living. As prehistoric people gained genetically more tool-making skills, they left enough artifacts that we can begin to tell our story.

First we insert a note of explanation about the activity of Homo Habilis and Homo Erectus for the sake of continuity of the creation process into the Stone Age:

The fossil remains of Homo Habilis, who lived over two million years ago, were accompanied by artifacts showing that he attempted to make stone tools; therefore he was called "habilis," or "handyman." His achievement was the cracked pebble. His offspring, Homo Erectus, seemed content to remain a hunter and gatherer for more than a million years while he wandered all over the world as Java man and Peking man. Neanderthal man and his cousins, our cave ancestors, led humans into the Stone Age of the last 500,000 years. This era came into being as Homo Erectus produced stone tools by fracturing and flaking larger flint stones. These improved stone tools reveal the gene's enhancement of the human psyche in the fight to become better. The tool artifacts show step by step how our psyche was and is being created for more perfection.

The Pleistocene, or recent, Stone Age is divided into early, middle, and late periods that occurred in concordance with the more recent glaciation cycles of the Ice Age during the half-million years. The Early Stone Age, comprising the first and second Ice Age cycles about 300,000 years ago, is documented by the remains of flint fist-hatchets found with bone fossils. Such a hatchet, about nine inches in length, could cut skins or meat. Early humans could cut wood limbs into clubs, spears or arrows and could craft stone spear points or arrowheads to attach to weapons for hunting or killing. Such artifacts are on display in museums all over the world. After all, the gene increased brain volume from the 1200 cc of Homo Erectus to the 1600 cc of Cro-Magnon, and it shows.

The second, or Middle, Stone-Age period covered the last two glaciation cycles of the Ice Age. A glaciation cycle begins with thousands of years of below-zero climate that continuously builds up glacier thickness to more than one mile. As the glaciers become top-heavy in the polar regions, they come crashing toward the equator, crushing everything in their path. After many thousands of years of glaciation came many thousands of years of warming, melting the glaciers and thus elevating the sea level. The melting uncovered many fossils and artifacts with which we now write our history of genetic enhancement of the psyche.

The last warming period came about 10,000 years ago—the period in which we live today. During both of the warming periods, Homo Erectus had gained enough genetic enhancement to be able to walk far and wide on two legs and use his arms (his other two legs) to do survival chores and subdue his adversaries. His fossils have been found in Java, in China, and in the Neanderthal Valley in Germany.

Discoveries of artifacts in caves from the last two Ice Age cycles show the genetic enhancement of the psyche by the way prehistoric people learned to survive in caves during severe cold years. Many of these caves were in France. In them have been found needles carved from bone for sewing clothing, and carvings of ivory. Carvings of furry musk ox on the rock wall, from the 30,000 years of the glaciers, are followed by carvings of reindeer on the rock wall during the warming period many years later.

In Grimaldi, Italy, along the Mediterranean coast, is a cave that has more than 100,000 years of accumulated layer upon layer of remains piled up 60 feet. The remains contain artifacts and human bones from the age of Homo Habilis and his pebbles, from crude stone tools to the flaked flint drills, knives, and axes of Cro-Magnon (early Homo Sapiens) 100,000 years later.

The most spectacular evidence of the credibility of creationary processes is the finding of elaborate stone-wall paintings near Avignon, France, along the Mediterranean coast. The paintings articulate both the Stone Age and Ice Age, and verify the creation processes that lead us to the concept that the spirit of supreme goodness (*numen summum bonum*—NSB) resides in every human soul. The Avignon paintings depict early humans living in caves while much of the world was too cold for them to survive during those more than 100,000 years. More important, this art verifies that the genetic creationary process of our psyche actively produced enhancement that resulted in magnificent paintings. It also shows that stone was the only thing available to them for such work that could survive for us to look at.

Access to the cave entrance is significant. Today it takes a scuba diver to reach the entrance because it has been below sea level under more than 100 feet of water, since the present warming time of 10,000 years has melted glaciers enough to raise the water along that French coast by about 300 feet whereas prehistoric people walked into the cave on dry land nearly 100,000 years ago when sea water was frozen in mile-high glaciers.

The Late Stone Age covers the last glaciation warming period, which started about 20,000 years ago. Its remains are in all of Europe. Life in the caves in isolation had done very little to help the genetic enhancement of soul, mind and intelligence. Escape from the caves to wide-open spaces where flora and fauna flourished provided new communication, travel and environments that greatly speeded up the creationary process of the psyche through genotype-phenotype environmental interaction.

This process enabled culture in Egypt, with its warmer climate farther south, to be about 2000 years ahead of the cosmologies of the cave people. To be able to attain enough mathematics, engineering and mechanics to build the pyramids in 3000 B.C., Egypt had to have at least 1000 years of preparatory training. Egypt's advanced culture of 6000 years ago leads into the history of the Orient (see "The Orient"). Evidence that the level of intelligence of humans 10,000 years ago was very high is seen in the construction of the Egyptian pyramids, the buildings of the Incas in Peru, and similar structures in Mexico and Central America.

Cave findings all over Europe verify the credibility of all three phases of the creation process that is the basis for this discussion of concepts of who we are and who God is. In the first phase, geology shows that the change from water to ice and from ice to water has come in cycles for more than three billion years. The cycles of severe temperature changes are an inorganic process in which the DNA molecule is not involved as it is in humans existing in creationary evolution.

The culture phase of the creation process is verified in these caves by the layered deposits of human and animal fossils over several hundred thousand years. Bones show the changes from Homo Erectus to Cro-Magnon (early modern man); stones show how the intelligence of the psyche developed implements from the crude pebble tool to the sophisticated, crafted stone tool, and cave walls show the genetically enhanced creativity that produced painted art.

How, then, do all these artifacts connect in significance to the near total absence of such verifying artifacts related to the Bible story? I will mention two connections.

The earliest evidence that the God-gene of the psyche grew in animal bodies in the Early Stone Age is the pebble-stone tool. A million years ago we were hunters and gatherers to stay alive like all the rest of our animal ancestors. The God-gene of the creation process had been working since Australopithecus lived in Africa, to grow the psyche gene in our animal bodies. The first evidence that such a psyche had gained reasoning power was the pebble that was cracked to produce a sharp edge to serve as a knife and scraper. Proofs are the pebble tools excavated by the side of fossil remains of the hominids of that age—Homo Habilis.

To appreciate the significance of such findings, we must realize that the only source of reasoning had to be evolved by the God-gene of the DNA molecule. To know that the gene directed the evolution of the psyche, i.e., the soul, mind and intelligence, in our animal body for the last three million years, we need to trace the remains our forefathers have left. To know how much the God-DNA has accomplished, we need to look at who we are. By our own free will, we can differentiate ourselves from our animal ancestors.

During the 20th century B.C., the empire of Babylon had a king named Hammurabi who was the first person in history to write a sophisticated code of law for his country. It was carved in 3500 lines of cuneiform on a stone shaft about eight feet tall and three feet in diameter. Around 10 centuries later, Moses came down from Mount Sinai with such a law code in abbreviated form as the Ten Commandments. Hammurabi had even depicted God handing the law tablets to Moses by sculpting the Sky God of Babylon in a cloud of fire handing the law tablets to the king. This sculpture appears on the top 18 inches of the stone shaft, which is on display today in a museum. There are no artifacts for Moses receiving the Ten Commandments on Mount Sinai.

Geology (earth structure), the Ice Age and the Stone Age are part of the inorganic process, but they are also part of the organic and culture evolutionary processes that created us humans—a process begun by the Bible God-Christ as the first cause of all creation.

PREHISTORIC HUMANS—
A MILLION YEARS OF CULTURE

Some of the circumstances and problems that prehistoric human beings faced are being disovered by scientists and archeologists. However, there are no written records of how prehistoric human beings developed from the mammals of the animal kingdom.

Findings collected for more than 5000 years outline past events. These visible facts are still scattered and poorly organized, but they are real facts that we can put our hands on. Scientific findings and deductions that testify to the genetic creation process leave very little room for the credibility of the Bible in explaining who we are and who God is.

The Bible and the Koran teach creation by teleology; i.e., creation was completed in totality at a point in time with no allowance for ongoing evolution into a better life.

The Bible teaches that creation was done *ex nihilo* (out of nothing). The Bible teaches that the spirit of supreme goodness that enables us to reach the divine can come only by way of Christ from above. The Bible teaches apocalypse, which says the world will come to an end and then all people will be judged to reach heaven or hell. The Bible teaches we are born in sin and therefore must be born again through Christ.

The Koran of Islam, the Muslim faith, has all the teachings of the Bible with one difference. Mohammed says he worships the God of Abraham with the same incarnation and eschatology. He repeats the Garden of Eden story, but he does not buy the born-in-sin idea, so he does not need Christ for salavation (though Jesus is considered a prophet). The snake and the apple do not speak to him.

More than one billion Judeo-Christian believers and nearly one billion Muslim believers have lived by this mythology. Genetic science answers all monotheistic believers by stating that human beings were created by the organic creation process, evolving from an animal body to a body possessing the psyche—soul, mind and intelligence—that the DNA gene added to our body over a period of three million years.

The God we present is based not on mythology but on findings that establish reality. The spirit of the Bible is retained, as well as God as the first cause of the genetic creation process according to Proverbs, John 1, Paul in Colossians 1, and Thomas Aquinas. The God-spirit appears after the soul has been added to our animal body in the form of the Jesus-spirit of love, mercy and forgiveness.

This chapter will present scientific findings and deductions that prove the evolution of the human being by genetic actions. This chapter should also show that genetic evolution of the human soul does not allow for biblical concepts of God on a throne in heaven, resurrection of the dead, creation teleology, apocalypse and creation *ex nihilo* by that format with which it created us as human beings in nature as detailed to us in the Bible.

The genetic creation process is an evolution of our humanism from our animal ancestors. In this case humanism is the addition of the psyche with soul, mind and intelligence. But the gene has done more than that; it has added the urge in our soul to practice the Jesus-spirit of love, mercy and forgiveness. Scientifically we can show that the process changed our physical characteristics from those of primates to those of humans. With increase of brain size came the activity of the psyche, namely, the God of genetic theology. Over a million years, by what geneticists call behavior genetics, God-genes developed the potential desire to be good, to overcome animal instincts that we carry forever in our genetic makeup.

That final concept of the spirit of supreme goodness—*numen summum bonum* (NSB)—in every soul ever created is God for us today. The metaphors of the Bible give way to the urge of the Holy Spirit in our souls.

Proof starts with Australopithecus, which was introduced when Raymond Dart, a university anatomy teacher, excavated a fossil specimen in South Africa in 1925. The name he gave it translates to "southern ape." At the university paleontology department, study revealed that the fossil was not an ape anymore but the first specimen discovered to show when the gene was on its long trek to evolve a human out of animal primates. Its date is estimated at three million years ago.

The predominant feature evidencing such a move was the bulging upward of the cranium instead of its being flat on top as in the ape. The volume of the skull had increased from the 390 cc of the ape to 600 cc. Other physical characteristics, such as the position of the pelvis and spine and the lock mechanism of the knee joint proved that Australopithecus walked on two legs.

Mary Leakey, daughter-in-law of a missionary in Tanzania, found footprints as fossils in stone that were the footprints of a hominid, showing the shape of a human foot and five toes. These fossil remains were dated about three million years B.C. To these two remains can be added other fossils, little Lucy and Skull 444, both from hominids who lived later.

For about two million years the Australopithecus tribe learned how to use primate forelegs as arms and hands to carry and make provisions for the sustenance of life, since they lived by hunting and gathering. Their canine teeth receded while their intelligence to use their arms increased.

Before introducing Homo Habilis, the next hominid, as we trace the DNA molecule with the God-gene creating humans from those early ancestors, we must describe some circumstances that existed during those early two million years.

The inorganic creation process of eternity came first. Tectonic plates that carry all continents had been in juxtaposition long enough, 500 million years ago, to start creation of our ancestors on all continents at the same level. This one land mass was called Pangaea. Then the continents separated about 250 million years ago, and from that time each continent carried the organic DNA creation to its separate destination. All hominid fossil specimens of the first almost two million years of the culture process showed up only in Africa and nowhere else.

Another example is that the gene of marsupialization started scientifically on Pangaea, and as the continents separated, the gene produced variations in marsupials — the opossum in Kansas and the kangaroo in Australia. These developments verify two concepts in creationary evolution processes over 500 million years:

1. They support the concept of Pangaea and its later separation into continents, since there are no apes in the Americas.

2. They support the genetic mode of operation as science articulates it, as a genotype-phenotype environmental interaction. Because of the

HOMO ERECTUS

Bones from the Homo Erectus, which existed one million years ago, have been found all over the world. These first of our ancestors were known as the Java Man, the Peking Man, and later the American Indian.

NEANDERTHAL

The Neanderthal or Cavedweller living about 100,000 years ago, started the art work at the Avignon cave, which is below sea level today, during the glaciation cycle of the Ice Age.

difference in Kansan and Australian environments, we have the kangaroo in Australia and the opossum in Kansas.

Such a circumstance is important because it explains the evolution of hominids solely in Africa. Later, fossils show that from the time of the traveler Homo Erectus, hominids were living all over the Eastern world. As explained previously, a lowered sea level because of freezing near the poles allowed Homo Erectus and his descendants to walk on dry land from Asia to North America. We can assume that hominids would have reached Australia in the same manner.

As glaciers moved south (the Ice Age of the inorganic creation process) to cover much of North America and Eurasia, the cold made cave dwelling a necessity for survival. The gene that increased Homo Erectus' intelligence through genotype-phenotype environmental interaction taught him how to build a fire to keep from freezing to death. Thus the inorganic creation process that moved tectonic plates and glaciers was part of the organic creation of hominids.

This evolution from a morsel of bacteria with its active DNA molecule to plants and animals to mammals and primates, our immediate ancestors, is illustrated in the October, 11, 1993 issue of *Time*. This process led the hominid Australopithecus to produce us as human beings—Homo Sapiens— over three million years.

These time periods are assessed by carbon dating, which is now corroborated by other dating mechanisms such as the spectrometer. Spectrometer dating is extrapolated by the laser released from argon gas in an atom, accumulating at a specified rate for a specified time, and is up to 98 percent correct. Carbon dating is based on extrapolating the radioactive carbon 14 deterioration rate plus its radio content today as compared to its original content to give the date of the existence of an object.

All encyclopedias, *World Books* and recognized publications in archeological sciences accept the above dating. We can justify an assumption that within the next 100 years, three billion nucleotide pairings in him will tell us exactly when Australopithecus lay down his bones in South Africa.

It took the DNA gene around 1.5 million years to advance from Australopithecus, Lucy, and Skull 440 to the next hominid in the evolutionary process, Homo Habilis. A Homo Habilis fossil was found by Mary Leakey in Tanzania, dated at more than two million years B.C. Brain volume had increased, the protrusion of eye-socket bones and jaw bones had receded, and canine teeth were smaller because this hominid had abdicated the animal method of tearing flesh from an animal carcass. Homo Habilis ("handyman") had learned how to make and use cracked pebbles to do such tasks with easily available arms and hands. With his bones were found cracked pebbles used for their sharp edges as tools to scrape and cut leftover meat from carcasses left behind by other animals.

Homo Habilis was the first hominid to show that the gene of intelligence in the psyche had been producing culture results in the creation process. Homo Habilis became extinct in about 300,000 years, but he left us with Homo Erectus. As the evolutionary creation process of the DNA molecule advanced from Lucy to Homo Sapiens, certain characteristics appeared:

1. The ability of locomotion, not only on two legs but with the free use of his hands and arms, helped the hominid not only to protect himself but to create a passage way to travel. This ability is especially evident in the hominid who appeared in China as the Peking man, in Java as the Java man, and in Europe as the Neanderthal man.

2. The intellectual capacity to make and use tools of stone, wood and bone protected him from other more fierce animals. He also used these tools in the quest for food to survive in his travels.

3. Growth in skull volume over two million years accompanied the acquisition of knowledge and skills. Adult skull volume grew from about 500 cc to over 750 cc in Habilis to over 1000 cc capacity in Homo Erectus to the 1600 cc of Cro-Magnon and humans today.

4. Reduction in the size of his canine teeth occurred as he discontinued tearing up flesh as he had for two million years along with other animals in order to survive as a species. He lived largely on plant food and on meat that he could scrape off carcasses left by other animals. He became smart enough to hide from wild animals, but he stayed close enough to study their behavior and habits so as to take advantage of whatever flesh could be taken from their bones.

Most of the species that hominids started with had become extinct, while the DNA gene enhanced enough mind and intelligence to enable Homo Erectus to grow in his psyche for more than 1.5 million years. From here on, most of the creationary enhancement was in the psyche (mind, soul, intelligence) instead of in the physical frame of the body.

5. His habitat changed from caves and trees to the open savannas. Here he could gather plant food of seeds and roots or even produce the

same. Here he could build a sod house with a grass roof to be able to live more safely. This change is verified by fossil remains.

6. Homo Erectus found life easier to live in pairs. He found life safer from wild animals if lived in organized groups such as tribes or colonies. Group organizations and building of fortifications became a mode of living.

7. The gestation time of life in-utero became longer, and the brain took longer to create all its expertise and specializations.

8. The infant development period became longer. An animal takes its first steps after the first breath. A human infant is dependent longer because it spends more time developing the mind and intellect.

9. Family living was necessary to teach the newborn an intellectual way of life through the gene of the psyche.

10. With this family life came the shared responsibility of the female to teach the offspring and manage the home and family while the male became the provider in hunting and gathering.

Tracing the sequential stages of the evolution of the psyche is more difficult than demonstrating physical changes of the fossils, such as skull volume of the brain. Capabilities of the psyche can be estimated by what the body produced and are best shown by the remains of tools and activities that are found with bone fossils (see "Stone Age" for details). Here we refer only to tools made of wood, bone and stone—tools that show the approximate level of intelligence of hominids at that particular time. Since wood and bone tools deteriorated, stone tools became the primary focus of scientific study, plus the artwork painted or sculpted on stone surfaces.

Homo Habilis introduced the cracked pebble. Homo Erectus developed sophisticated tools by flaking and fracturing larger rocks into stone axes, hammers, arrowheads, spearheads and cutting and scraping knife edges and hatchets. Prehistoric sculpturing and painting on stone give us additional results of the activity of the mind and intelligence.

Since much of the evidence of the evolution of the psyche and the body comes in the form of fossils, remains and artifacts, it seems appropriate to write about these and how they are interpreted. Fossils are remains of plants or animals preserved in the rocks of the earth's crust, or a petrified trace of an early organism, such as footprints. According to *World Book*, most fossils are found in sedimentary rocks. The oldest recorded organisms are morsels of bacteria with a DNA molecule in them, found in rock crevices, that identify the beginning of the organic creation process.

But what is the force or the potential ability that makes this gene do what it does? The question is not: How does it do it? but: How can it do it? That is one of the incomprehensibles of God's secrets. (The complexity of the origin of DNA and of its life was revealed in an exciting discovery at the Scripps Research Institute in La Jolla, California, as noted in "Creation.")

Homo Erectus appeared about 1.5 million years ago, following Homo Habilis, who became extinct. Homo Erectus was taller than his ancestors at over five feet. His forehead was higher, his face had flattened, and his teeth were aligned in a straight line with the canine teeth reduced in size. The activity of Homo Erectus showed an intelligent quotient that had never before appeared in the hominid. He was able to build a fire, starting it by rotating a stick of wood in the hollow of a log fast enough to make the friction produce enough heat to produce a flame. His IQ was also demonstrated by his ability to build stone axes, chopping tools and stone flaking knives and scrapers. The most assuring fact about Homo Erectus in our story is that his bone fossils have been found in large numbers all over the contiguous continents of Asia, Africa and Europe. With his fossils were found the tools he worked with. No fossils of Homo Erectus were ever found in the Americas—the ocean was too high in his time.

To illustrate the international character of Homo Erectus, we present the Peking Man found near Beijing (Peking), China. He was dated as living between 500,000 and 250,000 years B.C. This find was followed by a discovery of 30 more fossils of the Peking Man family. About five feet, one inch tall, they still had primitive anatomical features of heavy bones, large teeth, large protruding jaws, a wide face and heavy eye-socket protrusions. They were found in a cave with thousands of stone tools and indications that they were cannibalistic. We can assume that Peking man survived because he could build a fire and find caves, since during the more recent Ice Age cycles, the glaciers came down every 50,000 to 100,000 years. All these findings indicate that human life was cheap and easily expendable ages ago.

The other Homo Erectus who traveled far and wide was Java man, whose fossils were found on the island of Java in Indonesia. Dated at around 750,000 years B.C., he also had primitive anatomical features. He had large, protruding eye-socket bones and large protruding jawbones. The glaciation of the Ice Age and the lowering of the sea level enabled Homo Erectus to walk from island to island on dry ground.

But Homo Erectus was never found to have reached North and South America. He either never found the Bering Strait or else he tried to cross when the warming time had raised the sea level. Several thousands of years later, the offspring of Peking Man walked across into America as our Native American Indians. After World War II, many more fossils of Homo Erectus were found all over Asia, Africa and Europe but none in the Americas.

After following Homo Erectus for nearly two millon years, we need to present what the gene has given to us since Homo Erectus began. Changes in the gene during the time of Australopithecus, Homo Habilis and, most of all, Homo Erectus were physical and anatomical, but by the end of the Homo Erectus period the gene had filled in the psyche to a greater degree. During the first two million years of Lucy, Habilis and Erectus the psyche was still nearly empty. During the last million years, the genetic process was largely a process of enhancing the strength and quality of the psyche, and since the psyche cannot be fossilized, there are no artifacts or fossils to demonstrate that process. And since there was no writing until 5000 B.C., this genetic activity that is the most relative to our evolving from animal ancestry to people with the divine in our souls is most difficult to articulate.

The most damaging aspect of the concepts of religious life of the three monotheistic religions of Yahweh-worship, Christianity and Islam is that they are not compatible with the facts of science. None of the writers of the Bible and the Koran could know of genetic creation activity. However, the gene of the Jesus-spirit of love, mercy and forgiveness is universally present in every human being because the gene of the DNA molecule put it there genetically for everyone to put into operation on planet Earth.

The genetic creation process of the pysche and its affect on human behavior is being researched today as the greatest challenge of the scientific age. Many textbooks and treatises discuss how the the DNA molecule enhances quality of behavior and the psyche (bringing closer "thy kingdom come... on earth"). The headquarters of the Jesus-spirit is no longer with Christ above as traditionally thought; the spirit is moving in each of our souls, through the genetic evolutionary process of interaction, as the *numen summum bonum* (spirit of supreme goodness, or NSB) of genetic theology—the Jesus-spirit.

The genetic creation of our behavior by way of our psyche is an ever-ongoing process. In genetic science, this process is called genotype-phenotype environmental interaction. The paucity of fossils or artifacts that monitor the creation process of the psyche is partly due to the following:

1. The psyche cannot be fossilized.

2. Even a million years is a short period of time vis-a-vis the 3.5 billion years of creation of all organisms.

3. The custom of burying the dead during this time period obviates fossil formation.

4. There was no writing to record the activity.

5. We are just touching the tip of the iceberg in our knowledge of the genetic creation process.

But, finally, bone fossils would not tell us very much anyway because there is no way to fossilize the genetic product of the psyche of soul, mind and intelligence by way of the bones.

The artifacts of the Stone Age and Ice Age, and the painting and sculpturing found largely in caves are some of the remains of our ancestors that testify to the credibility of the creation process of the psyche—results that our animal body produced in prehistoric times, directed by the genes of our enhanced psyche. These stone findings, if judged by our computer-era perspective, seem much too crude, mundane, primitive and inconsequential to be of any value in telling us anything about the genetic enhancement of our psyche potential during that time period. But to accept the Stone Age as being extremely important in our story we must know that 2.6 million years ago:

1. We had nothing in the way of tools

2. We had no precedent of tools or tool-making. Our mind was completely void of such concerns because they had never existed. We had always survived like other animals by gathering and hunting.

3. We had no one to teach us how to make anything.

4. We had in our psyche all the animal traits to overcome, such as aggression, hate and brute strength of bone and muscle as means of survival.

5. As our *NSB* reached a higher level, we had a fear of attack by our animal partners of that time.

6. During all those years, the gene was striving for some higher quality in us that had never existed before.

7. Such quality was demonstrated in us by our immediate forefather, Cro-Magnon (early Homo Sapiens), whom we know from fossils of about 150,000 years ago.

8. The enhancement of the psyche by genotype-phenotype environmental interaction advanced only as the environment progressed. The high level of culture today increases the rate of enhancement of the psyche every day.

The crude primitive artifacts of our culture of the Stone Age are to be seen in museums all over the world. The Bible writers and worshipers have hardly a single artifact to prove divine authenticity of the Bible. We cannot even see the Ark of the Covenant or the plates of the Ten Commandments that God handed to Moses on Mount Sinai as the Bible relates so graphically in Genesis.

In contrast, King Hammurabi of Babylon in the Late Stone Age wrote, as we have related, the laws of his land—the Ten Commandments in more detail—in the form of 3500 lines in cuneiform writing on a stone.shaft. On the top 18 inches of the shaft he had a scene sculpted of the Sun God of Babylon, with a cloud of fire off his shoulder, handing the law plates to King Hammurabi. Such God-man communication was very likely observed by the Hebrews centuries later while in their captivity in Babylon. Hammurabi wrote this in the 20th century B.C. (some sources give 2050 B.C.), long before Moses floated down the Nile in a basket, was picked up by Pharaoh's daughter and grew up in the King's court. The stone artifact of the Babylonian king is today on display. We can justifiably assume that Moses modeled his Mount Sinai scenario after that of King Hammurabi, an event 1000 years before he wrote the Ten Commandments on Mount Sinai.

To review the prehistoric artifacts' evidences of the human culture creation process since Australopithecus and Lucy in Africa about three million years ago, we notice that for the first two million years, creation results were mostly identified by physical and anatomical characteristics. The creation of the psyche was much slower.

Culture is the God-created entity of humanism, far above and beyond the other two entities of the universe, i.e., the organic and the inorganic. Culture contains our true comprehensible God within us. It is the spirit universe metaphorized in the Bible and Koran as God, Christ and Allah.

In that process the first hominid walked on two legs and had an increase in brain capacity. Then, sequentially, fossil specimens showed the gradual disappearance of the large eye-socket protrusion and a change to a flat face from the large protrusion of the jaw of the primate.

The skull volume of the brain increased from 390 cc in the ape to 600 cc in Australopithecus to 750 cc in Homo Habilis to 1200 cc in Homo Erectus to a normal human brain volume capacity of 1600 cc of Cro-Magnon and us today.

The creationary enhancement of the hominid was from near empty of the psyche of Australopithecus to an intelligence capable enough in Homo Habilis to make and use cracked pebbles. Genetic growing was demonstrated by the ability of Homo Erectus to adopt pair living and group cooperative living and by being able and motivated to start human civilization all over the world.

In the development of Homo Sapiens, Neanderthal man appeared in Germany. Archeologists of the world community are not agreed on just where he belongs in the creation process. He had a skull volume of 1600 cc. and was much more robust than Cro-Magnon. It is postulated that since he depended on his great strength and less on his intellectual choices, this is why he became extinct after living more than 100,000 years, partly at the same time as Homo Erectus and Cro-Magnon (early Homo Sapiens), though whether he was a part of them is still in question. He disappeared during the late prehistoric time.

Neanderthal man had more of the primitive anatomical features of greater protrusion of eye-socket bones and greater protrusion of the upper and lower jaw. His brain case was long, low and flattened behind. His canine teeth were larger. The Neanderthal people are generally looked upon as the cave people who descended upon the whole contiguous world of Asia, Africa and Europe in prehistoric times.

Neanderthals have left memorabilia in remains that have contributed to our story of the creation of culture, and these deserve exposure. Where they were cave dwellers, stone paintings and sculptures are still present. They developed the custom of burying their dead by covering their bodies with stratified layers of earth and rocks. Indications are that such a custom was more instinct than intelligence. They hunted with wood spears capped with a sharp stone head. In their caves are found stone tools of the Middle Stone Age. Neanderthals became extinct before 25,000 B.C. as a subspecies of Cro-Magnon.

A Cro-Magnon fossil was first found in the Cro-Magnon cave in South France. Dating of this people's fossils indicates that they lived from 35,000 B.C. The brain case held 1600 cc; also, the skull was better formed than that of Homo Erectus and Neanderthal man and was positioned with the base of the skull more parallel to the spine. The skull of Cro-Magnon showed very little forward protrusion of the bony eye sockets and jaws, and the trunk lacked the barrel-shaped thorax of primates. But his superiority was most significant in his ability to produce culture achievements. He made highly sophisticated paintings and sculptures.

In a February 13, 1995 *Time* magazine is a nine-page feature article and a front-page illustration captioned "Secrets of the Stone Age." The article presents the handiwork of Cro-Magnon of the Late Stone Age, timed at 20,000 B.C. Cro-Magnon painted this art during the glaciation cycle of the Ice Age when the ice of the glaciers was over a mile high and the sea level was down 300 feet. Cro-Magnon could walk on dry ground into a cave opening that is now probably more than 100 feet below the level of the Mediterranean Sea, near Avignon in South France. A scuba diver, Jean-Mario Chauvet, discovered this cave art, unseen since the last glaciation period, which may well be more than 20,000 years ago. Cro-Magnon also sculpted statues of ivory and stone of female figures, usually with large breasts and wide hips, and often apparently pregnant. Such paintings could well have been a ritual to show appreciation of fertility.

Cro-Magnon lived mostly in caves and under rock overhangs. There is evidence that he built huts to live in. He hunted deer, bison and even mammoths, presumably with spears, in concert with a group of hunters. The painting shows the fears these people had of being attacked and killed by wild animals.

Cro-Magnon was taller than any of his ancestors; some fossils indicate that he reached six feet, three inches in height. Specimens were also found in the Grimaldi caves in Italy, and other such fossils were found in Wales and Belgium. We can assume that the rugged life in caves produced environmental circumstances that accelerated the genotype-phenotype environmental culture creation process to produce a more motivated, more energetic white race of people who formed the Indo-European people of ancient history as they contacted the Semites from the south.

We know very little about the religiosity of the Cro-Magnon of 20,000 years ago because religion is not fossilized and there was no writing until thousands of years later. But we can rationalize that those people were so busy staying alive that the idea of a God was low on their agenda, and as with the aborigines and indigenous people contacted by

Bishop Wilhelm Schmidt, the idea of a God was very vague and not important.

The culture creation process of us as human beings over a period of three million years is authenticated by the remains that resulted from the functions of life directed by the DNA molecule. Such proofs showing us how Homo Sapiens was created by DNA-molecule action are copiously documented in all encyclopedias, *World Books* and thousands of acceptable scientific publications.

The Australopithecus, Homo Habilis, Homo Erectus, Neanderthal, and Cro-Magnon remains that preceded Homo Sapiens are an oversimplification of all the details that took place during those three million years. We have every reason to expect that many of these details will be presented to us in the next 100 years. The recent cave finding near Avignon, France, is a good proof that such details will come to us. The paucity of authenticating evidence of the three million years of culture creation becomes credible when we consider that all these events took place before any writing. All these events of our creation are lost in total darkness except for the remains.

These remains have become more relevant since we have in the last 100 years learned that the DNA molecule with its genes has controlled and will control the nature of all life of plants, animals and humans. This has become a scientific fact. Science has even mapped a few of those thousands of genes in one human body under the electron microscope. Now a 15-year program called the Genome Project will add vast new information about how DNA functions. We have barely begun to open the door in this field. Science is learning more every day that DNA is the only life that exists and has ever existed.

Science bases its conclusions on factual calculation. In contrast, the Bible bases its conclusions of an intervening Christ in heaven on assumptions of an incarnation that "could be true" and does not need to be proved. (See "Incarnation" for further discussion.)

THE ORIENT—WHERE CIVILIZATION BEGAN

The history of the ancient Orient—the land east of the Mediterranean Sea, known as the cradle of civilization—throws light on the development of ideas about God.

The Middle East is the area on our planet where civilization began. Recorded civilization started there about 6000 years ago, or 4000 B.C., when human beings had lived through half of the warming age of the last Ice Age cycle. Since during the Ice Age cycle of more than 100,000 years, the northern half of Europe and Asia was covered with glaciers over a mile high, it is natural that civilization started in Africa, in the Nile area of Egypt. In the warming age of the last cycle of glaciers about 20,000 years ago, North Africa had rains and lush flora and fauna. That same area is now desert. It is in this set of circumstances that we present ancient history following prehistoric man in sequence.

The oldest cosmology of note is Egyptian. The first history writing was in the form of hieroglyphics on papyrus. The Egyptians had learned to split a water-reed plant called papyrus into thin layers and to record writing on such thin layers. With these happenings, history started.

While Europe and Asia were largely covered with ice, Egypt was coming from the age of hunting and gathering through the Stone Age to the age of agriculture. People had learned how to plant and harvest wheat and barley developed by the selection of seed from ancient weeds and grasses. They learned how to domesticate animals such as goats for a living.

These accomplishments had changed their hunting and gathering lifestyle so that they could choose to use their leisure time for civilized endeavors such as writing records. They also invented the first time clock and the year calendar, and they acquired mathematical and engineering expertise that enabled them to build the pyramids.

The agricultural accomplishments of Egypt are specifically referred to in the Old Testament of the Bible in the story of Jacob and Joseph of Israel. This story starts with an intrigue involving Joseph and with Jacob sending his sons to buy grain from prospering Egypt. The Joseph connection ends with a 400-year servitude of the Hebrews to the pharaohs (kings) of Egypt and culminates with the exodus of the Israelites from Egypt back to Palestine.

During the agriculture age Egyptian herdsmen were tending their flock in the Sinai and having their evening campfire. In the morning sun, they saw the glitter of copper in the ashes of their campfire. Copper changed people's lifestyle in Egypt; instead of making their tools of stone, they now made them of metal. Metal-age development became very important to Egyptian engineers, who produced the most spectacular legacy of Egypt, the pyramids. Very clear in my memory is the midday picnic my wife Mariam and I had with friends by the pyramids, at the foot of the Sphinx in 1950.

The pyramids were built about 3000 B.C. The engineer and architect who led this mammoth project was Imhotep. The expertise of these people who learned to build such huge structures 5000 years ago has puzzled the experts even today. It does indicate that the Egyptian culture is much older and much more advanced than we have given them credit for in our written histories.

Each pyramid covers 13 acres and rises up 500 feet. The structure was a mass of masonry consisting of more than two million limestone blocks weighing 5000 pounds each. The inside of these pyramids was beautifully furnished to preserve the bodies of many pharaohs (kings). It took 100,000 workers 12 years to build one pyramid.

Egyptian theology set the pattern for four other religions that followed Egypt in the history of antiquity. The Egyptians started with many gods, a situation that seems plausible. As Martin Luther of the 16th century said, "Whatever thy heart dost cling to and rely upon, that is thy God." The Egyptians had many things to cling to that were important to them in their far-advanced culture.

Over time, every succeeding culture seemed to drift to the practice of monotheism. In Egypt, Imhotep IV, who ruled many generations after the architect of the pyramids, was inclined toward academia. He advanced the concept of one god, Osiris. Osiris was born of the spirit, died and was resurrected to become the spiritual leader of Egypt. The May 29, 1995 issue of *U.S. News and World Report* reviewed a recent discovery in Egypt. At Luxor of the Upper Nile, a statue of the god Osiris was found standing at the gate of a chamber with the tomb contents of 40 Egyptian rulers.

Many centuries later Moses was trained in Egyptian culture and religion while he lived in the pharaoh's household after the pharaoh's daughter found him as an infant in a basket floating on the water of the Nile. Much later, Moses established and recorded a religious system very similar to Egypt's; it was the basis for the Judeo-Christian faith as recorded in the Bible. Like Imhotep of Egypt, Moses inherited a multi-god people who worshiped Baal. Moses' God ruled over the Israelites with an iron fist as the pharaoh did over them for 400 years while the Israelites were in Egyptian captivity. The God of Imhotep IV served all people of the world whereas Moses' God served only his own small group of people. Like Osiris of Imhotep IV, the Jesus of biblical record was of a spiritual birth, died, was resurrected and became a spiritual leader—a God to be worshiped.

When Imhotep changed his country from polytheism to monotheism, he destroyed all the idols of many gods. He even changed his name from Imhotep to Ikhnaton (or Akhenaten) because one syllable of his old name referred to one of the many gods. The new concept of one God was instituted in Egypt in 1400 B.C.

Ikhnaton had no son to succeed him. He had three daughters, and his third daughter married a nobleman who would succeed Ikhnaton as King (Pharaoh) Tutankamen. The Egyptian kingdom had faded enough that King Tutankamen was considered of minor importance, and upon his death he was buried in a smaller tomb in the pyramid, off to one side. When tomb robbers, who were probably the Assyrians or Babylonians who later conquered Egypt, were so aggressive as to rob the major tombs, rocks fell upon the passage of the minor tomb of Tutankamen, and therefore the King Tut that we have read about was saved from the robbers for us to see in a museum.

In summary, Egyptians were the originators and teachers for the Assyrian, Babylonian, Phoenician, Persian, and Hebrew cultures that followed. This enormous civilization served as a guide for the other four empires that will be reviewed. Egypt has been admired worldwide for 4000 years for the pyramids. King Imhotep as Ihknaton created one God for all the world, a new concept and a new age in theology. Finally, Egypt made the first attempt at writing, which in Phoenicia and Greece would be enhanced into an alphabet that we use today. These writings started all of recorded history.

During the second millennium B.C., four other cultures besides Egypt were created — Babylonian, Assyrian, Persian, and Hebrew. The Egyptian empire occupied the Nile River country and especially the river delta country, includng present-day Sinai. The Assyrian, Babylonian and Persian empires, succeeding each other following wars in the area of Mesopotamia, occupied the region of the twin rivers Tigris and Euphrates. These empires ruled from the Nile to India.

Before presenting the empires that conquered and occupied the Middle East, each for a time sequentially, I will tell about the cultures of Phoenicia, Sumeria and the Hittites.

Phoenicians, the "sea people," had close relations with Egypt. They had no temples, no kings, no gods, but they learned porcelain-making and tool-making; they built their own ocean vessels and had factories in Tyre, Sidon, Byblos and Carthage. They had a loosely organized culture that was engaged in a system of commercial trade with all countries of the Mediterranean Sea. Besides being important in commerce, they were experts in communications. They served all countries with their writing. They borrowed the hieroglyphics of Egypt and created the alphabet essentially as we have it now. Their alphabet formed the basis of the writing of the Greeks, who added vowels. The tragedy of writing on papyrus was its lack of being preserved, in comparison to the permanency of the cuneiform writing of the Sumerians.

The Bible says that King Solomon called in the Phoenicians to build his temple for him, "for you know, no one in Israel can cut timber like you Sidonians" (1 Kings 5:6c). Activity at the Phoenician port Byblos is the origin of our word "Bible."

The Hittites, who operated out of an area north of Mesopotamia, left very little of themselves. They seem to have been a warrior tribe. They made iron tools and weapons and won a war against Babylon and King Hammurabi but did not survive as an empire.

The Sumerians were another group of independent people. Like the Phoenicians, they never reached empire status. They were non-Semites who lived in Mesopotamia in the upper region of the Tigris and

Euphrates rivers. They lived during the wars of all the conquering empires but survived with their culture. The Sumerians are known primarily for developing cuneiform writing. This writing consisted of imprinting wedge-shaped figures arranged in groups in various relationships of position to each other. The imprints were made in soft clay and then preserved by heating the clay tablets with a burn as we still burn bricks. The significance of fired clay is that writings of antiquity are much more preserved in cuneiform writing than in alphabet writing on papyrus, which was very destructible. The earliest cuneiform writing of Erlich of Babylon was in 3000 B.C.—the first preserved writing in human history. Although the alphabet writing of the Phoenicians and Greeks appeared soon after cuneiform, the cuneiform writing had the advantage of survivability.

The second great empire in the Orient after Egypt was Babylon. Babylon was mostly composed of the Sumerians as a culture rather than as an empire. These non-Semites, a people of high culture, held their own from 3500 to 2300 B.C. After 2300 B.C., Semites started infiltrating into this Mesopotamia area. (In medieval times, this area of Babylon was called the Eastern Civilization, and the Nile country was the Western Civilization.)

In 2500 B.C., King Sargon led the Semites in defeating the benign Sumerians. He soon established a powerful empire. Legend has it that King Sargon was retrieved in a basket off the Euphrates and, like Moses many centuries later, became a leader of his people.

Another people, the Semitic Amorites, moved into Babylon about 2150 B.C. Out of this people came King Hammurabi, who is credited with many accomplishments. He was more interested in achieving academic results than war gains. Balanced double-entry bookkeeping and modern banking are accredited to his achievements. Moreover, King Hammurabi is recognized as the writer and establisher of a code of law that he ordered carved on a stone shaft eight feet high and about three feet in diameter with 3500 lines of cuneiform figures on it. Above the writing, a carving shows the Sun God handing the code of law to King Hammurabi. An important detail is the flame of fire flowing from the shoulder of the Sun God, designating who he was. Today the shaft is on display at a museum. This event in the twentieth century B.C. was repeated 1000 years later by Moses on Mount Sinai with God in a cloud of fire handing to Moses the tablets of the Ten Commandments, which are modeled after Hammurabi's code.

After Hammurabi died, Assyria soon conquered Babylon. Although defeated and occupied, the culture of Babylon survived because the rulers of the Assyrian military empire respected the culture and felt they needed it for their survival. Assyria became so powerful after 900 B.C. that it controlled the entire territory, including the Nile country and all of western Asia.

Even while Babylon was occupied, it prospered enough under occupation to come up with its own king, Nebuchadnezzar. He held off the army long enough to become king about 600 B.C. His most remembered act was destroying the Jewish temple in Jerusalem in 587 B.C. and sending Israel into captivity. He had confrontations with the Old Testament prophet Daniel, and his successor, Belshazzar, also confronted Daniel. The Assyrians ruled from about 750 to 640 B.C. but contributed little to civilization; the Babylonians did that for them.

During the last millennium B.C., the nomads from the North had developed into a hardy white race near the area of the Black Sea. These so-called Indo-Europeans are the relatives of Caucasian people in North America. They had come through the warming stage of the last cycle of the Ice Age. The rugged climate had made them very aggressive, and with the absence of a hot sun, this active, blue-eyed, blond white race migrated down from the glacier country in Europe. For many centuries they had come down to the warm grassland for the winter as herdsmen of their flocks. Their increasing presence around Nineveh, the capital of Assyria, caused its surrender more from attrition than military might in 530 BC. The Assyrians had relied upon the Babylonians for their culture and development, and their Semite army was too weak to govern the vast area of population.

After the fall of Nineveh, the Persians ruled from 530 to 300 B.C. The area that the Persians governed fell to them mostly by default and stretched from India in Asia to Greece in Europe to Egypt in Africa. The Persians were a rugged people with no writing, so they adopted both cuneiform and alphabet writing. They had stone tools, lived mostly on agriculture, and brought with them from the north country the first domesticated horses to aid in travel and cultivation of their croplands.

The Persians brought two new concepts to the Orient (land east of the Mediterranean Sea). The new concepts were:

1. The religious concept of the human soul as the home of all divinity. This belief, known as Zoroastrianism, was part of a faith of more than 20,000 years.

2. Installation of a government of many democratic states—an entirely new concept in the Middle East, and on earth, for that matter. Here are the beginnings of a truly spiritual religion and of democracy.

Middle Easterners were not ready for such religious concepts and prepared to follow the God of Moses, who had a concept of the spirit that they could perceive with their senses. However, the Greek philosophers Socrates, Plato and Aristotle kept such a religious concept and wrote about it. Zoroaster taught that every human had free will to fill his soul with good and light or to dwell in evil and darkness. For my dissertation in this book, Zoroaster and his idea of divinity is the high-water mark of our ancestors of the Orient. There is evidence at Avignon that Zoroaster"s idea had existed 20,000 years ago—16,000 years before the God-in-heaven myth was born. We can rightfully assume that this ancient concept in Avignon of good and evil in every human soul led Zoroaster to record this.

The Medes and Persians, our distant ancestors, ruled the first empire to construct a federation of herding tribes that became democratic states and members of a larger confederation. The structure of this confederation was written in cuneiform starting about 600 B.C. After the Assyrian King Esarhaddon died, the Mede and Persian tribes decided to join to form the Persian government. They stationed their army in units over the large area, and they developed a sophisticated system of banking and taxation. Persia was the last empire of the Orient. This area was later ruled by the Greeks and then was conquered by the Roman Empire of Jesus" time.

This perfunctory review of the empires of the Orient will be followed by more details of Hebrew cosmology as given in the Bible. History indicates that the Hebrew people never became an empire. They divided into Israel in northern Palestine and Judah in southern Palestine, and even killed each other on occasions.

II. GOD IN HEAVEN

The Bible—A Narrative of Metaphors

Old Testament—The God of the Prophets

The Hebrews—A Quasi-Jewish Nation

Incarnation—Embodying Spirit in Form

Teleology—Instant Creation Versus Evolution

Eschatology—System of the Death Process

Afterlife—Apocalypse Versus Natural Death

Islam—Religion of Allah and Koran

Trinity—A Farce of Athanasius

Resurrection—Incarnated Jesus-Spirit

Who Is God?—God is the Gene of the Spirit

Christ—Metaphor of Jesus

THE BIBLE—A NARRATIVE OF METAPHORS

The Bible, in science, is a narrative of metaphors that are incarnations of the spirit in the gene's evolutionary creation process of the soul containing the *numen summum bonum*, or NSB (spirit of supreme goodness).

The Bible is also a dictatorial document that has all the answers that a human being needed 2000 years ago to reach eternal bliss. It satisfied the fear of the animal genes that we carry in our genome forever. All animals have natively a fear for their survival. We share these fear genes of our animal ancestors. The Bible promises heaven to us fearful people if we pass the judgment of Christ when he comes down from heaven on the day when the world comes to an end. For a people who lacked all knowledge of the three-phase creation process, inorganic, organic, culture (cultural), the Bible served its believers very well, teaching obedience in exchange for a heavenly reward.

Today that document is still very valuable as a presenter of the soul quality within us that the gene put there, and therefore it should not be discarded. The veracity of the Bible system of Christ ruling in heaven and Satan punishing sinners in hell will be discussed elsewhere.

The really important point of discussion is the acceptance of science and-or the Bible. The struggle for survival of these two ideologies probably started over 100 years ago with Charles Darwin when his theory of evolution appeared. The struggle manifests itself with the charisma of the fundamentalist religious right—Bible believers in a ruling Christ from heaven in action as opposed to a God of the soul. When the Bible reverses incarnation from the metaphor back to the spirit of the gene that created the psyche containing the spirit (of Jesus) in common with the Bible spirit, the two ideologies are on the same level of truth.

The alternative to the Christ in heaven is what we may call the theology of genetics. In this theology, the God-spirit is active in the soul of every person. The Jesus-spirit of love, mercy and forgiveness was inserted into our animal body by the gene of the DNA molecule more than a million years ago.

This struggle between fundamentalist believers and the scientific community has been going on for many centuries with no resolution in sight. They both exist side by side with no attempt to outline procedure for such a resolution. Both adversaries have to make some concessions.

Science has to concede that it has to deal with certain incomprehensible circumstances for which neither mathematics nor scientific research will ever produce a formula that will delineate their form. Some incomprehensibles are time and space. When did time begin? What is beyond the view of the Hubble telescope? God is another incomprehensible mystery, for according to John 1:18 no one has ever seen God.

But the most relevant incomprehensible item today is the gene of the DNA molecule. It concerns the *Lebenkraft* in what the Apostle Paul calls "the power that holds everything together." It is in the gene chromosome that we can see under the electron microscope. It is the incomprehensible motivation that enables the gene to do what it does. In science we know that the gene is the only "item" that is alive today and that has been alive through all eternity. This life of the gene is the can-do quality. We are learning how the gene acts, but the can-do will probably remain one of God's secrets with the rest of the incomprehensibles of the God mysteries.

The Bible gives us a God who has a connotation of immortality, omnipotence and omniscience. This God was in existence in the human psyche long before the Bible was written. But we must credit the Bible for presenting a God who can take care of all the incomprehensibles of our scientific endeavors.

The concession of Bible believers concerning Bible metaphors is more difficult. The Bible community must concede that God-Christ, as the first cause of all creation and the custodian of all the incomprehensibles, does not reside in heaven. He lives and performs in the mind that the gene gave us in the culture creation process. We have presented scientific evidence that genetic action produced the Jesus-spirit of love, mercy and forgiveness as a gene in our genome in the culture creation process. That is a gene that aninals have not yet received in quantity.

The Old and New Testaments and the Koran are narratives of metaphors written by human beings directing the dramatization in temples and mosques and churches of the God-spirit that the gene of Christ the first cause gave us in the culture evolution over a time of more than a million years. The enhancement of the NSB that the genes had evolved into our souls did not appear as metaphors of the gods all over antiquity until cuneiform and hieroglyphics and alphabet writing came into being. As we have related, God metaphors appeared in Egypt, Assyria, Babylon, Persia, Greece, in ancient Israel and in Christianity and Islam as the incarnation was recorded in writing.

The Bible-God metaphors for the spirit in our soul are totally based on incarnation, eschatology, teleology, creation *ex nihilo* (out of nothing) and apocalypse. According to Christ as the first cause of evolutionary creation, such tenets of the Bible cannot exist. The veracity of the God-spirit metaphors as physical truisms comes into question more every day.

Before the Easter Sunday of 1996, three prestigious periodicals, namely *Time*, *Newsweek* and *U.S. News and World Report*, came out concomitantly with the same format. All had a full front-page picture of Jesus, and all had an eight-page discussion about the doubt by scholars that the resurrection and ascension of Jesus into heaven to take on the name Christ did take place as the Bible relates to us in detail. In fact, Paul writes to the Corinthians that "if Christ is not raised from the dead, then our preaching is in vain and so is your faith."

Another public demonstration of the question of the veracity of the Bible was presented by CBS's *Sixty Minutes* in the spring of 1996 in an interview with a fellow physician, Dr. Jack Kevorkian. He stated that the bigotry of the Christian and Jewish Bible and the Muslim Koran are at the root of most of the problems of life of the world today. If we look at the killings in Northern Ireland, Palestine and Bosnia, we must conclude that if we could get rid of the metaphors of the spirit of supreme goodness such as Yahweh, Christ and Allah, we could have peace. God is and was and always will be with us, and needs to be and will be. The solution is purely a matter of orientation as to who God is.

Even *The Living Bible* needs such reorientation. Since the Bible presents us with so many entirely different Gods, we have the duty to accept the God that can be possible in the field of science. In the Bible we have the God of Moses who created in teleology the world and humanity in a specified six days *ex nihilo* as told in Genesis. In Proverbs we have King Solomon's God, who worked side by side with "Miss" Wisdom in planning the "blueprint" for the creation of the universe.

In Genesis we are presented with the God of Abraham and Sarah in their tent in the desert, acting to bring about Israel and Islam. Writers of the first part of the Old Testament present us with an entirely different God who spent all his time killing and exterminating all human beings on earth because they were all enemies except his people the Israelites. This was so because none except the Israelites worshiped him.

In the New Testament, the Bible presented another God, wholly different, a God of "love your enemies." Also in the New Testament is another God—Christ who sits on the throne of heaven. He is the God in Revelation, the God of the apocalypse, who comes down to earth at a specified time to end the world and resurrect all the dead to life. He will then judge all of them to burn in hell forever or come with him to heaven to live in bliss forever.

The Bible presents us with still another God in John 1 and Colossians 1. That God is Christ, who is presented through two names representing the same being. Both John and Paul tell us that God and Christ are two names of the same One. More important, they say that Christ created everything, starting long before the earth was formed.

As we sum up the Bible connotations of God, we can list them as immortality, omnipotence, omniscience, omnipresence and divinity. Science accepts and meets the specifications of the Bible God of the first four above connotations when scientists credit Christ-God as the bearer of the first cause of all creation and of many other incomprehensibles. Such a concept of the Bible God was conceptualized by Thomas Aquinas in the 13th century A.D. when he declared that the cause of the creation of the universe had to be preceded by a cause that caused the subsequent cause, and that original cause is called God.

Science tells us that the organic creation process began with the morsel of bacteria that started genetic creativity, but science will never find a formula for the *Lebenkraft* that the gene possesses. That *Lebenkraft* we call God because science can never comprehend the power that Paul says "holds everything together." That God of the Bible we choose to worship.

A second of the many Gods of the Bible is Jesus, the human-born human being who showed us how the gene of love, mercy, humility, forgiveness and a simple lifestyle works in human affairs to produce heaven here on earth.

The conclusion is that this dissertation does not teach atheism; we worship a concept of God that unites two of the Bible's many Gods. The two Bible Gods that can and have survived are the God of the incomprehensible and the God of Jesus of love. The rest of the different Gods of the Bible have to be read as metaphors created by writers in their effort to incarnate the gene products of good and evil in our psyche. That involves the evil animal genes in our genome, to be corrected by the Jesus genes of love, mercy, humility, forgiveness and a simple lifestyle.

The Bible spirit is in science entirely credible when we completely reverse the incarnation of that spirit by all the writers of the Bible and the Koran. That eliminates the metaphors so that we can, by meditation, worship the Spirit that created the metaphors in the first place.

Recent archeological findings of the tomb of Caiaphas, who tried Jesus, and the stone marker of King David of the ninth century B.C. are hailed by a Fundamentalist as findings of much importance. He expects these findings to cut down the skeptics. What Fundamentalists are really saying is that the incarnation assumptions of the Bible can be sneaked in by showing evidence of the authenticity of the history of David and Caiaphas (see "Incarnation"). Scientists are not skeptical about what real history the Bible presents because that history is recorded in other history books of other cosmologies in more detail. Also, all the history of Bible times does not prove the truth and reality of the incarnation of the Holy Spirit into a form sitting in heaven that rules everything. Such a maneuver of the spirit into a form sitting on a throne is a repeat of a common event of antiquity of making an idol with form to activate idol worship in principle. To worship a metaphor of the Holy Spirit looks like idol worship.

Science will credit Bible writers for having served well a people 2000 years ago in presenting a form by which, in their imagination, they could reach the divine. It served a purpose in its time. Today scientific facts have no room for immaculate conception, resurrection from the dead, creation *ex nihilo*, teleology, incarnation, sin, hell or heaven as detailed to us in the Bible. The details of why this is so are discussed elsewhere.

The incarnation of the spirit of goodness through evolution of the DNA gene produced gods all over the prehistoric world. Dozens of cosmologies, including the Hebrew, incarnated the spirit that was started in their soul by their gene, into their own God. Such concepts of a God were later interpreted by Martin Luther: "Whatever thy heart dost cling to and rely upon, that is thy God."

OLD TESTAMENT—THE GOD OF THE PROPHETS

Since the Western concept of God started with the Old Testament, we shall dig into verses (from *The Living Bible*) on how God related to his human beings with their ethical, moral and spiritual problems. We look beyond the Bible metaphors to see the beauty of the forces of the spirit of the Old Testament prophets. They are an inspiration to the good; they overcome evil in our soul by our compassionate behavior.

We avoid all the details of God's goings-on in daily events in the life of his people in peace and war. God's action and domination of his people through anger, vengeance, fear, punishments and exterminations are completely irrelevant and obscene. Those events represent a corollary to actions of the neighboring warriors of Babylon, Egypt and Macedonia and are all metaphors of the spirit of animal genes.

Moses and the other Old Testament writers were aware that God had another purpose for being. That purpose was spiritual. This purpose started to show up in the Old Testament after the first 17 books of the Bible. The spiritual behavior of God in his relation to the affairs of his people is what we will try to fathom from several quotes from Old Testament writers.

Genesis 6:3: "Then Jehovah said, 'My Spirit must not forever be disgraced in man, wholly evil as he is. I will give him 120 years to mend his ways.'"

This verse tells us several things. Moses and his God had to be consistent. Since Adam had already eaten the apple of "born-in-sin," all humankind had to be called "evil as he is." God will give humans 120 years to mend their ways. Such a statement shows Moses and his God to be severely amateurish when God-Christ the creator had been mending the ways of humans for over two million years. Of course, 3000 years ago Moses and his God did not know what had been happening to the human race through the gene during all this time.

The most striking concept that appears repeatedly in the Old Testament is the concept of adversaries: Moses' God versus humans and evil. We have to conclude that such a concept is forced upon Moses and his people by the strength of the spirit of God's goodness that longed for identification. It was a quality in the human soul that Christ as the first cause of all creation had by genetic evolution over a million years planted into the minds of all of us, versus the evils that plague us of the animal genes within us.

Moses here introduces two Gods that satisfy his program. He presents a God of Adam and Abraham, of power, anger, fear and vengeance—a spirit of antagonism modeled after Babylon, Egypt and Persia. The second God he now presents is a God who has a spirit. As we trace this God through the history of the Bible we find that God is the *numen summum bonum* (NSB), or spirit of supreme goodness, that God the creator—a creator as presented to us in Proverbs 8, John1, Colossians 1 and other scriptures—has genetically placed into every human soul. The spirit was beautifully etched by Jesus on the cross in the final stage of his dying process. He gave up not his body but his spirit, as stated in all four Gospels.

Everybody who accepts that last word of Jesus on the cross has added to his/her soul the spirit of Jesus that will live forever. That spirit of mercy and love, extended even to the prostitute at the well or to the homosexual at Berkeley and even to his enemies, and Jesus' lifestyle of a simple humble life, was so great that he willingly offered to be crucified for its importance.

We need to worship that God-spirit that he surrendered to our soul while on the cross. That spirit cannot be found anywhere else but in ourselves. It would therefore seem immoral to worship the cross and his blood, let alone the Virgin Mary—an idolatry—and thus not to concentrate completely and only on the NSB that Jesus gave to all human beings that will live forever in our psyches.

In summary, Genesis presents both a God of anger and a God who is a loving spirit. Against that scenario we present a God-Christ as one, as the first cause of all creation as presented by King Solomon in Proverbs, by John in John 1, by Paul in Colossians 1 and by Thomas Aquinas in the 13th century. This second concept of God-Christ as representing all that is good, which has been the ideal of activity of the Judeo-Christian community for 3000 years, is offered to us in the life and behavior of Jesus.

Exodus 35:21: "Those whose hearts were stirred by God's Spirit returned with their offerings of materials for the Tabernacle...." Not God, but God's NSB induced that religious activity.

Numbers 11:16a,17: "Then the Lord said to Moses, '....I will come down and talk with you there and I will take of the Spirit which is on you and will put it upon them also....'" We add this to other scriptures that tell us that God is a spirit, and that God's spirit can move from soul to soul. Moses' God of NSB is the Holy Spirit in genes that have given the genetic chain such quality during the last million years.

Numbers 11:25: "And the Lord came down in the Cloud and talked with Moses, and the Lord took of the Spirit that was upon Moses and put it upon the seventy elders, and when the Spirit rested upon them, they prophesied for some time." We see here the fakery that Moses had to use to satisfy the culture. God could not appear because he had no form. John 1:18: "No one has ever actually seen God...." Therefore Moses had to fake God's presence in a cloud. On Mount Sinai the fake was a cloud of fire; another time, it was a burning bush. Therefore, if God has no form to perceive by the senses, he has to be a spirit.

The transfer of spirits to the elders was not a physical act. The transfer of spirits must be a prayerful communion of spirits. Such a prayerful communication of God's spirit and the spirits of all persons can be universally accepted as an effective mode of meditation. The God-Christ DNA molecule has over the ages built a genetic chain that creates in all persons at birth the spiritual capacity to receive God's will to attain the perfection of the heaven concept.

Much talk exists among church people that so-and-so accepted Christ and therefore he is saved. What they should really say is that he found the spirit of Jesus in his own soul because it had been there all the time. Your salvation is in your own hands to receive when you pray for it in your soul long enough for that spirit to activate itself through meditation.

In Numbers 11:29, Moses says, "I only wish...the Lord would put his Spirit upon them all." After Moses returned to camp (31-32): "The Lord sent a wind that brought quail from the sea, and let them fall into the camp and all around it. As far as one could walk in a day in any direction, there were quail flying three or four feet above the ground. So the people caught and killed quail all that day and through the night and all the next day too! The least anyone gathered was 100 bushels." Then in his anger God kills these people (with a plague) for their greed.

Again we see the theologies of Moses and of Plato, i.e., a God of doing and a God of the spirit. This is the dualism of God and Moses; in fact, we see two beings working side by side. God is again the starting point of all being and activity. Such activity in the Bible is all rhetoric. Therefore in the aforementioned scriptures, when human activity becomes reality, that reality does not come through God but through his God-spirit of goodness (NSB) placed within the elders. In the 3000 years of Judeo-Christian religion, the rhetoric always starts with God's activity—a God who has never acquired a form and always ends up as a spirit, unseen, and "in his image" producing the action.

We propose to start with what "is." We know there is a creation process. That process we choose to call God as per King Solomon, John, Paul and Thomas Aquinas. That God we see, hear, feel and taste all around us. That God, in one with Christ according to John and Paul, is the first cause of the three phases of the creation process. God as the creator has been universally accepted by theological thought from the beginning.

Here we need to introduce another concept, that of several incomprehensibles. Time is incomprehensible as to when it began and when it ends. Space is incomprehensible as to where in our universe it begins and where it ends. The basic cause of the DNA molecule with its genetic chains of chromosomes is incomprehensible, and so is what produces the smarts of the gene in its creation directives. God has always been considered to be incomprehensible. Therefore we propose to assume that all these incomprehensibles are made of the same stuff. They are "one being" and they exist in unison as God. God is solving the incomprehensible mysteries that science cannot handle.

The creation process of what "is" comes in three phases. First is the inorganic process, in which are all the elements listed in our chemistry textbooks. In the universe they are found as galaxies, stars, planets, satellites and debris. On planet Earth the inorganic creation process presents the atmosphere, the seas, the land and mountains. If we follow Newton's Law of Conservation of Matter and Energy, then this phase of the creation has no beginning and no ending—one of God's incomprehensibles.

The second phase of the creation process is organic. This phase in our present cosmos is scientifically estimated to be about four billion years along in the creation process from its inception. The active agent here is the God-Christ-DNA molecule of the genetic chain of chromosomes that executes every detail in the organic creation process of plants, animals and humans.

The third phase of the process, known as the culture phase of creation, was superimposed on the organic phase of the process during the mammal stage of the creation of animals. At that point in time about three million years ago, the God-Christ-DNA molecule of genetic action introduced the psyche into our ancestors, the mammals. Inherited physical characteristics have been observed to change over generations as they are affected by interaction with the environment. In scientific terms, change resulting from either a phenotype addition to genotype-environmental interaction or from mutation is the basic mode of genetic evolution of us human beings.

The psyche introduced into our animal ancestors has for all these ages grown to include our soul, mind and intelligence. God's spirit, or NSB, in the human soul became so strong 3000 years ago that a character like Moses was acceptable. Moses created God in his image (imagination). However, Moses turned the concept "in his image" upside down to be acceptable. Thus Moses had God create man in God's image. Again, we must state that human beings, *in toto*, have created their own God to satisfy their beliefs.

Two more concepts need to be made clear. First, the word "God" in this book includes Christ since they are made of the same stuff but more authentic; as John said, "Before anything else existed, there was Christ, with God" (John 1:1-2). Paul developed this in Colossians 1:15-17 (see "Creation"). These verses tell us several things. "For his [Christ's] own use" and speaking of the unseen spirit world denotes that the Christ-DNA molecule started the psyche with the soul in it. That change from mammals to humans is in full operation forever. Also, Paul does not say Christ was active in the beginning. He says Christ was there before God made anything at all. We credit God-Christ, as did Thomas Aquinas, as the first cause of all creation—another one of God's incomprehensible secrets.

This first cause of God-Christ in the inorganic phase of the creation process has no beginning. This is so because in physics the Law of Conservation of Energy and Matter tells us the inorganic universe has always been there. Such a concept is another of God's incomprehensible secrets, as is time, space and the smarts of the gene of the DNA genetic chain of chromosomes. It then follows that we use the name God and Christ interchangeably.

If we read the scriptures literally, then Christ and Jesus are two different beings. According to John and Paul, God-Christ is the first cause of the creation process. Christ and God belong to the unseen, hence the spirit. Jesus was human-born, and the Christ-DNA molecule had, through the genetic chain of chromosomes, created Jesus with a perfect God-spirit through the genes of Joseph and Mary.

When Jesus was dying on the cross and gave up his spirit, that spirit, surrounded by his teaching, lifestyle and personal choice to be crucified, transferred automatically into the psyche of every human being. Every human has the free will and personal responsibility to find that spirit of Jesus in his very own soul. In the Bible, Christ and God are metaphors of the Holy Spirit. Jesus was a human being, an actor of the Holy Spirit—Jesus is not a metaphor. Such a transfer of the Christ-spirit from Jesus to us genetically is called genotype-phenotype environmental (Jesus giving his spirit to us) interaction. Such interaction can actually be demonstrated in the laboratory of science.

And now we come once more to the hard questions. Why should we believe the concepts presented here? Science has many problems and uncertainties; how can science be credible? Judeo-Christian beliefs have given us so much meaning and hope in life, so why give them all up?

The last question can be answered first in that we give up none of the NSB of God, Christ or Jesus. The only changes are the dynamics of the spirit. Basically God, Christ and Jesus as savior are spiritual entities. Entities without physical essence can be found only in the souls of humankind. Heaven is not a place but a concept of perfection. Hell is not a place but a concept of evil such as situations in Rwanda or Haiti. Sin is part of our animal heritage, and to overcome such evil we must find the spirit of Jesus in our minds to overcome the evil of our animal genes within us.

On the question of belief: We can believe in Christ's creation process in the three phases leading to our psyches loaded with good spirits because we can see and feel this creativity in operation around us every day. How can science be credible when we see all its uncertainties? We need to place all these problems in perspective. The inorganic creation process has gone on forever. The organic process has been active for four billion years. The culture phase of the creation process, which is the introduction of the psyche to form humans out of mammals, has traveled more than three million years. The credible study of the Christ-genetic creation process is less than 100 years old. The odds are four billion to 100 or 40 million to one. This perspective presents us with adequate results to prove science as credible in detailing much of Christ's creation process as it is progressing every day.

Paul says in Colossians that Christ uses all these findings "to his own glory." Here is one: The two "bubble babies" were genetically cured of their immune deficiency and are now going to school like other children, as we will relate elsewhere.

Behavior genetics has been demonstrated in the drosophila (fruit fly) with a generation cycle of 10 days compared to a 25-year life cycle of humanity. In other words, you can accomplish in a drosophila in one year what would take 1000 years in a human. An insect can be genetically engineered to create a psyche that reacts either for or completely against accepted sex behaviors. Genes have been introduced into drosophila that made its male completely asexual. That gene insertion completely reversed the evil behavior of drosophila.

The May 1996 issue of *Nature* reports that at Johns Hopkins University a killer gene was added to a mouse, which then repeatedly killed all mice in its cage. Soon scientists will be able to identify that killer gene in human beings and then eliminate it from the human genome.

Dr. Hall and Dr. Stillman created a human being in a petri dish at George Washington University. In their in-vitro lab they cloned a human embryo. All of this was reported in the November 8, 1993 issue of *Time*. We add to this the mitotic DNA cloning by Dr. Wilmut in Scotland in 1996 with an adult mammal, a sheep, as donor of the DNA, to produce a calf. These two events happened in less than 10 years in the culture creation process that has operated for more than one million years. These events merit serious consideration for each of us.

Numbers 27:18: "The Lord replied, 'Go and get Joshua (son of Nun) who has the Spirit in him....'" Here God and Moses talk to each other as two buddies, and seemingly God wants his spirit to trust Joshua as the leader of Israel as Moses was preparing his own demise. The "Spirit in him" makes us read beyond the rhetoric to the real qualifying requirement as to what is in the soul of the person. It tells us where the values in every human lie.

This dualism of God as an activist and God as a spirit goes back more than 2000 years to the philosophies and theologies of Plato and Aristotle, a dualism of reality versus mythology, rationalism versus beliefs, and *Naturwissenschaft* versus *Geistwissenschaft*. We are trying to put both concepts in perspective. Aristotle taught 2300 years ago that the human soul alone led to a full life. Such life Jesus gave us later.

I Kings 22: 22-25 presents a scenario of communication of the spirits of Zedekiah and Micaiah concerning the strategy of war against Syria to recover the city of Ramoth-Gilead. One angel told the Lord: "'I will go as a flying spirit in the mouths of all his [Ahab's] prophets.' And the Lord said, 'That will do it....'" In response, Zedekiah said, "'When did the spirit of the Lord leave me and speak to you?'....And Micaiah replied, 'You will have the answer to your question when you find yourself hiding in an inner room.'" The concept of communication of spirits between each other and God's NSB instead of man praying to a God out there somewhere is the cornerstone of this new theology. It is meditation as prayer for churches of tomorrow.

In this theology God's spirit of goodness resides in every soul of all humanity. This NSB has been introduced in our psyche by the God-Christ-DNA process of creation over a million years. In the above planning of war by the armies of Israel and Judah against Syria to recover the city of Ramoth-Gilead, God, Ahab and Jehoshaphat do all the talking. The spirit determines all the action as it passes back and forth between Zedekiah and Micaiah.

To accept prayer by us as an interaction of God's NSB in the souls of all human beings is difficult for Western Christianity to attain. This is because we have for thousands of years prayed to a God in heaven. We have held on to the idea, albeit it was very fuzzy, that God had somehow continued to be a being of material essence and worked in an imaginary place called heaven. God responded metaphysically somehow to solve all our problems here on earth if we prayed to him who "art in heaven."

A new theology says that all good things that happen to human beings comes through the efforts of God's NSB, which appears in the souls of all humans. The word "God" is used here as a connotation in the Christian community of a spirit of supreme goodness. This new theology based on the human soul as the basis of God's *numen summum bonum* has been simmering since 400 BC. Greek theologian-philosophers Socrates,

Plato and Aristotle taught during Old Testament times that the human soul was the source of all goodness.

In recent years that simmer has turned up the heat. We have prayed in the conventional pattern to God to solve our problems of rape, crime, murders and legalized mass war killings. But God could not come down from heaven to help us much. All these circumstances are forcing us to go where the real strength of God's goodness lies, and that is our soul. We are finally forced to carry out our own responsibility. In the creation process God gave us the power and wisdom to solve all our problems. All we need is the motivation for our spirits to become responsible through meditation.

II Kings 2:15: "'The spirit of Elijah rests upon Elisha!'" After Elijah and Elisha crossed the dry Jordan (Elijah struck the river dry with his cloak), Elisha asked Elijah to give him all his prophetic power as his successor because Elijah was preparing for his own demise. Thereupon, the Bible says, "The spirit...rests upon Elisha!" This is a bare-fact transfer of the spirit of the soul of one prophet to the mind of another.

It seems appropriate at this point to define some earmarks of a spirit. First of all, spirit has no connection with the common perception of a mystic. Spirit is the vital essence or animating force in living organisms, especially man, often considered divine in origin; the part of a human that is incorporal and invisible, characterized by intelligence, personality, self-consciousness and will—the mind. Here is the capacity to carry out the will of God's goodness. At this point we feel Old Testament language is not capable of doing justice to this effort.

Nehemiah 9:20: "'You sent your good Spirit to instruct them....'" This is the climax of a nationwide revival celebration praising the Israelites' unseen God who had delivered them from Egypt, the wilderness, and other domination over 1000 years. However the real cap that had sustained them through all this suffering was not the unseen God but God's NSB that the God-Christ-DNA creation process had placed into each Israelite soul over a period of a million years. This sustained each one of them. That spirit came to them through meditation—continuous and contemplative thought, thinking about doing, planning.

Job 4:12: "This truth was given me in secret, as though whispered in my ear. It came in a nighttime vision as others slept." 4:15-16: "'As a spirit passed before my face—my hair stood up on end. I felt the spirit's presence, but couldn't see it standing there.'" Job presents a common problem all of us human beings have. Genetically we have the potential to be perfect in our soul. Like Job, we might find it by way of our dreams. Very often we find it hard to find the Jesus truth.

Job 32:9: "'Rather, it is the spirit in a man, the breath of the Almighty [the first cause] which makes him intelligent.'" Here Job finds himself in a court of law in the form of Elihu the Buzite, who seeks from Job a confession of sin and acceptance of punishment by God. The accusers were older patriarchs who knew everything. Elihu was a younger patriarch who came to Job's defense. 32:9: "But it is not mere age that makes men wise. Rather it is the spirit in a man, the breath of the Almighty which makes him intelligent." We know now that God the Almighty as first cause of the creation process gave that breath millions of years ago. What was there in Job's soul for ages, he found by way of a dream. Meditation takes place in Job's dreams.

Psalm 31:5,7: "Into your hand I commit my spirit." "...you have listened to my troubles and have seen the crisis in my soul." In this context David feared his enemies; therefore his spirit wants to be joining hands with the spirit of God's goodness to strengthen the spirit in his mind. The crisis in his psyche, science tells us, is conflict between the animal genes and the good genes.

Psalm 104:30: "Then you send your Spirit, and new life is born [created] to replenish all the living of the earth." The context in this verse is a response to David's worry as to what would happen when God takes time off for all the animals under his care. David did not know that God as first cause of the creation process determined billions of years ago what would happen to all life on that day when God started the laws of the creation process that will go on forever. Also, it is the spirit, not God, that directs all processes. David's spirit in his soul will have learned by now that the fate of all living organisms including man was determined by God the first cause four billion years ago when the gene acquired directives through genotype-phenotype environmental interaction.

Psalm 143:10: "....God, lead me in good paths, for your Spirit is good." The writer is asking God for help and salvation from evil. He says God can do so because God's spirit is good. This suggests that without God's spirit, God would be no good, or can one say that God does not exist without his spirit of goodness? We are trying to answer that problem by reality between the metaphor and the real spirit.

Proverbs 20:27: "A man's conscience [the Bible commentary says "spirit"] is the Lord's searchlight, exposing his hidden motives." Here the wise author identifies the unseen spirit in our soul that determines who we are. It is so important for each one of us to search our mind to find out who we are. The value of a human being resides totally in the quality of the contents of our psyche. Without the soul I have only animal value, fit to be slaughtered like any other animal.

Ecclesiastes 11:5: "God's ways are as mysterious as the pathway of the wind, and as the manner in which a human's spirit is infused into the little body of a baby while it is yet in its mother's womb." Some of these wise sayings suggest very strongly that the author knew of the thinkers of Athens, Greece, namely Socrates and his followers. They taught that the spirit of God's goodness came into the human soul through the creation process. The verse also helps me in placing God's name to the existing incomprehensibles, here especially to the incomprehensibility of the "smarts" of the genes that infused God's spirit of goodness into the soul of the intrauterine developing fetus in the genetic chain of chromosomes. The creation process follows a genetic blueprint of ages past as stated by "Miss" Wisdom in Proverbs 8.

Isaiah 11:2: "And the Spirit of the Lord shall rest upon him, the Spirit of wisdom, understanding, counsel and might; the Spirit of knowledge and of the fear of the Lord." These are sayings Isaiah received from God through visions. Here he presents the messiah not as a body to be crucified but as a purveyor of the spirit of wisdom, understanding, counsel and might, the essence of the "fear of the Lord" of knowledge. Thereupon he drifts into the conditional reflexes of the times of strong, angry armies taking joy in their victory of destroying all sinners. In those verses we have a head-on confrontation in an atmosphere of violence of an angry God who kills all human beings thought to be sinners and the promise of a messiah who will rule with mercy and love for everybody including sinners and enemies. Actually, Isaiah here presents the characteristic of fear inherited from our animal ancestry in those who have no developed psyche. He also presents the human being in whom the psyche infused by the God-Christ-DNA molecule is in charge.

The violent God of the Old Testament is presenting the behavior of our ancestors the animals. The animal has instinct only, without a developed psyche. The animal instinct has for hundreds of million years been interested in only one thing, and that is survival of its species. That instinct brings with it several characteristics. First, killing other species is routine for survival. The male dominates the family and especially his female mate. He rapes his mate by force when it is convenient and especially when she is in heat. Members of a species will not kill members of their own species exept when it concerns a male showoff who fights for dominance of his harem. When threatened, he becomes violent, and to him, killing is not evil.

Therefore in the hidden recesses of the DNA molecule we carry the regressive directives of our unpredictable animal ancestors. Each DNA molecule with its genetic chain of chromosomes carries millions of directives in our creation process. We are destined to carry these regressive directives in our genetic chain for future generations to come. They have to be overcome by God's spirit of goodness within us.

Even as I was writing this, a news report was that O.J. Simpson allegedly sliced his ex-wife's throat and also killed a friend. If so, obviously O.J. did not call upon the Jesus spirit of mercy but by his own free will reportedly let the animal instinct that is in all of us take over his behavior. Two primary animal behavior patterns surfaced in his alleged action, sex and killing. That suggests the necessity to domesticate the animal genes in every human male on planet Earth.

The animal gene of the orgasm that comes with copulation is the prime mover of the sex drive, especially in the human male. This gene was necessary for our animal ancestors for the survival of their species. Today that evil gene is unnecessary because we are already overpopulated. The evil gene can be treated in several ways:

1. As related in connection with drosophila, an opposing gene can be introduced into every human cell by a virus transfer that will neutralize that evil gene.

2. After experimentation with the killer gene of the Johns Hopkins University mice, an enzyme was located that can kill the gene by cutting the "H" atom bond of its nucleotides (the interferon enzyme in leukemia is an example).

3. The evil sex gene can be neutralized by surgical castration of all

males to domesticate males for cohabitation (as happened with the "Heaven's Gate" people).

In the April 1, 1997 *Wichita Eagle* appeared a report by the *Los Angeles Times* and the *Washington Post* that Dr. John Harrington of Case Western Reserve University, Cleveland, Ohio, had created an artificial chromosome gene. Scientists now expect a made-to-order gene (*Time*, June 12, 1995) that could, for example, be infused into an O.J. Simpson cell to change character and behavior completely. God is slowly coming down from heaven and living with us as the DNA molecule, and when he closes shop in heaven he will deincarnate resurrection and give us back our Jesus of love, mercy, forgiveness, humility and a simple lifestyle.

I remember at home on the farm that the family bull who sired all our cows was so domineering that we dared not enter his corral lest we be mauled. He raped his cows anytime he felt like it, and if he was disciplined, he became violent.

According to court records in the Simpson story, for eight years of their married life, O.J. allegedly acted out this animal instinct. One day he was threatened by an attorney and became violent; when people act instinctively, such violence can bring about killings that are acceptable as a solution. In Christian Fundamentalist jargon, he was not saved because he had not accepted Christ at the altar. In reality he had the potential of the love and mercy of Jesus in his soul; only at one moment it allegedly escaped him.

Therefore the problem becomes: Who are we? We have to decide daily who we are. We can't look to the cross and the blood of Jesus to help us. Instead, the priorities in our behavior in our psyche alone will save us. We are by our own will able to create the perfection of heaven or the evil of hell according to how we sort out these qualities in our mind. Having bared our soul to the depth of the moment, we can ask religious activity and the church's activity to continue to help us sort out in our soul God's NSB and the Jesus-spirit of love and mercy. The church's activity helps us to sort out our own spirit as it visits with other spirits.

However, church activity in the world of Western Christianity has an even more important role to play. This activity helps the environment to form phenotype interaction with the genotype to grow more genes that infuse God's NSB in our psyche and soul. The phenotype is the aggregate of genetic characteristics visibly manifested by an organism through environmental influences. The organism is us, the environment is Western Christianity, and together these two elements produce genes going into our offspring to have a stronger, more stable soul function. This spirit of God's goodness has been operating for more than two million years through genotype-phenotype environmental interaction, as the genetic mode of action in all of us.

Isaiah 34:16: "...and His spirit will make it all come true." Isaiah comes to this conclusion after imagining in great detail how the unseeen God will destroy Edom. To clear his conscience of a guilt feeling for such beastiallity of his God, he states who God really is—a spirit (a metaphor for our evil animal genes and our good Jesus genes).

Isaiah 42:1b: "I have put my spirit upon him [Jesus]; he will reveal justice to the nations of the world." Isaiah continues the above by conceding that the unseen God of Israel, the imaginary God, had not revealed justice like the spiritual God in the form of Jesus, who would correct all that fakery. Again God is a spirit, perceptually a spirit of goodness, as a metaphor.

42: 5: "...and gives life and breath and spirit to everyone in all the world...." This beautiful account cancels out Abraham's God, who brutally destroyed Edom, and brings out the real God as a spirit of goodness.

Since we have used the word "goodness" so often, one has to ask: What is the spirit of goodness? What is goodness? The first response is that any language is inadequate to delineate completely the qualities of goodness. Some of the parameters of goodness are love, truth, forgiveness, equanimity, tranquility, hope, mercy and compassion. In 42:1-7 Isaiah presents a system of justice which, by influence, has not existed during the rule of the God of Abraham, Isaac and Jacob. Having established justice, he adds the more important qualities of the soul. Isaiah seems to have a feeling that 2500 years later we will have what he predicted as the soul qualities that the Christ-DNA creation process had put into every human being, this quality of God's NSB, the quality of Jesus' love and mercy. Isaiah seems to be relieved that not much longer will he have to fake God's Noah flood or the destruction of Edom as a cure for sinners.

Also, in this scripture God passed his *NSB* into the coming Jesus to lead us to the correct behavior. Jesus transferred his spirit to us most effectively when, in the process of dying on the cross, his last words in all the

Gospels are recorded as: "I surrender my spirit." Any human who will seriously meditate under all these circumstances will be subjected to adding that spirit into his own soul. We should not be concentrating on any importance of the cross or the blood of Jesus. We want his spirit of humility, simple lifestyle, mercy and love, even love of enemies, to enter us. We can't rely on the metaphors of his crucifixion nor on the metaphors of God or Christ.

Isaiah 61:1: "The spirit of the Lord God is upon me...to bring good news to the suffering...." All God can give of himself to his servant who will bring good news is his spirit. In this context there is no mention of the son of God; the spirit is everything to Jesus and to us. This is what the God metaphor gives to the Jesus spirit.

Ezekiel 2:2: "And the Spirit entered into me as He spoke, and set me on my feet." Ezekiel was a 30-year-old priest in Babylonian exile when he had a vision-meditation from God. The vision came to him in the most outlandish, complicated forms of fire and multiple-headed persons. After all the exotic rhetoric, the substance that came out of all that was the appearance of God, the spirit. The God-spirit was not a matter of belief but a force to action. The God-spirit had been in the human soul for a million years, but because Ezekiel had been praying to that spirit within, he found it and it activated him.

Ezekiel 3:12: "Then the Spirit lifted me up and the glory of the Lord began to move away...." 3:10: "...let all my words sink deep into your own heart first; listen to them carefully for yourself. Then, afterward, go to your own people in exile, and...tell them...." Paraphrasing these instructions more than 2000 years later, we must find this spirit in our soul. We must anchor this spirit within us securely enough so that it can cover any and all animal evil that will come along, remembering that we will always have the presence of the spirit of our animal instincts to be overcome within us.

Ezekiel 3:14: "The Spirit lifted me up and took me away to Tel Ahib...." After this lifting of Ezekiel by the spirit, God comes back in the same format we see throughout the Old Testament, of fear and punishment by death. Ezekiel will die if he does not present the right message to the Jews or the Jews shall die if they disobey the right messages. In today's circumstances that kind of threat means a schizophrenic life.

Ezekiel 8:3: "And the Spirit lifted me up into the sky and seemed to transport me to Jerusalem...." Jerusalem seemed symbolic of heaven above. From above, God directed Ezekiel to look down, and again God pointed out to the prophet the sins of his people. Again the God of fear and cruelty had no other solution but to kill all sinners—the gene of our animal spirit.

Ezekiel 11:1: "Then the spirit lifted me and brought me over to the east gate of the Temple...." 11:5: "Then the spirit of the Lord came upon me and told me to say: 'The Lord says to the people....'" 11:6: "You have murdered endlessly...." The animal genes again killed. 11:10: "You will be slaughtered...."

Ezekiel 18:30b, 31: "Oh, turn from your sins while there is yet time. Put them behind you and receive a new heart and a new spirit." Of all the God-spirits that Ezekiel had in his vision, this one had real substance in it. This verse tells us that we have the capacity to build on this spirit more new spirits in our souls genetically in God's creation process.

Ezekiel 36:26: "'I will...put a new spirit within you.'" 37:14: "'I will put my Spirit into you....'" Repeatedly Ezekiel was told by God that God's spirit was "within you." That spirit was put there, unknown to the writer and his God, during the culture phase of the creation process which distinguished humanity from its animal ancestors in the gene of the psyche. All this happened in the million years of the culture creation process.

The Ezekiel story is a drama of three beings. Ezekiel was the producer and the writer. His two characters were God the actor and God the spirit. It seems he was obcessed with the spirit. The angry God did things, but the spirit of God always came up with loftier things.

Ezekiel died as all the rest of us will, but the God-spirit kept right on growing by way of the God-DNA molecule's culture creation process. Spirits exist in human souls that live forever from generation to generation. The God-spirit represents the gene's "blueprint" laid out by "Miss" Wisdom of King Solomon, which has elevated humanity from the animal stage to where we are now, and this God-spirit will keep on growing forever in the psyches of all human beings. Creationary evolution is an ongoing genetic process.

The God of Abraham, Isaac and Jacob, created by Moses in each other's image, died with Moses and the rest of the prophets. Jesus completely negated (killed) the God of anger, fear and vengance who, as genetic cleansing, killed in masses all human beings who opposed Israel. Jesus did all this by his God-spirit of love, forgiveness and mercy. A God of muscle who does things has to reach a demise like the end of the organic process of any living thing. The God-spirit is permanently engraved into the millions of directives that function in each DNA molecule of the genetic chain of chromosomes, of which there are millions in our bodies. These genes that have in their blueprint the directives of God's NSB reproduce themselves every time a human baby is born. They have done so for about three million years, and they will continue to do so forever as long as our species survives. They cannot die; they are as etched in stone. They personify our immortality in succeeding generations.

Daniel 4:9: "I know that the spirit of the holy gods is in you and no mystery is too great for you to solve." Here Nebuchadnezzar asks Daniel, whom he affectionately named Belteshazzar, to interpret his dreams. Our soul has all the tools to solve all problems through meditation.

Daniel 4:18: "'But you can tell me, for the spirit of the holy gods is in you.'" After the experience of Shadrach, Meshach and Abednego surviving in the fiery furnace, Nebachudnezzar, king of Babyon and at that time the greatest king in the world, had designated Daniel as chief magistrate of his court. When we consider that the Christ-DNA culture creation process had operated for three million years, we can assume that the God-spirit level of King Nebuchadnezzar's soul was equivalent to that of any other human of his time. Therefore even the king of Babylon, who had conquered Judah with his army and destroyed Jerusalem, was capable of digging into his soul and asking for the God-spirit by meditating as Daniel did.

Now we come to a pause on our highway to ask: Who is God? After all, God is our main subject for our genetic life. Two connotations in the Judeo-Christian culture fit into my discussion. They are the God of incomprehensible majesty as first cause of the genetic culture creation process and God as the spirit of goodness of Jesus.

In our human existence we have several situations that are totally incomprehensible, which I want to call "incomprehensibles." One is space. Can we comprehend where space begins and where it ends as we look at all the stars? We know we can see stars whose light took a miilion years to reach us. In mathematics we would say that space reaches its ends at infinity. In cosmology we are compelled to call the end of space incomprehensible.

Time! When did time begin? Moses thought it began about 4000 years ago. Science indicates there is no beginning and no ending. Time has always been there. To us, time is another incomprehensible. These two burdens we will have to load onto someone's shoulders. Our God alone is capable of carrying the mysteries of the incomprehensibles

The whole creation process is full of incomprehensibles. When did it start? What was the chief cause of the inorganic process that probably has no beginning and no ending? What caused an organic cell to appear on an inorganic base? And most important to us human beings, who or what gave the genes the "smarts" to infuse the psyche into mammals to start the creation process, to create us humans from our ancestors the animals?

The most complicated incomprehensible is "God." Who is "he"? No one has ever seen God, according to John 1:18. Moses says he saw God on Mount Sinai in a cloud of fire, thunder and lightning, or in the burning bush. But to be sure he would not be prosecuted, he warned his people not to snoop too closely lest God would kill them at Mount. Sinai.

We have identified God as the spirit of goodness in applying all the preceding Old Testament passages. God as the spirit of goodness did not show up in print until human beings like Moses appeared, more than two million years after the culture evolution started. God's spirit did not exist until there was a human soul that could host the idea of a God-spirit of goodness. If I were to ask the mule on our farm about the God-spirit, he would just look at me with no understanding. King Solomon, John, Paul, and Thomas Aquinas give us a second identification label for God, which for short is "first cause." "First cause" covers all the incomprehensibles. We can't find anybody but God who is responsible for time, space, the creation process and even the smart behavior of the genes in the DNA molecule in the evolution of humans. Again, God is (a) the spirit of goodness in our soul (NSB) and (b) first cause of all the incomprehensibles.

The conclusion of this Old Testament chapter is that the God spirit can live only in the human spirit and nowhere else. We have reviewed many Old Testament events as they took place, and in no case did God-Christ roll up his sleeves and physically solve our problem. Throughout the Bible, it was always the God-spirit that was activated. We assume humanity has the knowledge that a spirit cannot live on a fence post nor in any animal. The Jesus-spirit can surface only in the human soul by meditation.

Incarnation and eschatology are part of the Bible drama that dramatizes the imagining of how the God-spirit revealed itself in human existence. This dramatization has been very helpful in picturing for us the activity of the God-spirit of the gene of the DNA molecule for a million years. But the picture is only a metaphor of the spirit. Theology and science tell us that the picture of deism is not the real thing. The real thing, instead of deism, is the Jesus-spirit of that picture living in our soul.

This concept was strengthened at Easter in 1996 when *Time*, *Newsweek*, and *U.S. News and World Report* had full front-cover pictures of Jesus, accompanied by an eight-page feature article questioning the veracity of the physical resurrection of Jesus to become Christ. Science (*Wissenschaft*) identifies the physical resurrection of Jesus to become Christ as a metaphor for the gene of the holy spirit of Jesus living in us.

THE HEBREWS—
A QUASI-JEWISH NATION

The Hebrew nation and its theology as given to us in the Bible came into being with the decline and demise of all the cosmologies of the Orient (land east of the Mediterranean). The Hebrew home was finally a strip of land called Palestine between the eastern end of the Mediterranean Sea and the desert. Palestine was 150 miles long and less than 50 miles wide. It has poor, nonproductive limestone soil as my wife Mariam and I noted while walking over that area in 1950.

The Hebrews were a conglomerate of the descendants of Abraham who had intermarried with people of the neighborhood. It has been postulated that the Hebrews inherited a long hooked nose from non-Semitic Hittites from the North through intermarriage.

Enslavement of the Hebrews started after Jacob sent his sons to Egypt to buy grain from prosperous Egyptians, with the result that the family joined Joseph in Egypt. The Israelites spent 400 years in slavery there.

As a Hebrew infant Moses was taken in by the daughter of Pharaoh (King) Ramses II when he was floating in a basket on the Nile. Moses was trained into maturity in the Egyptian king's court during the latter part of the second millennium B.C. With that Egyptian training in hand, Moses became the leader of the journey of the Israelites to Canaan, a journey involving the miraculous crossing of the Red Sea. For 40 years Moses wandered around the Sinai desert trying to lead the people into the Promised Land. Joshua finally accomplished that.

During the years of wandering Moses created the Old Testament God of the Bible who created us humans "in his image." Factually it will always remain unclear whose image came first, i.e. the image of God or the image of Moses. Or can we say flat out that Moses was imagining a God speaking to him?

In this connection it is significant that King Hammurabi of Babylon (where the Jews were later in captivity) records a precursor of the event in which Moses talks to God on Mount Sinai. Hammurabi's Code, or laws for Babylon—the Ten Commandments in more detail—are recorded in the cuneiform writing of the Sumerians on a stone shaft now in a museum. At the top is sculpted the Sun God with a cloud of fire from his shoulder, handing the tablets of the law to King Hammurabi. This artifact is dated 20th century B.C. Many centuries later this identical scenario was presented as Moses with God and the Ten Commandments on Mount Sinai.

The Bible records God as acting and speaking to the prophets many times in antiquity as long as such activity seemed believable in the religions of the Middle East. But when such events became unbelievable, God quit talking to his people in that way.

The Hebrew nation never really reached the status of an empire. Historians estimate that early Hebrews wandered in the area for more than 200 years, from 1400 to 1200 B.C. They were then joined by the slaves from Egypt and entered the Promised Land. Meeting the Canaanites who lived there, they conquered some of them.

Two groups of Hebrew people evolved over time, Israel in North Palestine and Judah in the South. As recorded elsewhere, the writing of the Old Testament of the Bible uses sources from each of the two areas, called E and J. Each group's stories, although different in theology, were combined by Old Testament writers into the Old Testament story of the Bible.

The E material comes from Israel, whose people were more religious; in fact the Bible relates that Abraham had a social evening meal with God. The J material from Judah presented a more combative God in the form of the warrior Yahweh.

These two Hebrew kingdoms never actually qualified as Oriental kingdoms. Nearly always they were servants of other ruling kingdoms that in succession reigned over the entire region: Egypt, Babylon, Assyria, Persia, Greece and finally Rome. The Hebrews had no writing at first; they started recording in cuneiform and switched to the Phoenician Greek alphabets. This did not happen until after Assyria released them as Babylonian prisoners about 550 B.C. Then they began to record the E and J stories.

Technically the Hebrews became a kingdom when Saul became the first king of Israel. Theologically the little nations of Israel and Judah worshiped a warrior God, Yahweh, and were either fighting outsiders or each other. After more than 4000 years Israel is still fighting. Almost every day someone is killed in what was ancient Palestine. Much of this killing is promoted by religious bigotry.

Such behavior places doubt on the credibility of the Judeo-Christian religion. God and Christ out yonder somewhere have always been in trouble. Killing on a religious basis is between Jews and Muslims. In Sarajevo, it is between Orthodox Catholics and Muslims. In Northern Ireland it is between Roman Catholic Christians and Protestant Christians. We can cancel this bigoted killing by each individual worshiping God in his own soul instead of depending on the pulpit of a specific church.

Thus Hebrew culture has had a very spotted history of violence along with other religious groups. Maybe the gods should be universally discounted as deities to reach peace.

INCARNATION— EMBODYING SPIRIT IN FORM

The three Gods of the monotheistic religiosities, Yahweh, Christ, and Allah, have always been a part of the heaven-God concept.

The DNA gene infused a psyche into our animal body that called for a God of immortality, omnipotence, omniscience, beneficence and divinity as a metaphor. The Bible presented all those connotations in visual form for perception by the senses of uninformed psyches of human beings 2000 years ago.

Bible writers created the form of a resurrected ruling Christ in heaven with certain tenets that we had to believe or assume to be true or real. Those tenets are incarnation, eschatology, teleology with creation *ex nihilo* and a finis of apocalypse. These tenets of the Bible story of a God-Christ ruling from heaven will be discussed separately.

In our quest for who God is, incarnation gave us a workable answer. Incarnation is the assumption of bodily form, especially human form; bodily form assumed by a deity or supernatural being, a person, animal, or thing, in which some ideal, quality, or abstracted idea is incarnated. The Bible and the Koran of Islam relate the incarnation of the *numen summum bonum*, or NSB (spirit of supreme goodness), in the soul of our psyche that the gene of the DNA molecule has been infusing into our animal body for three million years.

In prehistoric times when there was no writing, the incarnation of God as the spirit of all goodness was very simple. It consisted of mundane elements of folklore. These could be a mountain like the Mount Olympus of the god Zeus, or a cloud of fire for Moses on Mount Sinai.

In the early 1900s, Pope Pius XI appointed Wilhelm Schmidt, an anthropologist who founded the Anthropos Institute of Vienna, to record the concepts that prehistoric people had of who God was. He wrote many volumes on *Ursprung der Gottesidee* (Origin of the Idea of God). He researched the Pygmies and indigenous people of Brazil, India and Tibet. In his 1912 writings he concluded that God-incarnation concepts were simple folklore forms that were extremely variable and non-controversial (they are reviewed elsewhere).

About 4000 years ago when cosmologies of Egypt, Assyria, Babylonia, Persia and Greece brought forth the cuneiform and alphabet writing of the Phoenicians and Greeks, the concept of incarnated gods was spelled out in writing all over the ancient world. The early incarnation of the NSB gene was polytheistic, but influenced by the pharaoh of Egypt, people drifted to monotheism. Their incarnations were rather nonspecific and showed great variation. Moses, who was trained and educated in the king's court of Egypt, to some extent incarnated his God after the Egyptian monotheistic God.

The Moses-God of the first millennium B.C. started the God of the Jews, Christians and Muslims. Believers in all three religions of the God of Abraham presented by Moses are basically worshiping a deity created by incarnation. They have to have faith to believe that a spirit of supreme goodness can be worshiped only after it has been incarnated into a form of living, personal, active God called either Yahweh or Christ or Allah. All three religions have mechanized the NSB (*numen summum bonum*) into a God of form who rewards much praying to that God in a place called heaven.

Such was the cosmology 2000 years ago. Today we know about our genetic makeup. Today, if the NSB in our soul can overcome genetic traits of the animal desires within us, we are already in heaven. We then, as a result of such overcoming of our animal desires, feel good about ourselves. In reality, we are then in the only heaven that exists or will ever exist. To look for a mystical heaven on the firmament as two billion people on earth do today is to miss the real heaven here on earth—and that is tragic. Our ego cannot admit that we are only a minute segment in the genetic evolution process of the creation of human beings.

This whole concept reminds me of a sign in the Netherlands along the road from Amsterdam to the international airport. It says, "Guk net in de luft—guk op den weg." Look not in the air—look on the road."

Judaism, Islam and Christianity all contain incarnations of God's NSB that the genetic creation process has infused into every human being over a period of some three million years. They are metaphors of the spirit in the Bible and the Koran. Many Jews, Muslims, and Christians believe in incarnated Gods who intervene in the processes of our daily affairs, especially in response to worship and prayer offered to them by human beings. The Bible and the Koran indicate that belief in and worship of the intervening God and his activity will be rewarded by a place in heaven with everlasting life in bliss. Believers think that their God alone can save from damnation to the fire of hell. The eschatology of death, resurrection and judgment to heaven or hell is essentially the same in all three religions, starting in the Garden of Eden. However, Muslims do not buy the born-in-sin idea of the Christians as etched in stone.

Evidence of psychogenesis in animal bodies in our culture is Australopithecus in Africa, who lived there about three million years ago. This fossil evidence is on display for any of us to look at. The evolution of the human with a soul can be traced step by step from Australopithecus to Homo Habilis, Homo Erectus, Neanderthal Man and Cro-Magnon, who had all the characteristics of us Homo Sapiens. (Further details of how fossil findings show how we evolved from mammals to primates to humans are related elsewhere.)

After the genetic process had infused the spirit of supreme goodness, the Bible tells us the story of the incarnation process of the *numen summum bonum*, which is God. The peoples of antiquity, including Moses, could not comprehend a spirit without an active body in heaven, so people created a God not only as the source of everything but, as the Bible says, "in his image," resulting in incarnation—a God who could be manipulated to fit the occasion.

In the time that the Bible was written, God was the center of all life. Today, science proves to us that the only being that is alive, and always was, is the small gene molecule of a larger DNA molecule. Therefore, the God who is the first cause of all creation has to be the gene.

Although the gene created the *NSB*, it also carried the genetic traits of our animal ancestors and will continue to do so forever. That animal trait within us has always striven only for the enhancement and survival of the species. The desires of the animal in us are mostly evil, such as lust, selfishness, greed, combativeness and outright desire to kill for species advantage. The Bible incarnated these evil animal genes into sin, Satan and hell. In real life, these genes of evil in our soul, where they live side by side with the spirit of supreme goodness, can be completely wiped out if we so choose.

Our capacity to activate the God-spirit against our animal desires was incarnated into the form of forgiveness of sin by Christ from heaven by some imagined process that we cannot accomplish by our own will. If the evil desires of the animal genes are sin, then we are born in sin, but it did not happen in the Garden of Eden with the snake and the apple and Adam and Eve. In science, sin is the action of the animal gene within us. Our way to heaven by the genetic creation process is directed by the gene of the God of the first cause of all creation. This gene has infused the soul of our psyche with the Jesus-spirit of love, mercy, forgiveness and a simple sustainable lifestyle. Therefore it is our responsibility to activate the God-spirit in our soul and pray to it for results, by meditation.

When those results of the spirit of supreme goodness occur and make us feel good, we have reached heaven because we feel good about ourselves. The tranquillity in our soul as a feeling that our best efforts have brought "thy kingdom come...on earth" is the only heaven we will ever see.

Arthur Foote expresses a Unitarian Universalist view: "All the gods, including the Jewish, Christian, and Moslem, have grown out of the human experience of something divine in human existence, our awareness of sacred reality" (AAU Pamphlet Commission Publication, 1995).

TELEOLOGY—INSTANT CREATION VERSUS EVOLUTION

Teleology is the branch of cosmology that treats final causes: finalism.

The Bible teaches that Almighty God created everything in the universe and on this planet out of nothing—*ex nihilo*—and that he did it in six days. Even when believers in this account compromise a day of Moses' God as 1000 years, that time is still but a moment in nearly four billion years of the God-gene process of organic creation.

The Bible creation process was not only *ex nihilo*; the Bible also says it was *ex finis*—finished—because on the sixth day God looked at what he had made *ex nihilo* and *ex finis* and said that it was good. The Bible gives no room for evolution of the enhancement of the soul. The *ex nihilo* and *ex finis* concept is very convenient for believers whose emotion has taken over the reasoning process of the intelligence. Such belief solves everything so that we can coast along in our emotional bed of roses without stirring up the mind. But for believers in this idea, many contradictions have to be resolved to make the concept real, possible and credible.

What about considering reality? What about scientific facts that report the evolution of everything? What about archeological findings that trace the organic process from plants to multi-celled life to animal life to mammals to primates to our human ancestors? What about Australopithecus Afarensis of Africa three million years ago, Australopithecus Africanus 2.5 million years ago, Homo Habilis two million years ago, Homo Erectus one million years ago, Homo Neanderthal half a million years ago and Homo Sapiens at the Cro-Magnon cave in France less than 100,000 years ago?

What about going back 3.5 billion years when a morsel of organic life began in the form of a bacteria in the rock crevices of Greenland? What about the Stone Age which has traces of the development and evolution of the human mind, starting with our ancestors using pebble-stone tools more than two million years ago, followed by the age of fractured-stone tools and then the copper and iron age of Egypt, with the glitter of copper in campfire ashes in Sinai more than 5000 years ago?

What about the scientific discovery in genetics that the gene of the deoxyribonucleic acid (DNA) molecule is, and always has been, the only living being in the history of planet Earth? What about the God-gene of the first cause of the creation process that produced the "blueprint" (*The Living Bible*) as presented in Proverbs 8:29 and 31: "I [Wisdom] was there when he [God] made the blueprint for the earth and oceans....and all his family of mankind!"?

All these questions are answered and recognized in all encyclopedias and scientific publications all over the world. How do all these known events stack up with the incarnation details told by writers of the Bible when they still lived on a flat earth? Add to that the fact that Bible writers presented humans as "in his image" as stated in Genesis 1:16: "Then God said, 'Let us make a man—someone like ourselves....'"

Maybe we humans need to raise our heads out of the sand and look around us to see what Christ and God as One, the first cause of all creation process, brought us with the gene of the DNA molecule. We know from visibly seen findings that, through genetic activity, this process is creating more rapidly in the culture phase than ever before. Almost daily we read of genetic breakthroughs (to be detailed later).

As related to us in the Bible, teleology assumes creation *ex nihilo*. With instant creation, the God of Moses created everything out of nothing. In the Bible, creation history goes back 4000 years. Scientific creation history goes back 3.5 billion years, an estimate that can be verified by scientific findings available for us to see. Such findings, mostly archeological, prove the Bible revelations are completely untenable. The Bible has no findings to verify its credibility.

Therefore the Bible story of the creation process and the scientific story of the inorganic, organic and cultural creation processes are not compatible. Since science, or *Wissenschaft*, deals with some things scientists know have taken place, the Bible and its believers have to recognize this and make some basic compromises to have credibility. The Bible was completely credible 2000 years ago because we humans did not know any better.

ESCHATOLOGY—SYSTEM OF THE DEATH PROCESS

E schatology is defined as the branch of theology that treats of death, judgment and the future state of the soul. To discuss eschatology, we need the Bible as a frame of reference to be able to draw conclusions. (Quotes are from *The Living Bible.*)

Isaiah 26:19a: "....Those who belong to God shall live again. Their bodies shall rise again!" I start with this verse because it identifies most clearly the basic eschatological concept of the Bible. It says that God decides which people he will raise from the dead to live forever in heaven.

Such a concept of resurrection of the dead was recorded so often in many other religions in antiquity that it was no big deal. Acceptance with no thought of verification was possible when communications were nonexistent and when registration of deaths, without autopsy, was thought irrelevant. Also, such resurrection events were recorded in absentia by the writers many years after the fact.

More important to negating the credibility of resurrection of a dead organism is our history of the creation process of millions of years during which a resurrection has never been verified; therefore according to science, resurrections have never taken place. The genetic process of the God-gene of the first cause makes the resurrection of a dead organism impossible.

John 5:28-29: "'....Indeed the time is coming when all the dead in their graves shall hear the voice of God's Son, and shall rise again—those who have done good, to eternal life; and those who have continued in evil, to judgment.'" For 2000 years, fundamentalist believers have been setting dates for this coming. They don't want to stand in a queue of over 50 billion Homo Sapiens who have lived on this planet in the last three million years. In Heaven's Gate, a group near San Diego set a date for March 1997.

Matthew 8:22b: "'Let those who are spiritually dead care for their own dead.'" Jesus is speaking to a man who wants to follow him after his father is dead. The significance here is that Jesus speaks of a spiritual death instead of a physical death. The value of all human-born beings, including Jesus, is measured entirely by the quality and activity of the Holy Spirit, which I like to call the Jesus-spirit as an entity.

2 Corinthians 5:14: "...because Christ's love controls us now. Since we believe that Christ died for all of us, we should also believe that we have died to the old life we used to live" [the animal ancestor life]. We agree with Paul that it is not Jesus as a personal savior but the Jesus-spirit of love that controls us. The body of Jesus, the cross, the crown of thorns, or his blood are of little consequence, but in his last word on the cross it was his spirit of love, mercy, forgiveness and a simple lifestyle that he offered to us to store in our soul.

Romans 5:12: "When Adam sinned, sin entered the entire human race. His sin spread death throughout all the world...." Here Paul gets all whipped up repeating the system of death, sin and judgment of the soul. This idea is related in Genesis 3:1-14. In the Garden of Eden, Satan in the lowly snake causes gullible Eve to entice Adam to eat the apple of sin. Science says No to that sin—it is all animal.

Job 7:16a: "I hate my life." Job hates not the devil but the animal-trait genes that he carries in his soul. 17:19: "Why won't you let me alone...?" 17:12: "O God, am I some monster, that you never let me alone?" We carry those animal genes always. 6:29a, 30b: "...I am righteous....Would I not admit it if I had sinned?" Job did not accept this Garden-of-Eden sin idea, yet he could feel the evil desires of his animal genes in his soul. In his agony, Job gives us a very specific experience indicating that the Garden of Eden and Satan never existed. We know now that the monster he felt within himself was the animal genes in his soul that we all carry forever. Job had no time for blaming Satan for his own sinful desires as did other believers of that time. He knew that there was a "monster" within him, which we now recognize as the gene of our animal ancestors.

Romans 7:9a: "Christ rose from the dead and will never die again." 6:5: "For you have become a part of him...." 6:6: "Your old evil desires were nailed to the cross with him...so that your sin-loving body is no longer under sin's control...." Paul starts out with the death on the cross of the animal body of Christ—death which was final for the body—but the everlastingly important item was his spirit, as Jesus himself tells us in his last response on the cross as recorded in all four Gospels. Our evil animal genes are nailed to the cross with his body when his spirit enters our soul to control our behavior. Romans 8:11: "And if the Spirit of God, who raised up Jesus from the dead, lives in you, he will make your dying bodies live again after you die, by means of this same Holy Spirit living within you." Confusing—but nothing works without the spirit.

Hebrews 2:14b: "...for only as a human being could he die and in dying break the power of the devil who had the power of death." Here Jesus is called a human being as Arius contended when he opposed Athanasius, who dictated the Trinity that we have accepted as true gospel.

1 Peter 3:18: "....He died once for the sins of all us guilty sinners....But though his body died, his spirit lived on." What can be more specific to tell us that the resurrection of Jesus was spiritual? Why should we want to hang onto a resurrected animal body even if such a process were possible?

1 John 4:16b: "God is love...." Therefore we have to accept the fact that the love in our soul is God. Also, therefore, God can live nowhere except in our soul.

Revelations 20:5: "This is the First Resurrection...." 20:7: "When the thousand years end, Satan will be let out of his prison." 20:10: "Then the devil who had betrayed them [God's people] will again be thrown into the Lake of Fire burning with sulphur where the Creature and the False Prophet are, and they will be tormented day and night forever and ever." I call the sequence of sin, death, resurrection, second coming and judgment of souls to heaven or hell the "system" of eschatology of the mythical incarnated God and Christ of the Bible. However the Jesus-spirit of love, mercy, forgiveness and a simple lifestyle is presented to us by Jesus himself (as I detail elsewhere).

The Bible begins with this system in the Garden of Eden, continues through slavery in Egypt, the flood and many other happenings, and ends in Revelation with the same "system" of a God of anger, vengeance and death that is yet to happen to us soon. We have waited for 2000 years for his second coming. So far, we have not had the 1000-year reign, during which time Satan is to be in prison, before the second coming. So for the time being we can forget about the "system." What is significant is how this "system" came to us that has controlled our behavior for 2000 years.

Revelation 1:1-2: "This book unveils some of the future activities soon to occur in the life of Jesus Christ. God permitted him to reveal these things to his servant John in a vision; and then an angel was sent from heaven to explain the vision's meaning. John wrote it all down— the words of God and Jesus Christ and everything he heard and saw." 1:3c: "For the time is near when these things will all come true." 1:8: "...says God, who is the Lord, the All Powerful One who is, and was, and is coming again!"

The eschatology of the "system" in Revelation was given to John in a vision by God through Christ, who was given permission by God to create such a vision. The Gospel writers have already made it clear that God and Christ are one and the same, and here God had to give Christ permission to give a vision to John. This is just one inconsistency of many in the Bible because there are so many writers who incarnate God in their own perception.

In deference to the Bible, the Bible writers were not historians. They had no intention of relating realities; they were interpreters of the incarnation of the Holy Spirit in a form as God. This was a time when the Jesus-spirit could not be conceptualized as a divinity in our souls; therefore incarnation as a vision can be justified.

I hope that in our creation process we can gravitate to reality. The angel that God sent from heaven to explain the vision to John is becoming more unacceptable as we accept reality over what was believed 2000 years ago. We don't need symbols or incarnations to pray to the Jesus-spirit in our soul. We can enhance the quality in our psyche. God the Creator is enhancing gene production every day. The God-gene has over millions of years given us the psyche of soul, mind and intelligence to enable us to establish the kingdom on earth if we have the will to do so by meditation.

The eschatology of the Jew, Muslim, and Christian hits at the core of the make-believe of a deity who does everything. These religions today are religions of incarnation. The Jews hang the God-spirit of goodness (or what I prefer to call the Jesus-spirit) on Yahweh. The Muslims hang that same spirit on Allah, and the Christians hang that same spirit on Christ the Resurrected One. Thereby we can manipulate that spirit.

There is nothing evil about using such crutches, and it still seems necessary to continue to pray to such images as models of a deity as long as we are unable to recognize such a deity in our soul as the reality. Under the prevailing "systems" of eschatology in all three religions, we are helpless without praying to some divine model out there somewhere. We cannot reach heaven until "he" has a second coming. We are still waiting until we follow the Jesus of love for life and the living.

Why is a deity out yonder necessary? Why do we have to carry the extra baggage of angel-messengers of God to tell us where we are going? Why do we have to wait 2000 years plus 1000 years of the reign of a deity before God comes down from heaven to judge us to heaven or to hell? That eschatological "system" of sin, Satan, hell and finally a savior will be with us conceivably for another 1000 years before we can reach heaven, when in fact, with the God-spirit in our soul, we can reach heaven every day of the week right here on earth. We don't have to wait.

AFTERLIFE—APOCALYPSE VERSUS NATURAL DEATH

Religion is universally a response in human beings to fear of the unknown afterlife. Eschatology is the study of the theology of death, resurrection, judgment and after death, the life of the soul. As we review the hereafter concept of the major cosmologies and their perspectives of death and afterlife, we will see that their eschatologies have much in common.

In the animal kingdom of our ancestors, death was and is an inevitable step—one end point in the sequence of the genetic creation process. But when in the last three million years the DNA molecule had infused the gene of the psyche into our animal body, we had to deal with the death of two beings, the body and the soul. The death of the body was no problem; it was still only an inevitable end in the sequence of bodies of the creation process. But the soul that lived in that body demanded recognition. It made heroic efforts to avoid death as it does today in us—a system of apocalypse.

Death involves the physical end point of the body, but it becomes a psychiatric process of the soul—termination. The psyche demands immortality. It does so with justification because it (we) are immortal as the gene replicates us into the same genes of our offspring forever. But our immortality is much more than replication into our offspring. The soul gives us the opportunity to add quality and quantity to the gene chain of the *numen summum bonum*, or NSB (spirit of supreme goodness). Such a process is called genetic behavior creation and is known as the genotype-phenotype environmental interaction that we have described elsewhere.

The enhancement of the quality and quantity of the spirit gene that we contribute to the gene of our offspring is probably minuscule in amount, but whatever it is, it makes additions in the genetic chain in all generations of our progeny forever. That process gives us our immortality that the Bible talks about. We have the privilege of carrying that DNA molecule from our parents to our offspring. Even more important is that we have the opportunity to add the environment to genotype-phenotype interaction to determine the value of the gene that we give our children. It is therefore most important how much of the spirit of goodness we put into that environment in this genetic behavior process.

Behavior genetics and the concept of the evolution of the soul were unknown in antiquity. Wilhelm Schmidt's *Ursprung der Gottesidee* (Origin of the God Idea) had a simple beginning: Death was simple, physical and final in folklore of aborigines (primitive indigenous people) all over the world.

In the Chaco of West Paraguay, South America, where I did medical and surgical work for many years, the Lingua and Chalupe Indians were entirely indigenous when we started in 1940. They actively put death behind them quickly and completely when it happened in their small group. They had no tombstones. They burned all their grass huts to destroy the spirit of death and moved to a new location for a new start.

Because the recording of civilization started in Africa, we will try to offer the afterlife concept of African antiquity. The hunters and gatherers of that time were too busy trying to survive to give much thought to the past or the future. They accepted the physical death of the body, and they felt a vague idea of a spirit passing from one generation to the next. They felt that the spirit of the dead body was spending itself among the spirits of the surviving bodies. Their acceptance of reality became ever more complicated as succeeding incarnations of that spirit were delineated in the writing that was developing in antiquity.

After the gene of the psyche in the bodies of the hunters and gatherers became stronger, the NSB was incarnated into a heaven with God, and the gene of the evil desires of our animal bodies was incarnated into Satan residing in hell below. We were developing an afterlife existence in two worlds: one in heaven above and one in hell far below.

The two-level world of heaven and hell surfaced all over the world during the second millennium B.C. The world on high was ruled by polytheistic gods of various forms in Assyria, Babylonia, Palestine and Greece. Baal was in Judah and Zeus in Greece. But their peoples were too busy making a living to consider afterlife.

The Egyptians had already around 3,000 B.C. built the great pyramid tombs for their rulers, providing for their needs in the afterlife in and around the crypts in the pyramids, for they were enamored with death and afterlife. They supplied mummies in the sarcophagi with rations to use when they were resurrected. They left us with the importance of mortuary practices that are still evident in mausoleums in the United States and elaborate granite buildings to house the dead in cemeteries in Latin American countries. Pyramid-building probably took place 2000 years before Moses and the recording of God's creation of the world in the Old Testament. Being farther from the Ice Age glaciers, the Egyptians were nearly 1000 years ahead of the Mesopotamian area in their culture.

The Egyptian concept of afterlife seems to be entirely physical; there was no mention of a soul in the hieroglyphics of Egypt when the pyramids were designed and built by Imhotep. But about 1000 years later, Imhotep IV was the first ruler of the ancient countries to establish the concept of a single God. With the introduction of monotheism and the cuneiform writings of the Sumerians and the alphabet writing generated out of the hieroglyphics of Egypt into an alphabet created by the Phoenicians and the Greeks, we read of a "system" of eschatology that became a concept in all cosmologies to be considered. This idea was the physical incarnation of a spirit. It was a physical process of death, resurrection, judgment and God's reward of either heaven or hell. The process carried the spirit along with the body in this transformation to actual physical places of heaven or hell.

While this eschatological "system" of death, resurrection, judgment and rewards in physical places on this planet was being promoted, another eschatology appeared. This eschatology started in Persia in the second millennium B.C., was shaped by Zoroaster in the sixth century B.C. and was advanced by the academy of Socrates, Plato, and Aristotle during the first millennium B.C.

It taught that the human being is composed of a physical (animal) body and a soul that houses the spirit. In the fourth century B.C., Aristotle added all the ingredients of the genetic evolution of the psyche and soul by stating that the *numen summum bonum* (NSB, or spirit of supreme goodness) became stronger as it interacted with the environmental complexity of the day. This theory is now known as behavior genetics.

Socrates and the Athens Academy taught that God's NSB lived only in the human soul. Moses, who grew up and was educated in the court of the pharaohs, on Mount Sinai changed the many gods of Baal to Yahweh, one God patterned after the one God of the Egyptian ruler Imhotep. Along with Babylon and Egypt, Moses advanced the concept of a single God who lived in heaven, from where he ruled everything. To that one God was later added the New Testament eschatology of death, resurrection, judgment and reward of heaven or hell.

After the early African eschatology came the Sumerian influence in the area that is now Iraq: the empire of Assyria and Babylon. These people began to think of human existence as composed of body and soul. During the second and first millenniums B.C. they began to fear the underworld. They developed belief in two worlds, one under and one above. But since there were no writings then, the specifics of their concept of afterlife never became fixed. Death was final, and heaven and immortality took second place to the fight for physical survival.

In the eschatology of Israel, the concept of death, resurrection and judgment became a "system." In modern Judaism, the problem of how to perceive the body and soul working out the finality of heaven and hell is as divisive as it was for Plato in the prophets' time of the fourth century B.C.

In Christology, eschatology is patterned after that of Judaism plus the added concept of salvation through Christ. According to that eschatology we can reach heaven not on our own but only through Christ's forgiveness after we have confessed our sins and asked for forgiveness. That forgiveness is possible only if we believe in the physical resurrection of Christ and the resurrection of us physically on judgment day—apocalypse.

It can be said that the afterlife is a compromise of the soul concept of Socrates and the Bible belief in a resurrection of a physical body. The essence of life and afterlife in Christology is birth in sin, salvation of the soul by a magical process of Christ's response to our prayer to him for forgiveness of our sin by confession, then death, and then resurrection of our physical body to be judged on judgment day when the world comes to an end. We are then rewarded with heaven or hell forever. This concept will be evaluated elsewhere.

The Chinese belief in divinity is often called ancestor worship. Traditionally Chinese communicate with their ancestors' soul-spirit (which they actually are carrying in their genes to the next generation).

In reality they are praying for the enhancement of the NSB of their ances-tors' souls, which in the scientific concept of the genetic creation process appears in all progeny forever. Even more amazing is their practice of spiritual communication of all spirits of goodness of the world in the past, present and future. They were not concerned about a heaven above or a hell below. They were making heaven here on earth by calling upon the function of the spirit of the soul. There is no born-in-sin, salvation by magic, heaven or hell out yonder. That extra baggage they did not have to carry because they realized the genetic process of the NSB.

In Tibet the struggle to reach the divine is through Buddhism. At death one reaches the light of one's life and the internal power to deter-mine destiny. By disciplining the mind through meditation, one controls the body. Tibetan Buddhists teach in essence that death is a release from the responsibility of making the spirit gene overcome the evil desires of the animal gene in us.

They believe in rebirth from one generation into the next generation. The parallel in today's genetics is the replication of the DNA product in the creation process. Geneticists would say that my genes are reborn in my daughter even before I die and that my genes give me immortality.

(Tibet is significant to me because Mariam, my wife, for three years had Mary Taring, "daughter of Tibet," as a classmate at Queen's Hill School in Darjeeling, North India, within viewing distance of Mount Everest. After China took over Tibet, Mary established across the moun-tains a Tibetan refugee orphanage called Happy Valley. Invited to spend a day with her there, on June 21, 1972, we witnessed the priest calling people to the temple with his long alpine horn. Mary had written a book, *Daughter of Tibet*, which she autographed for us. She said Buddha is not a god but a teacher.)

Islam has an eschatology modeled after its predecessor, the worship of the God of Abraham. It is essentially of death, resurrection, judgment day, and reward at the world's end of either heaven or hell as in Judaism and Christology. However there are significant differences. Muslims believe that God represents everything that "is." With that concept they come much closer to the genetic process than Christology. Also, they have the Garden of Eden in their eschatology, but they do not teach that humans are born in sin due to the snake and the apple. Their light of the divine is a vision of God. Evil is the absence of the vision of God's goodness. Again, that concept comes much closer to the concept of the genetic creation of the NSB in our soul that can correct all evil. They have no need for Christ as a God.

Hinduism of the Far East is similar to Buddhism in some ways. Ghandi said, "Truth is the means of purification of our soul." "Truth is the ladder by which man ascends to heaven." "Truth makes the sun rise." To make himself understood by one billion Muslims and the West's one billion Christians, he uses the metaphor of a ladder and heaven in reaching the perfection of a conceivable heaven here on earth by the spirit of truth in our soul. Hinduism teaches that divinity is reached through many cycles of rebirth from one generation to the next. The path to reach perfection depends on the temperament, ability and opportunity of our soul that we choose to put into play in the genetic creation of our soul. India has no Hindu tombs or monuments. Physical bodies have no value, so they are all cremated. There is no place for resurrection of a dead body to life. The NSB of Ghandi is: "Truth is heaven."

In the Eastern countries of India, China, Japan and Malaysia, their religions don't need any scientific writing about who God is and who we are because they are already in tune with the God-gene in the concept of the soul.

ISLAM—THE RELIGION OF ALLAH AND KORAN

I slam, like Christianity and Judaism, is a monotheistic religion. All three religions start with Abraham of the Old Testament and claim to worship the same God.

Islam and Christianity have lived side by side, and their adherents have killed each other for nearly 2000 years. Each religion has grown to a world membership of about one billion. The two faiths have some similar qualities: Both promise their members the coming of eternal bliss in the same heaven. Both have theological concepts that will lead them to a demise of their Gods as humans learn about the evolutionary, genetic, culture creation process of the psyche (soul, mind and intelligence) in our animal bodies.

In Christianity the human soul reaches heaven only through the resurrected Christ's forgiveness of the sin in which it was born. In Islam, humans can reach the same heaven without Christ by following the teachings of the Koran. When these two Gods, Christ and Allah, judge each other's followers to assign them to hell or heaven, nobody reaches it! We should expect such a failure because both Gods are created by us humans to give us eternal life and save our egos forever, according to religious mythology.

The three monotheistic religions in essence depend on incarnations of their deities and their processes. Judaism incarnates God as a ruler in heaven. Christianity incarnates God and the resurrected Christ. Islam incarnates Allah and the Koran as God's writing. In Islam, the Koran leads to God as Christ leads to God for Christians.

Roots of Christianity can be seen in the messiah prophesied by Isaiah in the Old Testament. Christ the Messiah was born by divine conception and started Christianity. Islam traces its roots to Ishmael, the son of

Abraham by his concubine Hagar, under God's directions to Abraham's household. Mohammed, the founder of Islam, did not need Christ as a forgiver of sins.

These religions operate under a common tenet of incarnation and an eschatology of death, resurrection, judgment and rewards of eternal heaven or hell for souls when the world comes to an end. The incarnations assume that the spirit of supreme goodness (*numen summum bonum*, or NSB) comes to us by a being with a form called God who rules on his throne sitting in heaven. The ideas of incarnation also include concepts of souls as bodies that go through the stages of eschatology according to religious beliefs and assumptions.

To understand how these ideas differ from my theology, I will explain that contributing influences on me were Zoroastrianism, Socrates and the Academy of Athens in the fourth century B.C., Hinduism and Buddhism in the Far East, and noted theologians of the last century. My theology teaches that the God of the Bible is the first cause of all creation, as detailed by King Solomon in Proverbs 8 with "Miss" Wisdom, and in John 1 and Colossians 1. It also teaches that the NSB of God the creator resides in our soul and nowhere else. The God-gene put it there—the spirit.

Muslim mystics came near to accepting the concept that God exists only in the souls of human beings. A saying attributed to Abu Said ibn Abi Khayr, who died in 1049 A.D., is: "If men wish to draw near to God, they must seek him in the hearts of men" (Margaret Smith, *Readings from the Mystics of Islam*, p. 49). In the Koran, the writers accept the theology of the Athens Academy with three exceptions. They do not accept Socrates because Socrates says (a) there is no resurrection, (b) the cosmos has no beginning and no ending, and (c) all men are mortal.

Islam teaches that these three concepts of Socrates and Aristotle are false because they do not show belief in divine law. Aristotle says the soul and its spiritual contents are not a commodity that can be sold over the counter like a tomato. The soul's NSB directs human response and feelings about me, you and everyone else on earth through our meditation.

It is a quality or value that God's gene has infused into our animal body. The immortality of that genetic value cannot be incarnated into Christ's resurrection process so that it can be preserved for us forever; it has to be passed on to our progeny to have its effect forever. The genetic directive of the NSB cannot be incarnated in a Koran that will carry it to

God for safekeeping, for us to pick up as a commodity when we reach the heaven of Islam. Rather, the effects of my soul's activity have to, and will, live religiously and genetically in my offspring forever.

Islam, Christianity and Judaism have a common origin in Abraham and a common eschatology of death, resurrection, judgment and a reward of eternal heaven or hell for our soul when the world ends. Mohammed's concepts vary from those of the Bible. These variations came about in the evolution of God, who changed in essence from one religion to another.

Late in the second millennium B.C. the God of Moses in the Old Testament was a totalitarian ruler of anger and vengeance, exterminating all human beings who did not obey him. Obedience, not love, was his mode of operation, e.g., the flood and other events. Then during the first millennium B.C. the genetic process of the NSB demanded a change. The Old Testament processes did not produce tranquillity, so we have the Psalms and other tranquilizing literature. But to really produce a new deal, Isaiah prophesized a messiah. That started a new era of a Christ born of divine conception in Mary's uterus. He was crucified and resurrected, and ascended to heaven, carrying all good souls to heaven for safekeeping.

All the above led to Islam about 600 years later. Mohammed made the most drastic change in God. Mohammed relates the existence of the Garden of Eden and of Adam as the first prophet of God, but he did not buy the concept that humans were born in sin by way of the snake, Eve and the apple, so he did not need Christ as another God for humans to be saved from sin. Mohammed says in the Koran that, since he was the last prophet after Adam, Abraham and Christ, he was obligated to write the Koran to lead his people to God in heaven (as Christ in his resurrection did for Christians). Mohammed wrote the Koran as God told him what to write, to show everyone the way to God in heaven by way of the Koran instead of through Christ.

Islam, the third member of the incarnated God of Abraham's family, retained essentially the same eschatology of the Bible. While Christology added to the Old Testament Christ, through whom we reach heaven, Islam added the Koran, through which we can reach God in heaven—a distinct change in the concept of who God is.

Islam made an even more relevant deviation from who God is in our Bible by introducing the concept of Socrates, Aristotle and the Greek

Academy that God's spirit of supreme goodness resides in the souls of all humans. As mentioned earlier, Islam accepts this idea except in three areas: teleology, resurrection and immortality of the human body. Islam teaches that immortality has been established while Aristotle says the human physical body is mortal and physical resurrection of a dead body is not possible in God's universe. Islam teaches that the world will come to an end to fulfill its prophecy whereas Aristotle and the Greek Academy taught that the inorganic creation process of the universe has no beginning and no ending. (The Greek Academy in the fourth century B.C. was the beginning of all colleges and universities of today.)

Islam made other concessions in the theology processes. It taught that law was more important than beliefs in God and that behavior was more important than beliefs. It stressed the importance of education and knowledge. In this respect Islam has had an advantage over Christology. Christology has gradually become an adversary of the scientific community, more so than Islam. Islam teaches that to worship God out of fear or to receive a reward is not credible. Islam at last approached the concept of Aristotle that the soul contains the ability to reach "heaven" if it chooses to do so by the spirit.

Muslim worship is based on prayer, fasting, almsgiving, pilgrimage and faith. Islam has a keeper of hell called Malek. After the death of a Muslim, while in the grave the corpse is interviewed by angels concerning divinity. After death the corpse somehow goes through seven heavens before coming to the gate of the Mansion of Immortality.

The problem of why one billion Christians and one billion Muslims cannot follow God's NSB in their souls is because of concepts in the Bible and in the Koran. In each case the spirit of supreme goodness is incarnated into the God-Christ of the Bible and into the Allah of the Koran. After that personal soul-spirit has been properly incarnated into a God form, that form can then be manipulated to perform for its beholder any function that will fit the circumstances. That form can tell a Rev. Hill that he may kill an abortion doctor and his companion. That God form will take all the responsibility for that killing and absolve Rev. Hill of that crime because he served his God-image in Tallahassee, Florida.

The Muslims who tried to blow up two of the tallest buildings in the world were instructed to do so by the hierarchy of Islam from Mecca by way of the Koran. The suicide bombers of Gaza were promised a special place in heaven by Sheik Abdullah Shami if they would sacrifice their lives to send enemies to hell. That action killed more than 200 American soldiers in recent years.

Such God-manipulated crimes have been going on for several thousand years from incidental killing to terrorism to open warfare. But the gene that gave our soul this spirit that was incarnated into all these gods also gave us a mind and an intelligence that has the capacity to change the emotional incarnate God to a God with the gene who created our soul—a soul that has within it the Jesus-spirit of love, mercy, forgiveness and a simple lifestyle to sustain life on our planet.

Why is Islam important to this dissertation? Because:

1. Judaism, Christianity and Islam started with the God of Abraham and continue to worship God today.

2. Christianity and Islam came into being side by side and today each has about one billion members.

3. Christology and Islam both espouse incarnation and an eschatology of death, resurrection and reward to heaven or hell for human afterlife forever.

4. In methods of how to reach the same God and the same heaven, they completely cancel each other out. The basic steps that the two largest organized religions have to reach the same goal, judge each other out of existence: (a) Christianity has only Christ who can lead us to God in heaven; (b) Islam has only the Koran to lead to God and heaven; (c) Judaism is still waiting for a messiah.

The "clinical" diagnosis of these three religions is that their illness is an endemic one of incarnation and an eschatology of death, resurrection, and apocalypse and judgment. As to prognosis, the symptoms indicate the demise of the three monotheistic religions after a period of incubation. The spirit of the soul is forever the cure of this disease.

TRINITY—A FARCE
OF ATHANASIUS

The Holy Trinity has always been high on the agenda in the religious practices of the Christian community for nearly 2000 years. Most Christians accepted it as a concept come from heaven, etched in stone. This creed did not come from heaven or from God or Christ, not even from the Bible, but from Athanasius, the bishop of Emperor Constantine.

The history of the origin of the Trinity presents a controversial story. The picture of the in-fighting of Athanasius and Arius to determine who our God is, is not pretty. The antagonisms divided the Christian church in the Middle East, an area of Egypt and Turkey that is largely Muslim now. The polarity between the followers of Arius and Athanasius as to the nature of Jesus was so divisive that Emperor Constantine, in the Turkey area of the Eastern Roman Empire, called the Nicene Conference to take a vote over the controversy.

Athanasius, bishop of Alexandria, was born to Christian parents about 293 A.D. in Alexandria. He taught that Jesus was equal to God. He also taught what we call teleology. *Telos* is Greek for "end." This concept of the creation said God created the universe and man on command out of nothing. God regulated this creation from his throne, and we would see the world come to an end when he so decided. Athanasius was called the Bishop of Orthodoxy. He did not believe man had a soul that could lead man to divinity. Salvation to divinity could be achieved only by the grace of Christ crucified, resurrected and ruling from heaven above.

Arius, a Greek theologian, is thought to have been born in Libya about 256 A.D. His teachings were somewhat of a take-off of Aristotle's teaching in Athens around 300 B.C. Arius taught that Jesus was a lesser deity than God because he was born of a human being. He also taught that man had a soul that directed him toward divinity. He quoted "Miss" Wisdom as presented by King Solomon in Proverbs.

He also quoted John, who said that Christ with God created everything, starting before the earth was formed (John 1). Because he taught these concepts, conflicts continued.

All this strife alarmed Emperor Constantine. He called a meeting of all the bishops in the area for May 20, 325 in Nicaea to take a vote to settle the matter. At this meeting Athanasius received the most votes, partly because the Emperor favored his bishop. It was not at all certain that Athanasius had a larger following than Arius.

The Nicene Creed that Athanasius unloaded onto Christianity has been repeated in church services for nearly 1000 years. Basically it says we believe in one God and one Lord Jesus Christ who was the Son of God. Jesus came down from heaven for our salvation. He came as a man, suffered, rose, ascended to heaven and will come to judge the living and the dead. Almost as an afterthought, Athanasius introduced the Holy Spirit, a concept that was an important compromise of Arius' belief in a soul. It is also stated that Athanasius determined the date when the Church was to celebrate Easter. The doctrine of the Trinity is that God the Father, God the Son and God the Holy Spirit are deities to be worshiped.

Later, Constantine recognized Arius as more credible and ordered Athanasius, the champion of orthodoxy, to recognize Arius by serving him communion. When Athanasius refused to do so, Constantine and the synod of Tyre (now Lebanon) disposed Athanasius into exile in Gaul (France). Constantine ordered the bishops of Constantinople to restore Arius to communion, but Arius died on the day of the ceremony.

Why is this religious history so important? For two reasons:

1. It tells us how flimsily the concept of the Trinity got started, a concept that we now regard as inevitable.

2. It could very well be that the highly emotional charge to the blood, cross and physical resurrection would not have developed as it has by Christian Fundamentalism of today without Athanasius.

The confrontation of Arius and Athanasius in 325 A.D. is a forerunner or a continuum of the reality of modern scientific findings versus the fundamentalist bigotry of the believers of Athanasius. In 325, the question was whether Jesus was a deity equal to God or whether he was a human-born king. Did he belong to the incarnated deity?

Today the question is: Who is God? Is he the incarnated Almighty who sits on the throne in a place called heaven where he rules over all the details of our life, or is he the first cause of all creation and also the spirit of goodness that resides only in the souls of all human beings, albeit in variation of quality and quantity according to our freewill decisions that we make as to how much we want to be worth.

To the Fundamentalist, God is alive and active, answering all our prayers to him and intervening so as to rule our lives. To the scientist, the gene of the DNA molecule is the only life that is or ever has been. This gene is God in action as the first cause of all creation.

This gene exists because we can see it in action under an electron microscope. We do not have to incarnate it because it already has form. This gene has been working on one of its projects, infusing a soul into our animal body, for three million years, starting with Australopithecus, whose fossil Raymond Dart excavated in South Africa.

During these three million years, this gene has created a soul in our psyche, the urge to be good that we call God's *numen summum bonum* (NSB, the spirit of supreme goodness). Such a spirit is presented to us innumerable times in our Bible, as related previously. Although the God-spirit is often presented as an incarnation, the Bible writers credited the spirit and not the incarnation as worthy. The incarnation as a spirit deity is and has been universal in many religious groups all over the world. (This idea is discussed elsewhere.)

To summarize: The author of the Trinity, Athanasius, was a bishop of Emperor Constantine, not a historian. His duty was to interpret to the emperor what the Church was to believe and worship. In the Trinity, Athanasius told us that Jesus was equal to and on par with God. Arius, also a bishop of Greek heritage, taught that Jesus was human-born and therefore carried the divine spirit in his soul to be presented to all humanity as a model of divine living.

Zoroaster, a Persian theologian, was the first one to teach the concept of the God-spirit that resides in the souls of every human and is there available to make us more divine if we choose to be so.

Socrates, the Greek theological philosopher, was condemned to death in 399 B.C. because he preached against his government for worshiping an incarnate god. He taught that the spirit of God resides only in the soul of the human body. He also taught that the human soul has all the "tools" to correct its problems on a freewill basis without praying to an incarnate God out yonder somewhere.

Jesus Christ was crucified partly because he brought the spirit of God on the throne a bit too close to the soul that takes care of our daily problems. He showed love to the prostitute at the well instead of stoning her in the Jewish fashion. Of course, Jesus had to be presented as a deity of Athanasius instead of as a human being acting out the spirit of God, as taught by Arius, because the prophets of the Old Testament had already incarnated God's spirit in some of their writings. Must we worship an incarnated deity as the Jews, Muslims and Christians do to raise the emotional level high enough to get our own good will into action, or can we accept our freewill responsibility to activate the good will of the God-spirit and follow the Jesus-spirit of love, mercy, forgiveness and a simple lifestyle as Arius presented to us, to survive on the good earth God gave us?

If Arius had won, we would now credit what Aristotle taught in 350 B.C., after the Old Testament prophets had tried to transfer the God of anger to the God of love. Aristotle did not have to worry about any other god, so he came much closer to the idea that God resides in the souls of humankind.

RESURRECTION—
INCARNATED JESUS-SPIRIT

Resurrection of Christ after the crucifixion has been the corner-stone of worship of Christology for 2000 years. Easter, along with Christmas, has been the most celebrated holiday. It is based entirely on the belief that Jesus arose bodily from the dead to live again as the savior who saves us from all sin.

In the evolution of Christology this sacredness has gained in importance far beyond what it was at 29 A.D. when, Scripture says, even his followers looked upon resurrection with joy and doubt. The celebration of Easter goes far beyond considering the credibility of the possibility that the dead can return to life in three days. The Fundamentalist is talking to Christ in heaven by long distance, reinforcing his belief that Christ is there waiting for him. Fortunately, doubters can always use the Easter egg and Easter bunny at celebrations.

During those early years a resurrection from the dead was commonly invoked by all other cosmologies. It occurred in Egypt with Osiris, in Assyria with Sargon, in Babylon with the gods of Hammurabi, and in Greece with Zeus. The concept of the resurrection of Jesus to become Christ in heaven was modeled after all the above-listed cosmologies of that time.

In fact, resurrection was so generally expected that Matthew 27:52-53 says (King James Version): "And the graves were opened; and many bodies of the saints which slept arose, And came out of the graves after his resurrection, and went into the holy city, and appeared unto many." The imagination included earthquake and the temple veil rent apart. All this is said to have happened, yet there is no evidence of such happenings. The angel rolling the stone (28:2) is also way out of character since God visited Abraham in the tent 1000 years earlier.

Resurrection of Jesus into a ruling Christ was accepted because:

1. All cosmologies accepted the process of resurrection as a common occurrence.

2. It was a convenient method of raising the prominence of the resurrected one.

3. It allowed the resurrected one to function forever as a god.

The scenarios of the attempt to verify the resurrection of Jesus are questionable. John 20:17: "'Don't touch me,' he cautioned, 'for I haven't yet ascended to the Father.'" That passage conjures up different interpretations, but Jesus definitely says he is not physically touchable. Luke 24:39: "'Touch me and make sure that I am not a ghost! For ghosts don't have bodies, as you see that I do.'" But Luke was honest enough not to subject the onlookers to perjury; he did not record a response of touching that did not occur as verse 41 indicates: "Still they stood there undecided, filled with joy and doubt."

The concept of resurrection has a long history dating back to 2000 B.C. In origin, resurrection beliefs were largely Oriental (i.e., from the land east of the Mediterranean) and were that man could take on the nature of God with immortality. In most instances in the cosmologies of the Orient, the god was portrayed as a young hero who had been murdered treacherously and then miraculously brought to life again. That same story was attached to Dionysus, Osiris, Orpheus, Attis, Adonis and many others.

In Egypt more than 2000 years B.C., people reasoned that if it was the fate of the God Osiris to be resurrected after death, then a way could be found to repeat that fate for all people. It was therefore necessary to bury them properly in the pyramids with Osiris, and sooner or later the soul in the hands of God Osiris and the properly entombed body would arise to live again, hence the pyramids.

Evidence of this was reported in the May 22, 1995 *U.S. News and World Report* in "Tales from the Crypt," a nine-page description and illustration of tombs built by Pharaoh (King) Ramses II in the Valley of the Kings in Luxor, Egypt. The crypt has the remains of 40 sons of Ramses in separate tombs with a statue of God Osiris at the end of the hallway. They have waited 4000 years to be resurrected.

The basic question is: Does the Bible give any verifiable facts stating that a physical resurrection of Christ on Easter morning took place? Or is the resurrection of Christ from the dead and the ascension of a physical Christ to heaven and the physical presence of God-Christ on the throne in heaven answering all our prayers a spiritual operation?

If all the activity after the crucifixion death of Jesus is only the action of the spirit of Christ, then the aims of this dissertation have all been met because a spirit is in the soul of mankind. A spirit cannot attach itself to anything else or to any other place. It then follows that a Christ-God as a material being never existed.

Why is that concept so important? Because the God-Christ spirit resides in our soul only, and only we are responsible for our reaching the divine state called heaven. Therefore it becomes our responsibility to determine how much of the Jesus-spirit of love, mercy and forgiveness we activate in our soul.

This writing proposes that the physical resurrection of Christ on Easter morning probably did not take place for the following reasons:

When my wife Mariam and I visited the Holy Land, our idea of sanctity was deflated when we were told that Catholic Christians and Protestant Christians each had their own entirely different burial place for Jesus. They could not both be right; they could both be wrong. But basically that shows how superficial the whole resurrection story is.

There is a movement in our scientific America that the resurrection of Jesus from the death on the cross into Christ, the ruler of our psyche from heaven, is a myth. For Easter Sunday in 1996, *Time*, *Newsweek* and *U.S. News* all had a full-cover picture of Jesus and a feature article discussing the possibility of accepting the resurrection as a myth instead of as a fact in history. The concept of Jesus' resurrection from the dead occurred in ancient times because all cosmologies during the first millennium claimed their heroes were resurrected and lived forever, so Jesus was no exception.

Science tells us that a resurrection of the dead back to life cannot happen in God's creation process. We have a history of 3.5 billion years of the God-Christ DNA creationary process, and not once has a dead cell come to life. The Bible story of resurrection is nothing but a carbon copy of the resurrection stories of all the cosmologies of the first millennium B.C., starting with the God Osiris of Egypt 2000 B.C.

The Bible has no positive statements that verify the details of the resurrection. The Bible tells us of two confrontations of a physical Christ on the resurrection day with his family and followers. In one confrontation, Christ cautioned not to touch him, and in the other confrontation, Christ showed them his wounds, but there was no response of touching. Also, we can hardly trust the veracity of the scenarios when we consider that they were written about 50 A.D.

The Bible does contain several references to the fact that the resurrection was nothing else but a spiritual activity that the writers tried to incarnate into a physical body form as follows:

I Corinthians 15:45-46: "The Scriptures tell us that the first man, Adam, was given a natural body but Christ is more than that, for he was a life-giving spirit." Here Paul tells us we have two parts in our being; i.e., within our human animal body is Christ (Jesus-spirit), a life-giving spirit. Paul presents us with a perfect metaphor of what we now know actually happened in this scientific world. Three million years ago we had an Adam body; then God-Christ, the first cause of all creation process, inserted into that animal body the gene of the psyche with its soul, mind and intelligence, creating in us a life-giving spirit. That process started with Australopithecus in Africa and has been recorded. This is congruent with the concept that each human being has a small kingdom of God within his own soul as Luke says in 17:21b: "'For the Kingdom of God is within you.'"

Acts 17 contains a theological controversy between Paul and the people of the Athens Academy when Paul had an encounter with Epicurean and Stoic philosophers (17:18). Epicurus (342-270 B.C.) followed Aristotle in the theology of the Academy. The Epicureans presented the God of culture (genetic evolution of the soul), while Paul believed in the God of Christ and resurrection—a resurrection of Jesus and of all believers from the dead to be judged. They thought Paul was a dreamer for talking about resurrection (18) but invited him to speak.

Paul condemned "Epicurus" for worshiping an unknown God (17:23): "....I wish to tell you about him" [an image of God]. He presented God as the first cause of creation, as the One who decided "beforehand" (17:26), before Adam, to determine human destiny. In contrast is Socrates' God of cultural genetic evolution, which Aristotle called soul enhancement, in direct proportion to the complexity of the environment present. The encounter of Paul with the Epicureans and his response conjure up some perceptions of who God is:

1. God is much bigger than the Bible metaphors of Christ and resurrection.

2. God is an ongoing process of creation.

3. God does not rule on a day-to-day basis.

4. The genetic evolution of the soul was a concept realized by Aristotle more than 2000 years ago.

5. That concept has been rejected by Christology until today.

The overwhelming significance of Acts 17 is that it confronts the two concepts of divinity that existed side by side during the first millennium B.C. The Bible taught that God-Christ ruled from above in heaven. Socrates taught that the spirit of God resided only in our soul and nowhere else. That debate between concepts of the divine is what this book is all about. To Bible people believing in incarnation, a Jesus-spirit in our soul was incomprehensible; therefore they had to incarnate that spirit into material being, resurrected into a physical form, and sit it on a throne in heaven and call it God and Christ. Actually, the apostolic writers present us with a complete metaphor for our present scientific thinking:

1. They present God-Christ as the first cause of all creation processes.

2. They present Adam as an animal body in the organic creation process three million years ago.

3. They present the gene that Christ inserted—the psyche with soul, mind and intelligence—that could host the life-giving spirit that we can live by if we choose to do so.

4. They sensed that the gene created the soul ages ago (three million years ago in Africa).

Galatians 5:24-25: "Those who belong to Christ have nailed their natural evil desires to his cross and crucified them there....let us follow the Holy Spirit's leading in every part of our lives." Ephesians1:14: "His [Christ's] presence within us...." These passages tell us several things about the activity of the Jesus-spirit in our soul but do not tell us that the spirit is handed to us from Christ in heaven. They say Christ is within us and not on a throne. They say sin is an evil desire of nature, changing the concept of "born in sin." We were born in sin through the fact that we were born in the culture creation process with the genes of our animal ancestors with all their evil desires. That is the nature that Paul refers to here. That is a sin that is scientifically verifiable.

The crucifying of our natural sin on the cross with Jesus is a consequence of what really happened in our scientific world 2000 years ago. When Jesus, in the process of dying, surrendered his spirit of love, mercy, forgiveness and a simple lifestyle, he gave us the tools to overcome all the evil desires and acts that the animal genes of our animal ancestors try to force us to follow.

Luke 1:15b: "...he [Zacharias' son John] will be filled with the Holy Spirit, even from before his birth!" Birth is defined as an act of producing offspring. That birth process begins with copulation when the sperm with the Y chromosome gamete meets the X chromosome gamete of the ovary to form the zygote of the new offspring. But Luke says that the Holy Spirit was there before the birth process. Therefore, by applying the reasoning of Thomas Aquinas, we reason that the gene of the spirit had millions of predecessors in its evolution. It did not come from Christ in heaven as the Bible often infers.

Finally, "let us follow the Holy Spirit's leading in every part of our lives." Paul's advice is congruent with our scientific reality. The advice is necessary because the animal genes in our soul were part of our beginning, and they will be with us forever; therefore we will always need the Holy Spirit in our soul to correct the evil desires of our animal ancestry.

Resurrection is a metaphor for the spirit that Jesus surrendered to us in his demise on the cross.

WHO IS GOD?—GOD IS THE GENE OF THE SPIRIT

Who is God? Dare we ask? Or have believers manipulated the qualities of God to favor their own beliefs?

Through all of human history, about 5000 years, every nation, every culture, every religion, every church, every denomination (indeed, every individual) has chosen its own handle on who God is and what God does. These handles define in detail all the dimensions of their God. Such handles were necessary when the earth was thought to be flat and humanity was thought to exist in a three-story structure: life on a flat earth, life in heaven far above, and life in hell below in the fiery furnace. These concepts were necessary to motivate believers to worship the spirit of God's goodness and love. Some of these handles still seem necessary for us today to practice the spirit of God's goodness and love.

Yet all these religious handles have caused untold misery, suffering, bigotry, devisiveness, killings and wars—in the Middle East between Jews and Muslims, in Yugoslavia between Orthodox Christians and Muslims, in Iraq between Muslims and fellow Kurds, in Northern Ireland between Protestants and Catholics, and in Central America between religious and social factions.

The major religious handles are Judaism, Christianity, Islam, Hinduism, Buddhism, Confucianism and Shintoism. But before we compare the definition of God to the handles of these major religions, we must lay down some premises of who God is, that can be acceptable to scientific knowledge:

1. God-Christ as one is the first cause of all creation according to the Bible in Proverbs 8, John 1 and Colossians 1.

2. The creation process is active in the inorganic, organic and culture phases and is ongoing.

3. Humans are the progeny of the animals, having developed in the culture phase of evolution.

4. Humans were created in the culture phase when the God-Christ gene started the psyche with soul, mind and intelligence in our animal bodies three million years ago.

5. The Christly spirit of Jesus resides in our souls only.

6. God in heaven and the resurrected Christ "in his image" are spiritual only and nothing more; they are metaphors for the spirit.

7. Science has to concede that only God-Christ can qualify to contain the incomprehensibles in nature. Science is not able to write a formula of the mystery of God-Christ the Creator—the incomprehensibles of time, space, God and the gene.

Judaism and the Old Testament put the first historically recorded national and specific handle on God. The Old Testament, which is the history of the Jewish religion, is the first document presenting a God with a spirit of goodness. Historically the Old Testament lays the foundation for Christianity and to some extent for the beginning of Islam and Hinduism.

The first 17 books of the Old Testament record the history of the nation of Israel and relate the behavior and actions of God. This handle specifies a God sitting on the throne in heaven with a hands-on style of daily operation of his kingdom. As Jehovah he was so powerful that he killed all his created human beings who were enemies of his exclusively chosen people the Israelites. They were enemies because they did not worship the God of Abraham. This angry God is based on Psalm 78:62: "He caused his people to be butchered because his anger was intense." (Quotes are from *The Living Bible*.)

I Kings 22:19: "'I saw the Lord sitting on His throne, and the armies of heaven stood around him.'" Isaiah 13:3: "I, the Lord, have set apart these armies for this task [to destroy Babylon]...to satisfy my anger." 13:9: "For see, the day of the Lord is coming, the terrible day of his wrath and fierce anger. The land shall be destroyed, and all the sinners with it."

God says of vengeance in Deuteronomy 32:35: "Vengeance is mine, and I decree the punishment of all her [Israel's] enemies: Their doom is sealed." Isaiah 63:6: "'I crushed the heathen nations in my anger....'"
God allowed slavery in Leviticus 25:44-45: "'However, you may purchase slaves from the foreign nations, living around you, and you may purchase the children of the foreigners living among you....'"

God repeatedly exterminated people of his own creation because he said they were enemies of his chosen people the Israelites. Genesis 19:24-25: "Then the Lord rained down fire and flaming tar from heaven upon Sodom and Gomorrah, and utterly destroyed them, along with the other cities and villages of the plain, eliminating all life—people, plants, and animals alike."

The story of Noah and the flood details the extermination of all the people and all life on the planet except Noah and his family and animals in the ark. Genesis 6:17: "Look! I am going to cover the earth with a flood and destroy every living being—everything in which there is the breath of life. All will die. But I promise to keep you safe in the ship, with your wife and your sons and their wives." Genesis 7:23: "All existence on the earth was blotted out...." God destroyed it all, leaving alive only Noah and those with him in the boat.

Many other exterminations by God of human beings can be listed. The world of God as described in the first 17 books of the Bible was one of forced obedience to Jehovah. For 1000 years God ruled over humans by force as was done by all kings of the neighboring countries at that time. Such a rule by anger, vengeance and retribution was probably necessary to be acceptable to people then.

The next five books of the Old Testament record the most beautiful poetry and literature. The horrible handle of power and destruction changes to a handle of truth, love, wisdom and the spirit of goodness. But Proverbs goes far beyond the platitudes of love and the spirit of goodness, presenting us with Wisdom personified as a woman. It is a beautiful description of metaphors for the DNA molecule that has been God's method of creation for thousands of millennia in the organic phase of creation.

Proverbs 3:19: "The Lord's wisdom founded the earth; his understanding established all the universe and space." Proverbs 8:1: "Can't you hear the voice of wisdom? She is standing at the city gates and at every fork in the road, and at the door of every house." The DNA gene's creationary evolution applies to everyone—all four billion of us on earth today. When Solomon spoke these words, God the Creator was the only source to tell us what would take place 3000 years later. Solomon presented us with "Miss" Wisdom when the earth was still thought to be flat. We can justifiably present her as a corollary of the DNA molecule of the genetic chain of chromosomes that has been creating everything alive for millions of years. God is still doing so today, every day.

From Proverbs 8:22-31 (see "Creation") we must infer that Wisdom and her corollary DNA were active when creation began thousands of millions of years ago and not in seven days as is recorded in Genesis. Doesn't Wisdom relegate the Genesis story to the fiction of imagination? The description by Wisdom of God's "blueprint" for creation could not be closer to a corollary of DNA, which has been designated by the scientists as the architect of the present process of creation of organisms. "Miss" Wisdom updates us from the mindset of a flat earth and seven-day creation as envisioned 3000 years ago to the present concept, scientifically substantiated by the electron microscope, of the DNA molecule of the genetic chain of chromosomes that is the basis of creation of all living plants, animals and humans.

This creation process in the inorganic phase we are obliged to call God. Scientists tell us it is an ongoing process that has no beginning and no ending. It has gone on forever and will go on forever. This revelation of God's wisdom 3000 years ago in our religious journey on this planet speaks of the mystery of God in creation. Solomon tells us that God's wisdom created everything.

One must consider the time in which the first part of the Old Testament was written. Kingdoms were thought to be ruled by the sword of a mighty God that humans called the ultimate source and power of the universe. This God also served as a source of religious devotion. Knowledge was not adequate enough to acquaint the prophets with the true reality of nature.

How can we establish a mindset in which these two elements of the God concept are both contained in one process? As Martin Luther, generally looked up to as the founder of Protestant religion, said, "Whatever thy heart dost cling to and rely upon, that is thy God." Then, logic follows, we can agree that God is the process of creation. Proverbs 8, John 1 and Colossians 1 tell us this is so, and the theologian Thomas Aquinas said in the 13th century A.D.: "The fact that God exists can be proved in five ways":

1. The first way is motion, which we see all about us, perceiving it through our senses. Whatever is moved must be moved by another being. Such a Being is understood by all to be God.

2. Causality is the second way Aquinas identifies God with the creation process: "Causes follow preceding causes, and so if we proceed into the past into infinity and there had been no cause, there would be today nothing." Since that is not the case, there had to be an initial cause. "Therefore," he says, "we have to posit a first cause and effect. All men call this Cause God." The "first cause" is incomprehensible to science.

3. The third way is the possibility and necessity of a being. An original being was necessary; otherwise there would be nothing. All men call this Necessary Being God.

4. The fourth way is found in the perfection of things. Aristotle said: "Whatever is supreme in any line of perfection is the cause of all degree within that line of perfection." That being which is the cause of all perfection operating among us as Supreme Being we call God.

5. The fifth way is the order which governs nature. There is an intelligent being by which all natural things are directed toward their purpose. This Being we call God.

Such order is demonstrated by the balance of the centrifugal force of the tectonic plates on the earth's surface rotating at 1000 miles an hour, against the gravity (centripetal force) that keeps them in place instead of flying out into space with our continents and crashing into any of the planets or stars. This order or power that holds everything together, as the Apostle Paul puts it, is one of the incomprehensible scientific burdens that God carries for us. God will take care of them.

The big question then becomes why we have been worshiping a God of form that nobody has ever seen? Only Moses was to have communicated directly with God, but he had to do that through a cloud of fire on Mount Sinai, along with smoke, thunder and lightning. Why do we not accept God as the power, wisdom and spirit of goodness in the creation process that Solomon described 3000 years ago in "Miss" Wisdom and that Thomas Aquinas detailed to us during the 13th century A.D.?

Through all ages of recorded human history, worship was always attached to the specific handle of the god of that worshiper. The spirit of God's love and goodness (NSB) was not a concept in and of itself to be worshiped. Such was the case in Old Testament times, and it has remained so to the present time.

The one exception, recorded in Proverbs, is Wisdom working side by side with the spirit of God in creating the planet and the human family on it. They worked together since ages past, long before the earth was formed. Proverbs 3:19: "The Lord's wisdom founded the earth; his understanding established all the universe and space." Proverbs 8:12: "...for wisdom [DNA evolution] knows where to discover knowledge and understanding."

Such a knowledge (*Wissenschaft*, or science) is what genetics is all about. That is our God.

CHRIST—
METAPHOR OF JESUS

The Christ who was crucified as Jesus, resurrected from the dead and ascended to heaven from where he answers prayers, has been the essence of Christology that has been worshiped for 2000 years.

From a scientific viewpoint we have quoted the Bible, stating very specifically that Christ as God was the first cause of all creation. These same quotes by John and Paul also state that Christ and God are the same being. Such a first cause in the creation process of Christ and God is the incomprehensible quality that is competent to create everything. That quality is entirely without form, having no material content. Science can accept the name Christ-God with the incomprehensible gene as one. It is an incomprehensible secret mystery of Christ, of which there are many.

In the same Bible we have Christ presented to us as a human-born being who is crucified, resurrected from the dead and ascended to heaven to rule on the throne with God. In the crucifixion event Jesus was totally human—he carried his own cross, bled and spoke about his being. He was human, as Bishop Arius taught at the Nicaea Conference of Constantine in 325 A.D. (detailed elsewhere).

The crucifixion story of Jesus, the authenticity of which was questioned by *Time, Newsweek* and *U.S. News* in their issues of Easter week 1996, reveals several factors:

1. The crucifixion of Jesus is generally accepted as factual in view of the history of 2000 years ago when crucifixion was a means of capital punishment.

2. After Judas embraced Jesus to betray him, Jesus said (Matthew 26:56): "But this is all happening to fulfill [satisfy] the words of the prophets...." Bible writers determined many centuries previously that the messiah would be crucified, rise in three days, and be enthroned in heav-

en; the details of ascension to heaven would be added later. They were inspired by the "in his image" of an incarnated God. Jesus was captured by the scripture of the Bible.

3. Before Jesus surrendered his spirit, as a human he absented God from him (Matthew 28:46): "...'Eli, Eli, lama sabachthani,' which means, 'My God, My God, why have you forsaken me?'" That was a human response to be expected; Jesus' humanism lived in his soul side by side with the divinity of the imagined God.

4. Finally Jesus surrendered his spirit (to us) and died (Mark 15:37).

5. Matthew 28:51-54 records that at the moment of death, "the earth shook," and the Temple curtain split in two because of an earthquake, "tombs opened, and many godly...came back to life ...." These events exaggerate imagined happenings through Bible rhetoric. Of course, dead people coming to life is impossible to have occurred in the actual inorganic and organic evolutionary world that God created.

The most common concept of Christ is one born of the divine who performed miracles, was crucified and resurrected, and who ascended to heaven where he sits on the throne beside God ruling the events of the world and answering our prayers. He is to return when the world ends to judge all human beings, who will be resurrected, to determine who goes to heaven and who shall burn in hell.

Three biblical concepts of who Christ is can be accepted by scientific knowledge. The Bible tells us that "Christ" is God by another name, so in this writing "Christ" and "God" are used interchangeably as referring to the same being. The Bible tells us that Christ is the first cause of all creation, in Proverbs as Wisdom and in John and Colossians as Christ and God as one.

We are delighted that science can accept the concept of an incomprehensible God-Christ as cause of creation. The Bible is a noble attempt to animate and incarnate the *numen summum bonum* (NSB, or spirit of supreme goodness) into a form called Christ-God in heaven. We wish to go by the Bible as far as the science of today will allow us to do so.

In this discussion we equate Christ with other incomprehensibles such as time, space and the gene of the DNA molecule as it operates in the ongoing creation process. Science, it now seems, will never be able to define when time started or where space ends or who God is, and more relevantly, what power started and controls what the gene is creating.

Therefore Christ-God is an appropriate name to give to circumstances that are above and beyond what the scientific mind can comprehend.

God has always existed and will continue to exist forever. He has always represented the solution to the unseen and to the fears and uncertainties that confound us here on earth because our minds are limited, in contrast to God of the first cause. Such a concept of God came when the DNA molecule introduced the first gene of the psyche with the soul, starting with Australopithecus in Africa three million years ago. The soul enabled us for the first time to feel the Jesus-spirit. We acquired the feeling of the spirit of supreme goodness. We also acquired fear for our survival and the condition of our destiny and death. Our animal ancestors had no such fears. They did and still do react instinctively against any physical harm.

That soul consciousness of the spirit of the divine, as well as the fear of evil, created all sorts of gods all over the place in antiquity. These have recently arrived as Yahweh of the Old Testament, Christ of the New Testament and Allah of the Koran, plus Satan, all constructed to solve our problems.

The God-Christ of the first cause of the creation process of the Bible is an accepted concept of knowedge because science allows it to be so. In addition to God-Christ taking the burden of solving the incomprehensibles, God-Christ has certain connotations in all cosmologies of immortality, omnipotence, omniscience, beneficence and divinity. The gene of the DNA molecule covers these ancient connotations of God as infused in our psyche—immortality, omnipotence, omniscience, beneficence, divinity.

The gene is immortal because it keeps on replicating itself and has done so for several billion years, and science says it will continue to do so. That makes it immortal and omnipotent because it knows where it is going through its control of the incomprehensible directives of God the first cause.

The gene is omnipotent because it can create anything that God the first cause has on the agenda for it. The proof of such omnipotence is the millions of species that have been created. Nearly all species have become extinct, to be replaced by new improved species. Then the DNA took a "detour" from physical creation to culture creation.

The gene is omniscient because it knows in advance where it is going in the creation process. The proof of such omniscience is demonstrated with the introduction of the gene of the spirit into our animal ancestry starting three million years ago.

The gene is beneficent because it enhanced the human quality in us from Australopithecus to where we are today at a soul level far above our animal ancestors.

The gene is divine because it gave us a soul that can host the spirit and activity of supreme goodness. What a beautiful process that has given our animal body the quality of feeling, appreciation, sympathy and more! It has given us the Jesus-spirit of love, mercy, forgiveness and a simple lifestyle, all of which will save us from extinction and bring "thy kingdom come...on earth."

The existence of Christ as a human-born Jesus is well documented in the Bible. His life and service have no controversy with scientific knowledge. Scientifically Jesus had the right psychic soul genes in the genome he received from Joseph and Mary so that he could qualify as the Messiah of the Old Testament prophets to represent the divinity of the Old-Testament God to all people.

In all his teachings Jesus never once called himself the God that Athanasius taught at Constantine's Nicaea Conference in 325 A.D. We therefore accept the teaching of Arius of the same conference, who taught that Jesus was a human-born representative of God among people on earth. He was crucified and surrendered his spirit to all humanity in his process of dying on the cross.

The intervening resurrected Christ sitting on a throne ruling and judging all humanity is as such totally unacceptable by scientific knowledge for several reasons:

Resurrection, i.e., the returning to life of a dead Jesus to a living Christ, is physically impossible according to the laws of science laid down by the God-Christ of the first cause of all creation. Genetically it cannot happen. For that reason no evidence verifies resurrection as a physical action.

However there is no controversy with the concept that the resurrection was of a spiritual nature only, a concept that tells us that the form of a Christ or God on a throne never existed. A spirit can live and function only in a human soul and nowhere else. A spirit cannot perform any activity from a location anywhere in the universe. (For quotations from the Bible on a spiritual resurrection see "Resurrection.")

Finally, the Bible story of God-Christ ruling from a throne in heaven comes with a concept of incarnation, eschatology, teleology, creation *ex-nihilo* and apocalypse. Not one of these concepts is scientifically possible. Incarnation is defined as an assumption that a spirit has taken on a physical form that can perform from a place called heaven. For 3.5 billion years the DNA molecule has created forms of plants, animals and humans. It has created a human form that can host a spirit, but a spirit has never produced a form.

The religion of Christ, Yahweh and Allah depend on an eschatology of death, resurrection and a judgment day that sends humans to heaven or hell. But scientific and commercial travel and communications show no evidence that a place called heaven or hell exists on this planet or in its planetary system. More to the point, resurrection of a dead cell to a cell with life has never happened in several billion years of DNA creation. Science says it cannot happen in our God-gene creation process.

Christ, Yahweh and Allah stand on teleology, which teaches finalism. Creation started abruptly out of nothing, and after a short period of creation it stopped abruptly as finished. Science teaches that the creation process is ongoing. Science completely nullifies the creation process of teleology.

Christianity also teaches apocalypse, the sudden end of the world. At that event all the dead will rise from their graves and be judged by Christ, who will have just arrived from heaven to judge all humankind. Human beings have been enhancing their soul quality by the gene for over a million years, and science indicates that the universe can go on forever. 1 Peter 4:7 says, "The end of the world is coming soon." That was said almost 2000 years ago.

At this point, *if we could just let Christ remain Jesus, then we could go about our business of enhancing the quality of our soul spirit.*

III. GOD IN SOUL

Soul—Divine Principle of Life

Soul God—Soul God Versus Heaven God

Knowledge Versus Faith—Faith is in our Knowledge

Zoroaster—Reports 20,000 Years of God in Soul

Greek—Socrates Versus Heaven God

Salvation—Jesus-Spirit Through Meditation

SOUL—DIVINE PRINCIPLE OF LIFE

We are repeatedly presenting the human soul as the complete and only container of the spirit of God and Jesus.

Drawing from John 1 and Colossians 1, I write of God and Christ as one being and concept. The names represent one deity and are used interchangeably. Because of this concept, Jesus seems to be a separate being from Christ. Jesus is not a Bible metaphor, whereas God and Christ are metaphors. Jesus was human-born—born genetically to qualify as the possessor of the total spirit of God to act out on earth what the God-spirit stood for by his teaching and lifestyle. On the cross during the process of his demise, his last words were, "I commit my spirit." From that time forward the spirit of Jesus is combined with the God-spirit to live in the souls of all human beings, though too few find him in their soul. So God and Christ are metaphors, but Jesus is human, presenting to us the spirit of the soul.

Human existence started with life in a three-phase creation process. Life consists of a body of organic cells cooperating to continue metabolism, to replicate itself and to perform certain functions of motion and sense perception to which that body reacts. Such a process applies to all animal and human gene activity. The soul of humans is the quality that evolves out of the mind and intelligence to come up with a higher quality of life. It has raised us above the animal psychic and soul level. That soul quality aims to make life better. It is the "gene" of the Jesus-spirit that God-Christ the first cause has evolved.

Since all Bible worshipers rely on faith to reach eternal bliss, it behooves us to critique Bible rhetoric for its credibility and for how it functions in the presence of scientific facts today. With such an overload placed upon the soul, we want to document some of the things the Bible has to say about the soul (in *The Living Bible*).

Genesis 2:7: "The time came when the Lord God formed a man's body from the dust of the ground and breathed into it the breath of life. And man became a living person." In these early creation events, Moses had God do all the speaking. This God rhetoric, a paraphrase, fits quite well into today's concept of creation. God started with dust. Dust was early in the inorganic first phase of the creation process, so we are wisely led to accept the biblical dust as part of the inorganic creation process that has existed forever. Then the Moses-God makes the body which creation's first-cause God had already made more than a billion years before Moses in the organic phase of creation.

Next, very aptly, the Moses-God used his breath—an unseen thing that is a metaphor for the gene that infused the soul with the God-Jesus spirit into the human psyche ages ago. It was at a point in time of the culture creation process of the soul that that soul over a million years created the third concept, the "Jesus-spirit" of God. It could fathom the God of the *numen summum bonum* (spirit of supreme goodness), or NSB. Here, then, we see the concepts of the God of Moses, of the God who is the first cause of the creation process, and of the God of NSB who came during the culture phase of the creation process of God the first cause—a metaphor that is producing the human Jesus, a reality.

In Genesis 49:6, Jacob says: "O my soul, stay away from them....For in their anger they murdered a man, and maimed oxen just for fun." Jacob found the God-spirit in his soul.

Deuteronomy 11:13b: "....and if you will love the Lord your God with all your hearts and souls, and will worship him." Here we have a command condition of a dictatorial God. Soul in this verse is not the one the creating God infused into our psyche, a spirit of God's goodness. No; here the soul is a separate being that sometimes needs to be punished. In this verse the soul is really not that important; obedience is demanded so that rain can come.

Job 12:10: "For the soul of every living thing is in the hand of God, and the breath of all mankind." Again God determines the soul in everything, even the "dumbest beast" (12:8). The Moses-God commands everything. He is not our God of the NSB; he is a dictator, daily manufacturing everything, according to the reply of Job to Zophar in 12:14-15a: "And how great is his might! What he destroys can't be rebuilt. When he closes in on a man, there is no escape. He withholds the rain, and the earth becomes a desert...." He is a God of revenge and not like the God in our soul, the *numen summum bonum*. Rather, he is a day-to-day ruler, a metaphor for the animal desire to control our spirit.

Ezekiel 18:2-4: "Why do people use this proverb about the land of Israel: The children are punished for their fathers' sins [the animal genes]? As I live, says the Lord God, you will not use this proverb any more in Israel, for all souls are mine to judge—fathers and sons alike—and my rule is this: It is for a man's own sins that he will die." The Old Testament is almost devoid of the soul function. The obvious reason for this lack is that God determines everything in his mode as an almighty person. People don't need directives for their soul because he personally directs everything; he directs the spirit. In this passage God finally introduces the inner self as responsible for a person's sins, and the only solution is death. Although God in the subsequent rhetoric tells us how to live by good deeds, he says he is still the sole judge of our life. The "fathers' sins" are our animal genes in action. The solution is not God ruling. The scientific solution is very simple: It all lies in our soul's response.

Matthew 10:28: "'Don't be afraid of those who can kill only your bodies—but can't touch your souls! Fear only God who can destroy both soul and body in hell." The New Testament starts by separating the soul from the body, a Platonic concept which was changed by Aristotle to mean that the soul lives within the body. Five hundred years after Aristotle, Matthew presents them as separate beings that God can kill separately. Again God is shown as threatening with fear the destruction of both body and soul in hell. Here God does everything from killing to numbering the hairs of our head. He is the same old impossible giant of Moses' time, a metaphor for our animal genes of combativeness and fear—the animal spirit.

Mark 14:34: "And He said to them, 'My soul is crushed by sorrow to the point of death; stay here and watch with me.'" Jesus said, to his credit and sacredness, that the soul is at stake, not his bodily life. His death on the cross and his blood are part of the body. His burden is his spirit in his soul that he offered for our souls. His worry over the death of his body is a part of an ancient belief in which he had to die and be resurrected in three days, and in which Jesus is forced to become Christ in heaven.

John 12:27-28a: " Now my soul is deeply troubled. Shall I pray, 'Father, save me from what lies ahead'? But that is the very reason why I came! Father, bring glory and honor to your name.'" Here are two Gods talking to each other before the crucifiction. What are their priorities? They are to glorify their own name. These verses present the soul God and the honor-Father God.

To identify the real God as instructed by King Solomon, John and Paul, one must look in the Bible for the God of the first cause of the creation process. This God goes back forever in time. This God, as the Christ-DNA molecule in the third phase of creation (the culture phase), started three million years ago to produce genes in our ancestors the mammals that created the psyche containing soul, mind and intelligence. When those qualities of the psyche became strong enough, prophets all over the world sought to create a being that ruled everything by incarnation. As stated in Genesis the creations were "in his image." They all failed because they did not really exist. Soon the surviving God of the spirit of goodness (*numen summum bonum*, or NSB) established residence in every human soul born on this planet and created NSB incarnate through the genes of Joseph and Mary—Jesus.

The Jesus-spirit of a simple lifestyle, mercy, forgiveness and love even for enemies that lives in our souls is most worthy of our worship. By prayer we will find these qualities in never-ending abundance for the survival of this planet so that we can have "thy kingdom come...on earth." (We elaborate the last statement elsewhere.)

Luke quotes Peter's sermon in Acts 2:31-33: "'David was looking far into the future and predicting the Messiah's resurrection, and saying that the Messiah's soul would not be left in hell and his body would not decay....and we all are witnesses that Jesus rose from the dead. And now he sits on the throne of highest honor in heaven, next to God."

Acts 2:30: "But he [David] was a prophet, and knew God had promised with an unbreakable oath that one of David's own descendants would [be the Messiah and] sit on David's throne.'" Here David is repeating the resurrection concept of Egypt, Babylon and Assyria. In this verse is not a Jesus born of a virgin who had an immaculate conception but a Jesus claimed by the prophet David to be his descendant by the way of Joseph, Mary's husband. Immaculate conception and a Virgin Mary clearly cut out Joseph and his sperm from the progeny of Jesus. Therefore we have to address the Bible: "You can't have it both ways. In fact, this situation completely screws up the credibility of a virgin birth."

We accept God as the first cause of the whole creation process in its inorganic, organic and culture phases as it is presented to us in Proverbs 8, John 1 and Colossians 1. We accept God as a spirit of goodness in our soul as portrayed throughout the Bible and as presented to us by Jesus in human form. We accept God the father of the Old Testament as an image and only as such. The reality of such a God that appeared to do everything manually for his people never existed. He was merely an image of man. He even says so in Genesis. To the extent that this image is carried over into the New Testament, the New Testament becomes complicated and captive to the Old Testament.

In Acts 2:30 even King David had a healthy respect for the sacredness of the soul. However, he had a problem with the body of the soul—he did not want the body to decay. The chronological review in the Bible of the function of the human soul is a sorry spectacle. This is so because it is completely dominated and controlled by the mighty God presented to us by ancient writers in the J and E sources, modeled after other gods in that time and area. They were all gods of fear, anger and vengance, and they all destroyed human lives *en masse*. Such gods of Babylon and Egypt are all gone, but the God of Abraham, Isaac and Jacob is still alive and very active in the Judeo-Christian community. Scientific findings of the Christ-DNA creation process will change that, too.

The genetics of controlling and determining our behavior as human beings has become a science specialty that is producing textbooks on that subject. The genetic process that deals with the development of the soul gives us our feeling of the quality of a meaningful life. The Bible gives us a perfect being in Jesus to show us how the gene of the Jesus-spirit of love, mercy, forgiveness and a simple lifestyle can overcome the inadequacies of the animal genes that we carry in our soul. Jesus surrendered his spirit to us in the process of dying on the cross in his last words: "I commit my spirit."

Our value as human beings is measured by the quality and quantity of the Jesus-spirit active in our soul. Our animal body has no more value than that of chickens that we butcher by the millions every day. Murder is not a matter of killing our body but a matter of killing our soul. Jesus did not say on the cross that he was giving up his body. He said, "I commit my spirit." Such a soul-body concept applies to abortion before the soul appears after the fetus takes its first breath or in old age when the soul has left the body.

In this book, the word "soul" is repeated hundreds of times for several reasons:

1. Repetition gives emphasis.

2. There are many approaches that prove the existence and function of the soul of the psyche that the gene has given us.

3. It is important because, after all, these souls have created thousands of gods on this planet, precisely those of Yahweh, Christ, and Allah.

4. The soul is a verifiable entity that can be proved by its activity in us as the spirit.

5. Finally, we take a tip from the Bible. If God can be referred to thousands of times, then the soul, creator of God, deserves more. As Martin Luther pointed out, what people depend on is their God.

The soul is our life because:

1. Dictionaries and encyclopedias define the soul as the rational, emotional and volitional faculties in man, as forming an entity distinct from the body. Theologically it is the divine principle of life in man.

2. The Bible gives us a beautiful, complete essence of the soul in Jesus' love, mercy, humility, forgiveness and a simple lifestyle.

3. In "Christian science" the soul is God.

4. In the Old Testament, God and the prophets are confused between the God of vengance, retribution and extermination of humans; and the God of the divine goodness of "love your enemies."

5. In the New Testament, Jesus teaches love, mercy, humility, forgiveness and a simple lifestyle, which the genes of the Jesus-spirit gave us as human beings through the genetic evolution process to lead us to meditation.

6. Princess Diana and Mother Teresa were revered worldwide for their beautiful souls filled with goodness and compassion. Mother Teresa did her work for the God in heaven. Diana did her work for the God in her soul. Her funeral "sermons" had no mention of heaven, God or Christ. The response for Diana was so enormous in England, in the millions. Mother Teresa may receive sainthood from the pope.

SOUL GOD—SOUL GOD VERSUS HEAVEN GOD

A basic question is why belief in the one God in heaven of Yahweh, Christ and Allah survived and grew in world-controlling strength and dominance when belief in the God in our soul, taught by Zoroaster and Socrates, hibernated for more than 2000 years.

To answer that concern, we have to look at ourselves and how we functioned over the last 10,000 years. Were we knowledgeable enough to accept the God in our soul from Greek teaching, or did ignorance or low intelligence require that someone prescribe a God for us who took care of all the goodness in our lives? Obviously, we chose the Bible God who ruled everything from above and promised heaven forever.

What makes the metaphors of the biblical God confusing are the many variations presented of his being and behavior patterns. Versions of this manipulated heaven God are:

1. The God of Moses, who created in teleology and *ex nihilo* the earth and everything in it. This God managed to have humans born in sin because of the snake and the apple (metaphors for our animal genes.)

2. The God of Abraham, who came down to visit, eat and consult with Abraham and Sarah in the tent.

3. The God of the Exodus, who turned water into blood and separated the water of the Red Sea.

4. The God of Judah in Palestine, who was Yahweh, an exterminator God who killed all his created humans who were not his chosen obeyers, e.g., the Noah flood and Sodom and Gomorrah.

5. The more benign God of Israel in northern Palestine. When the fighting stopped, writers combined their source materials, E and J (for Ephraimitic, or northern, and Judean, or southern, originally based on

the way God was referred to—Elohim and Jahweh, or Yahweh) to write the Old Testament.

6. The God of David and the Psalms, a God of beauty, benevolence and comfort.

7. The scientifically acceptable God of the first cause of all creation as identified by Solomon in Proverbs 8, by John in John 1, by Paul in Colossians 1, and verified by Thomas Aquinas, as related elsewhere.

8. In the New Testament, the God of Jesus of Nazareth, a human-born model of love and supreme goodness, who taught: "Love your enemies."

9. The resurrected Jesus who becomes a hostage of the Old Testament—Christ in heaven ruling and judging all human beings.

10. The God-Christ of the apocalypse, who comes down from heaven at an appointed time to end the world, resurrect all the dead from their graves and judge all humanity to either burn in hell forever or ascend with him to heaven and live in bliss forever.

We relate again that in 1900 Pope Pius was surfacing the same question when he asked Wilhelm Schmidt, an anthropologist in Vienna, to contact aborigines in Brazil and Australia and other indigenous peoples all over the world and try to determine what their concept of God might be. These peoples had no writing and they had no indoctrination. In 1912, in the twelve-volume *Ursprung der Gotteside* (Origin of the God Idea) Schmidt detailed his findings. He reported that their gods were simple, nonspecific and vague. They only sensed that a great power existed that caused everything. They had no temples, no formal worship. They had no deity to worship, no beliefs in virgin birth or resurrection or judgment. To them, birth, life and death were steps in the process of nature.

In the last 10,000 years, three things happened:

1. The gene of the DNA molecule was identified that enhances the quality and capacity of the soul to host the God-spirit of goodness.

2. The great increase in population of antiquity produced groups and organizations of people who then concentrated on the specificity of their gods.

3. These people developed cuneiform and alphabet writing, which served to nail down the varied specifics of their gods, documented in the Athens Academy as the ideas of Socrates and Plato, and documented in the Bible as Judaism and Christianity and in the Koran as Mohammedanism, or Islam.

The infusion of the psyche with the soul, enhancing the genetic process in our animal bodies, greatly accelerated after more people fellowshiped with each other and read each others' writings during the last 6,000 years. Such acceleration of soul enhancement has a scientific basis because each human individual is exposed to an increase in the quantity and quality of the environment, thus adding to the evolution of the psyche. This is so because scientifically the culture creation process comes about largely through genotype-phenotype environmental interaction. (We discuss elsewhere the increased level in our souls and Zoroaster, Socrates and Aristotle as creators of culture.)

The God-spirit of Bible metaphor had its beginning long before writing came into use. To indigenous primitive people God was a vague force who made things happen. The very existence of things suggested a God who caused those things to take place. Movement of a tree's leaves in a breeze was thought to be caused by a God as a mover. They knew nothing about atmospheric matter moving tree leaves while that matter moves through space to equalize variations in atmospheric pressure. The running of water downstream was thought to be caused by a God-mover because they did not know about gravity.

But the most unbelievable fact is that in the 1500s civilized Christian people taught that God in heaven moved the sun and moon across the sky every day. In the 1600s the Church threatened Galileo with torture because he taught how the earth really functions. That same ignorance of some Fundamentalists is still trying to combat scientific reality. But in October 1996 Pope John Paul II recognized the validity of evolution.

Such a weapon against the God of science is actively promoted in the United States by the Christian Coalition. To preserve this ignorance of the existence of the real world is the theological and political kingpin of the right-wing fundamentalist Christian. This fact was illustrated on the front cover of the May 15, 1995 *Time.*, which had a full-page view of the face of Ralph Reed, leader of the Christian Coalition. He was quoted as saying he would take over politics. Such tactics have for 2000 years protected the survival of the heaven God over the soul God of Socrates.

The political protection of the Bible God started with the Roman Emperor Constantine at the Nicaea Conference on May 20, 325 A.D. With his rebellious Bishop Athanasius, Constantine ruled that world religion should believe in two gods, God the Father and God the Son. At the same time, Arius, a more intelligent bishop, taught in the Socratic mode that Jesus was a human-born being and a role model of the God-spirit working within us to guide all worship. Later, Constantine's nephew Julian, Emperor of Rome and a very intelligent philosopher, ruled briefly 361-363 A.D. He taught the philosophy of the Academy, advancing the concept of God in the soul. He believed with Socrates that the God-spirit of his soul could reach heaven without the intervention of the forgiveness of Christ. He was also the most capable emperor. Unfortunately, Julian was killed at Strasbourg in a war against invaders from the North. This was the last time in Roman history that the Socratic concept challenged the God-Christ-in-heaven concept of the Roman Empire. It seems conceivable that Greek theology might have survived over Christianity if Julian had lived.

After Julian, Justinian became the Roman Emperor of the Eastern half of the Roman Empire with its center at Constantinople. He built churches for the Christians instead of temples. He stopped the Greek concept of God in the soul by closing the Academy in Athens in 529 A.D. and embezzled its funds since he was the king of the world.

The final protector of the God incarnate was the papacy for the next 1000 years. Because of many wars and the division of the Roman Empire into an eastern half based in Constantinople and a western half based in Rome, political leadership became so weak that the priesthood took over leadership. For the first time the papacy became a nation that still exists today. The eastern half became the Orthodox Catholic Church of Eastern Europe and Russia.

Emperor Justinian in cooperation with the pope gained control of the beliefs of the largely uneducated masses of the Roman Empire. Monks established monasteries all over the Middle East and Europe where Justinian ruled. Much effort was exerted to evangelize the barbarians from the North and the German and Huns from the East. The monks taught that the pope controlled for all members of the Church the quality of their afterlife in heaven. For more than 1000 years, such promise of everlasting bliss in the afterlife has kept Christianity's concept of God in heaven functioning with great success.

Augustine, a most respected bishop of the fourth century in Carthage, North Africa, accepted the Socratic concept of God in the soul. He was a very popular church leader, and his untrained followers convinced him to work for the Christian Church as established in Rome; "without Socrates" he served as their bishop.

In 732 A.D. Charles Martel (Charles the Hammer, whose title was Mayor of the Palace), the first Frankish king, in cooperation with the pope used the sword to save Christians from being overrun by the Moslems. In 800 A.D. Charles Martel's grandson Charlemagne (Charles the Great) was crowned by the pope at Rome as king of the Roman Empire, which included most of Europe. Charlemagne was king of the Franks 748-814 A.D. As emperor he ruled all of Central Europe extending to the Slavic country of Eastern Europe and Russia, dominating the Orthodox Catholics, from 768 A.D. until his death in 814 A.D.

That thousand-year interlude of Christology history is followed today by unbelievable repetition. Orthodox Christian Serbs have killed thousands of humans into mass graves in the Bosnian Civil War—"ethnic cleansing." The Christian concept of God, like the Old Testament God, is still forcing believers to kill for their faith. Such killing of human beings to assure the survival of fundamentalist beliefs is going on in Northern Ireland, Palestine and Bosnia; and in the U.S., hate is directed against abortion doctors.

Many human beings are praying for the time when we dismiss out of existence hell with Satan and heaven with Christ, and worship Christ as the incomprehensible spirit of creation, and worship God in our soul as the Jesus-spirit of love, mercy, humility, forgiveness and a simple lifestyle. It is only when we recognize the evil behavior of our animal genes from within that we can oust "Satan" and subdue the crime gene within us in a process of meditation.

KNOWLEDGE VERSUS FAITH— FAITH IS IN OUR KNOWLEDGE

The sanctity of faith has high priority for Bible believers. Without faith there is no Christianity according to New Testament writers. It has to be the faith of a little child who is without knowledge. Faith in a biblical picture of Christ ruling from heaven above is based entirely on an emotional assumption of the incarnated spirit of Christ ruling from heaven as a physical reality, even to the extent that Christ will come down from heaven to judge everyone when the world ends.

In the genetic creationary process of God-Christ as the first cause, faith is entirely in ourselves. We need faith in us to motivate into action the Jesus-spirit whose genes reside in our soul.

We discuss how faith applies to biblical theology in contrast to how faith applies to the theology of molecular biology. Faith is confidence in or dependence on a person, statement or thing as trustworthy; trust; belief without needing proof; belief in God or in testimony about God as recorded in scriptures or other religious writing. It is a system of religious beliefs: the Christian faith.

In the Christology of fundamentalist believers, the word "faith" has become a sanctity. Faith has been sanctified to the extent that it must include Christ in heaven ruling from a throne. To these believers faith is the essence of a heavenly Christ who is the only path to salvation from hell. When fundamentalist believers lose that faith, they come up with nothing. The divinity of their being becomes a complete spiritual vacuum. In a Harris Poll quoted from the Wichita Eagle of September 9, 1995 only eight percent of the Wichita State University students polled in this Christian nation were concerned about Christ judging them to hell in life after death; 92 percent were concerned about their life here on earh.

When followers of the genetic theology of the Jesus-spirit in their soul lose faith in themselves, they still have existing a soul that can always be reactivated since they have the free will to do so. They will always have the genes of the Jesus-spirit within them to be prayed to in meditation.

For more than 5000 years more than a billion Judeo-Christian believers lived by the mythology of some prophets' image. Equally amazing is the fact that nearly one billion Islamic believers have lived by the same mythology. In fact, both groups of believers start with Abraham's God image. The New Testament says in John 1: 18 that "No one has ever actually seen God," yet all these believers are sure their personal God and Savior exists somewhere "out there." That is the faith-in-God-in-heaven theology in which Jesus, a human-born person in the Bible, becomes a hostage to the Old Testament to become Christ.

Faith has no biological physical or procedural qualities; it is an emotional demonstration of the metaphor for the unseen—the Jesus-spirit. When combined with bigotry and pride, faith leads to wars and killings as in Northern Ireland, Palestine and Bosnia today. But the same emotional drive of the faith of fundamentalists generates strife and misery and suffering within their own groups. One glaring example is Klaas Epp.

In 1874 Klaas Epp and my grandfather, J.E. Schmidt, lived in Molotschna, Russia. Grandpa came to Kansas in 1874 to seek religious freedom, but Klaas Epp migrated to Central Asia to meet Christ, who was coming down from heaven to form his kingdom. Starting on Thursday, July 3, 1880 Epp traveled with his large church group on foot and by covered wagon and on camels for four years. He and his fellow church members had calculated that according to the revelations of the Bible, Christ would come down from heaven in 1889 in Central Asia. The trek was overfilled with strife and dissension, and many died on the way. Christ did not show up, and many of the survivors are still looking for the second coming at Ak Metchet. Klaas Epp died in 1913, and the 1917 Revolution killed most of the Molotschna Mennonite men in Siberia, with their Bible offering their only hope for a better life to come.

With humility I must fault the Bible and the pride and bigotry of my fundamentalist-believing ancestors for the suffering and death of many in Siberia because they let pride in their faith overtake their humanism and treated their Russian workers disrespectfully. I remember Grandpa telling me that at harvest time the proud rich Mennonite farmers would make the heathen Russians eat in the barn while they ate in luxury. If they had practiced the Jesus-spirit, their fate in Siberia might have been avoided.

More recently pride in faith drove "Heaven's Gate" believers to unproductive mass suicide. They had the same faith from reading the same Bible about a non-existing resurrection and heavenly Christ—a faith followed by millions of Christians—that enabled them (as they believed) to rush the date of their resurrection

We present things we can see and put our hands on that tell us about the God-Christ of the first cause of all creation, that tell us how we were created, and that tell us that God, who designed DNA, inserted the psyche into our animal body to develop us as human beings. These facts are not yet well organized because detailed DNA study is less than 50 years old compared to 3000 years of the life of the Bible. In the 21st century creative use of DNA will produce unbelievable results.

The evolution of human beings has been going on for millions of years. The first evidence that a human existed on this planet are footprints of a hominid walking erect on just two legs. Mary Leakey, daughter-in-law of a missionary couple in East Africa, found the footprints, which are dated as having been made more than three million years ago. This finding introduces us to a concept that our time of life on this planet is but a fraction of a second of the time that God the DNA molecule spent in the whole time of the creationary process.

Again we repeat that in the Bible, Proverbs 8, John 1 and Colossians 1 tell us what Thomas Aquinas in the 13th century called God the first cause of all creation. Here the incomprehensible God is equated with other incomprehensibles of time and space and basically the quality or power that makes the DNA gene "tick."

Also basic to our story is the concept of the inorganic creation process as it affects the development of prehistoric humans. Pangaea, the supercontinent thought to have originally included all of the continents, and movements of tectonic plates in the earth's crust were in this inorganic phase. The organic creationary phase starts the physical making of animals and human beings. The culture phase is what lifts human beings from the animal level of existence, from animals to a whole family of early people called hominids.

The development of hominids from the animal stage to human beings is our subject here. All true scientists who can look at volumes of scientific and archeological findings objectively agree that such an evolution of animal to human has taken place over the last three million years. We are here not concerned about what happened in the last 3000 years as that has been documented adequately since the beginning of writing in cuneiform and alphabet characters of the Sumerians and Phoenicians respectively, and in the Bible and the Koran and the records of many other cosmologies.

What we are attempting to do is substantiate what really happened in the process of how we as human beings became what we are from what we once were—part of the animal kingdom in God's DNA organic creationary process that started about four billion years ago according to scientific findings. These facts prove the culture creation process. Pope John Paul II in a statement October 1996 said the Church accepts evolution as real and true.

Our perspective is comparison of two different concepts of God and existence. Judeo-Christian believers have for more than 3000 years prayed to God as a personal savior. We pray to him in heaven out there somewhere, believing he can change our circumstances of the moment at all times. Through reception of our prayers out there somewhere, forgiveness comes to us for all our sins, saving us from evil and damnation. We have a vague belief that somewhere God has a heavenly abode where we can live in bliss forever after we die. All these beliefs are called faith.

The God this book presents is based not on unseen belief but on real findings that establish reality against mythology. As we have just stated, God-Christ is the first cause of all creation. In this creationary process God used genes to introduce into our animal ancestors the first directive supplying the psyche of the soul, mind and intelligence about two million years ago. During those two million years, by what geneticists call behavior genetics, the God-Christ genes added holy qualities into that soul, and we assume that those qualities are the desire and potential urge to be good, to overcome the evil animal instinct that we forever carry in our genetic make-up. That urge to be good that was planted in our souls is the final concept: the spirit of goodness in every soul ever created. The problem is that not all people find that spirit of Jesus in their souls.

In summary, faith is the essence of the divine in biblical theology, and knowledge is irrelevant to faith.

In the genetic evolution of the psyche with God in the soul, by the God of the first cause of all creation, faith has no correlation in any of the three phases of the creation process. This is so because all the steps of the evolutionary creation process are based on verifiable facts; therefore faith has no meaning. However, each individual soul has to have faith in himself and in his soul so that he can motivate the Jesus-spirit that it possesses into action. In genetic theology, we demand faith in our knowledge of truth and the reality of God's Nature.

Faith (i.e., fundamentalist faith) and knowledge are the two opposing concepts that cause controversy between religion and science in our life today.

ZOROASTER—REPORTS 20,000 YEARS OF GOD IN SOUL

During the Stone Age a non-Semitic people called the Indo-Europeans, who seem to have been the ancestors of Caucasians in antiquity, was moving out of the caves.

These herdsmen living in the Caspian Sea area had no writing, no tombs, no monuments and no temples. During winter months they herded their flocks southward into the Mesopotamia country of the Semites. According to history the Semites of Babylonia, Sumeria and Assyria around 3,000 B.C. regarded these Indo-Europeans from the cave country to the North as highly energized barbarians. In spite of that, these people introduced a beautiful religion at Avignon around 20,000 B.C., that was taught later in the sixth century B.C. by Zoroaster, their spiritual leader.

Their doctrine taught that the divine resides in the soul of every human being and that divinity has the capacity to grow, to correct itself and to function independently of any other deity. Zoroaster taught that the spirit of evil as well as the spirit of good resides in our soul. Scientifically we now know that the evil spirit in our soul is nothing more nor less than genetic traits, i.e., the evil and selfish desires of our animal ancestors. The gene has infused in our soul a *numen summum bonum* (NSB), or spirit of supreme goodness, to overcome evil animal traits if we choose to make that happen. The responsibility is all our task—again, a process of meditation.

The herdsmen from the Ice Age caves of the North were called Aryans. Coming into contact with the Semites of Babylon and Assyria repeatedly with their herds, the Aryans soon learned and applied the writings and culture of the Semites. These aggressive direct ancestors of the Western world soon conquered all the empires of antiquity and became the most powerful empire, Persia. Since the Persian Empire reached from the Nile to Europe and India, remnants of Zoroastrian theology were seen in the Parsees of India and the Platonic Academy of Athens. (I discuss Greek "theophilosophy" elsewhere.)

Parsees number only about 150,000 near Bombay. They still regard the soul of every human being as the temple of God's spirit of supreme goodness. They see the human body as the animal that carries the soul. When that body dies, they park the dead body on their towers of silence (cylindrical structures open to the sky) to be devoured by vultures. Parsees are highly respected.

The four virtues of the cave people and Zoroaster are liberty, justice, friendliness and sincerity. He taught that our duties in life are:

1. To make him who is wicked, righteous;
2. To make him who is ignorant, learned;
3. To make him who is an enemy, a friend.

The *Zend-Avesta*, the holy book of Zoroastrianism, says that Zoroaster was prophesied centuries before his birth as the "savior." He was born of a virgin, saved as an infant from a jealous ruler, was admired for his youthful wisdom, preached at 30, was tempted by the devil, cast out demons, cured a blind man and preached a God of truth and goodness. All this was said to have happened between 700 and 600 years B.C. It therefore had an influence on teachings of Judaism, Christianity and Islam.

In connection with Zoroaster of the Parsees, it seems proper to look at Mahatma Gandhi. Gandhi is recognized as a saint of all ages. He lived by the good he found in Judaism, Islam and Christianity because he was interested only in the NSB that these religious incarnations tried to depict. He lived by the spirit of Jesus' Sermon on the Mount. He was not the least bit interested in the mechanics of the Old and New Testaments of the Bible nor of the Koran. It is Gandhi's sincerity and passion for truth that the two billion worshipers of the Bible and the Koran must attain before they can reach heaven, which can exist only on this earth.

Bill Moyers has presented the divinity of the NSB as worshiped by Buddhists, Confucianists and Hindus. Their meditation-worship of the spirit in their soul is congruent to the genetic theology of the Jesus-spirit of love, mercy, humility, forgiveness and a simple lifestyle. We accept that Jesus-spirit after we deincarnate the Christ of the Bible. Such a deincarnation relieves us of the subterfuge of traditional faith and beliefs.

Resurrection of the dead Jesus to a living Christ in heaven is an incarnation of the Jesus-spirit that he surrendered to us while dying on the cross—the creation of a metaphor that metamorphizes a spiritual process into a physical, biological, animal form so that people ignorant of scientific reality could perceive that spirit with their animal senses.

Such a deincarnation of the Jesus-spirit completely reverses my highly revered father-in-law P.A. Penner's evangelistic efforts when he became the first General Conference Mennonite Church missionary to India in 1900. To his credit is the super-good service of successful leprosy work among his beloved, miserable Indian people in Champa, India. He was knighted by the British Empire for his service in treating leprosy.

In Christian missions in India, Christ was the only source of the divine, but in Veda, the oldest sacred writings of Hinduism, the divine is heaven-originated here on earth by our spirit. A reversal of the mission of the divine in India was revealed in the January 9, 1995 Wichita Eagle in a multi-page illustration of Veda meditation in the "Heaven on Earth Inns" movement by Maraishi theology of the U.S. Their headquarters is in the Camelot Parkside Hotel, Tulsa, Oklahoma, which Maraishi bought for $1.5 million.

Why does this reorientation occur of who God is and who we are? The basic reasons for such reorientation as truth and reality are obvious and operational today. What is not clear is how we can preserve some of the beauty that Christianity has given us in the Jesus-spirit in music, art and literature, especially in respect to biblical metaphors for the Holy Spirit in the soul of every human being on earth. The challenge for us today is essentially to reorient our concept of who God is and who we are in our daily worship of the divine NSB and to save the beauty of the Bible.

In summary, the God of goodness that we pray to is in the souls of everybody alive. Satan is nothing more than the animal genes that we have inherited. They have to be overcome by the Jesus-spirit in our soul through meditation.

GREEK—SOCRATES
VERSUS HEAVEN GOD

Greek civilization starts at the Aegean Sea. The Greek culture came from the north in Europe whereas all the cultures related so far except Persia had their origin in the Orient (east of the Mediterranean).

The early people of the Aegean Sea were from the local area until 3000 B.C. when hordes of Europeans invaded Greece. The invaders, who had survived the last cycle of the Ice Age, were considered barbarians. These people had no writing, partly due to severe climates. They had not had the time to gain culture. But the harsh climate had through the genetic process made them very aggressive, and they conquered the Persian Empire. Soon they applied the cuneiform and alphabet writing from the Hittite and Phoenician cultures respectively. The Greeks showed their psyche potential by adding vowels to the Phoenician consonants to make words complete. From that time on, the highly cultured Aegeans were known as Greeks.

Then came the legendary poet Homer, author of the *Iliad* about the war against Troy and the *Odyssey* about the wanderings of Ulysses. Even before Homer, legend has it that the early Greeks looked at all the activity of nature and concluded that a spirit caused all that activity and the essence of nature, and that spirit should be worshiped. What a noble concept in 1000 B.C. compared to an angry God of the Old Testament!

In spite of Homeric influence on religion and literature the average Greek clung to the God called Zeus who lived on top of Mount Olympus. Zeus was less actively hands-on than Moses' angry, vengeful God who exterminated his people when they were disobedient—by fire in Sodom or by flood in the Noah story—but Zeus also ruled with an iron fist and swallowed his adversaries. The Greek Zeus went through the same processes as the Bible God of life, death and resurrection. However Zeus avoided the myth that he created everything and that he regulated every detail in war and peace. While Zeus lived on Mount Olympus the God of Moses sat on his throne on the firmament 3000 years.

During the first millennium B.C. the aggressive Greeks from the North became rich noblemen who ruled over the common person with tyranny, enslaving their subjects. But a time always comes for everything, so in 594 B.C. in Greece came King Solo, a rich nobleman. He ruled by his code of law, a constitution that did away with tyranny—the first constitution on this planet that gave every person a vote.

While Yahweh killed the two-headed sky-dragon Leviathan and cut to pieces with his sword all his adversaries in order to gain complete sovereignty as the God of heaven and earth, during the first millennium Pericles in Greece declared Athens the "School of Greece." The Greek God Zeus lost credibility to the concept of the God of the Persian prophet Zoroaster, who had taught many centuries earlier that God was a spirit in the human soul. Such a concept of God was now promoted by Socrates, Plato and Aristotle. This Zoroastrian religious concept is so important in this writing that we will discuss it more fully later.

Socrates was born about 469 B.C.to a stonecutter and lived his life in the marketplace when Greece was on the pinnacle of its power and success. Athens was still celebrating the victory over Persian rule. The Parthenon was being built, and everybody was living high off the hog. Socrates did not accept all that affluence but condemned the state for its hypocrisy and pretensions. He debunked the stuffed shirts. Later when Athens was in a war with Sparta and lost its democracy, its rulers were very nervous in 403 B.C. They blamed Socrates for their misfortune because he preached against the state's multiple gods of Zeus. He was tried in court and was condemned to death.

On the morning of his death Socrates counseled his companions about the immortality of the soul: "No man has anything to fear of death who has filled his soul with temperance, justice, nobility, and truth." Other thoughts of Socrates are: "The soul resembles the divine and the body the mortal." 'The soul is the unseen, the body the seen." "Our souls must also have existed without bodies before they were in the form of man and must have intelligence." Socrates taught that to realize the essence of goodness, truth and love, we must order our intellectual vision so as to have the most exact conception of the essence to be considered (i.e., meditation).

Scientifically we know that soul qualities in us are carried by the genetic chain of chromosomes from one generation to the next generation and are therefore immortal and live forever. We are immortal and live forever in that chain of genes in the chromosomes for the infinitesimal addition we have made to that genotype through phenotype soul interaction. Socrates taught that knowledge is recollection, but the soul must have existed before such recollection to produce something to be recollecting; therefore the soul is immortal.

Plato, born in 427 B.C., was a student of Socrates. He was greatly affected by Socrates' death and established the Academy of Philosophy in Athens in 387 B.C. in his honor. This academy was an active institution of Greek philosophy for nearly 1000 years. Plato was essentially an extender of Socrates' thought. He taught that rational insight is inborn. He also said: "The power and capacity of learning exists in the soul already." Plato agonized over the differentiation of soul and body. How did they operate together? To Socrates that had been unimportant compared to the sanctity of the human soul. Plato seemed to have some problem with how the soul was connected to the body, but his student Aristotle straightened out Plato on that little problem.

Aristotle is considered by many writers to be the major philosopher of all time. For more than 2000 years we have had the privilege of looking at the concept of Zoroaster and later of Aristotle and his elders, which is that God is the first cause of all creation, and that all the divine can be found only in the soul of humankind. Aristotle was born to a physician of the king in 384 B.C. in Macedonia about 200 miles north of Athens. When he was 18, he entered the Athens Academy to study under Plato. Later he tutored the future Alexander the Great. Like Socrates, Aristotle was suspected of government intrigue so he went into seclusion but continued his writing.

As a mathematician in an exact science, Plato confined himself to law whereas Aristotle taught that in order for the soul to live, it must grow. Aristotle was a staunch naturalist who saw soul and body as they are. He rejected Plato's dualism of separate soul and body and taught that soul and body were created simultaneously and made to form one single functional reality. Aristotle taught that the soul is the entire vital principle of any living organism, the inner form that guides the life and development of the whole. He said the important thing about life is growth and development. He saw that intelligence increased in proportion to the complexity, structure and mobility of form.

A biologist, Aristotle reasoned that creation is an ongoing process. He said the unmoved mover, a non-material being or force (this would correspond to DNA directives, the incomprehensible mover of the gene), is the nature of the continuous activity of the universe, and that he was satisfied to call it God. He said God was a pure being, free of material substance, eternal, immobile and spiritual. God was a thought, a concept of goodness, and yet God represented the power, wisdom and capacity to propel the creation process forever.

The survival of the animal species of Homo Sapiens in nature called for evil aggressiveness. Since Moses did not know about the genetic chain by which we carry this trait of our animal ancestry, the Bible knew no better than that we were born in sin. Aristotle says we are born in a soul that contains the God-spirit of goodness. This nature according to Greek theology of 400 B.C. exists in us from birth and it is up to us to find that God-spirit.

The soul is the inner form that guides the life and development of the whole. Aristotle taught that the divine can be found only within the soul and that everyone is responsible by his/her own free will to enter heaven through finding and extending the Jesus-spirit of love, mercy, forgiveness and a simple truthful life. It is there because according to Gospel writers John and Paul, God-Christ created such a holy spirit. Scientifically the psyche (soul, mind, intelligence) rests in the genetic chain of chromosomes. God used the DNA molecule to get that job done.

Socrates taught that the goodness of the soul must overcome the body since the body is a source of endless trouble for us. He listed the lusts that come with the body inherited from our animal ancestors millions of years ago. The Bible calls this condition "born in sin"—a condition that science calls the genes we inherited from our animal ancestors.

Job 5:7: "Mankind heads for sin and misery...." Job made this "sin" statement when the earth was still flat and God still sat on his throne on the firmament and physically ruled the universe. We have since learned that "sin" is a metaphor for the evil that erupts in us when the evil instincts of our ancestral genes overpower the God-spirit of goodness that

God the first cause has placed in our soul. Since according to Socrates our animal body can cause us trouble, we must overcome such trouble before we can set our spirit of goodness in action. A concept of stirring the spirit of our soul into flames of action is given to us from the Gospel writers.

The Bible tells us in Proverbs, John and Colossians what Thomas Aquinas aptly defined: that God and Christ, the first cause of all creation procedures, are one and the same. They are identical. This God-Christ established a system of evaporation and condensation and precipitation of water that gives us rain. Job talks about the cycles of the atmosphere's activity. This system of God's creation process of the inorganic universe has been going on forever. We need to forget a mythical God on the firmament who acts in the fancy of our imaginations.

Romans 6:16: "Don't you realize that you can choose your own master? You can choose sin (with death) or else obedience (with) acquittal)...." This scripture passage presents us with the real problem in our theology. The spirit that the Bible presents to us is almost always worthy of our worship and should never be destroyed. But the procedures and incarnations presented to show how this spirit acts have been and are a hindrance in the spiritual enhancement of our soul, which is through meditation, not obedience based on fear..

In antiquity all spiritual values had to be incarnated for two reasons. First, such everyday handles offered an attractive way to hold on to such values. Second, this process put all the burden on God and relieved man of the responsibility of his obligations. We just pray to God out there somewhere, and he will answer all our prayers. He will do everything we "command" him in our prayer. Paul condemned Epicurus, a successor of Aristotle, for worshiping an unknown God. In his letter to Titus, whom he had taught "eternal life" (1:2), Paul quoted a Cretan poet (1:12, *King James Version*): "'The Cretans are always liars, evil beasts, slow bellies [lazy gluttons].'" To soften the blow in the same letter he entered a subterfuge in the commonly accepted controversy he had with those demanding circumcision.

In contrast, Socrates taught that we have the ability and responsibility to get rid of anger, lust and fear so that the soul can work effectively. Under the Bible system only a distant God can forgive us before we put our God-spirit of goodness—the *numen summum bonum,* or NSB—into action. In reality, we will never rid ourselves of such a "sin"—the animal instinct that we carry in our genome forever. While Socrates was in prison in Athens, waiting to be executed by the state for not believing in the mythical gods who were the resurrected offspring of the Greek God Zeus, he had many dialogues about the sanctity, function and immortality of the human soul. He taught that reason provides the only foundation of morality and the good life, and he taught people to examine critically all beliefs, pretenses and hypocrisies. To him the soul was immortal.

Socrates had a total absence of any desire for possessions. With his bald head, round face, protruding eyes, thick lips and big snub nose, he was all soul and a forgettable body. In his prison cell he encouraged his friends to be of good cheer because everyone who has adorned his soul with truth, love, the good life and who feels good about himself has no fear of death. As sunset drew near in that prison cell Socrates bathed, asked God's goodness to bless him and reached for the poison without hesitation or fear.

Since the Phoenician alphabet had just become available to the Greeks, the Athens Academy was very active for nearly 1000 years until 527 AD. Very likely this activity also accounts for a better and fuller account of Greek theology than is available of Hebrew theology as the Hebrew Bible was actually written many decades after the events that it describes. It can be assumed that Emperor Justinian closed the Academy in 529 because Christianity could not survive if the Academy continued to preach Zoroaster and Socrates' God-in-soul religion.

Nearly 2000 years later, Thomas Aquinas, a most respected theologian, referred back to Aristotle to set Bible believers straight about God and the creation process. He backed into such a concept somewhat. He said there had to be a first cause to start the creation process, so there had to be a God. John and Paul had probably already taken note of such a concept in Greek writing from nearly 400 B.C. across the northeast corner of the Mediterranean Sea.

Greek theology and philosophy of God in human beings teaches us several things:

1. God reveals himself in our souls—and there only.

2. God is a concept of goodness without form—a spirit.

3. Our soul is within. It is unseen as mentioned by Paul :in Colossians 1:15-17: "Christ is the exact likeness of the unseen God. He existed before God made anything at all, and, in fact, Christ himself is the Creator who made everything in heaven and earth, the things we can see and the

things we can't; the spirit world with its kings and kingdoms, its rulers and authorities; all were made by Christ for his own use and glory. He was before all else began and it is His power that holds everything together." (That power holding everything together is today the incomprehensible directive activity of the genes of the DNA molecule.)

4. Christ-God is the first cause of all creation, an Aristotelian concept repeated by John and Paul, and then by Thomas Aquinas of the 13th century.

5. Soul growth increases with the complexity of life. We recognize this genetically today as the genotype-phenotype environmental interaction in the evolution of humans.

6. A biologist outlined the evolution of life that Darwin later named. This biologist was Aristotle of the third century B.C., more than 2000 years before Darwin.

A final comment centers on the concept of Zoroaster that the human soul is the only place where we can find the spirit of God's goodness. The human soul started to show up in the creation process as it entered into the bodies of our mammal ancestors three million years ago. This idea can be proved more scientifically every day by scientific findings and will be discussed in more detail.

Zoroaster also taught that God was the first cause in the entire creation process of the whole universe and everything that "is." We can rightfully assume that the Zoroastrian concept of God has existed to some extent in our human ancestors for hundreds of thousands of years before writing came into being so Zoroaster and Socrates could relate it to us.

SALVATION—
JESUS-SPIRIT MEDITATION

The dogma of the salvation of our soul has deep roots in the Christology of fundamentalist believers today: If I am saved, everything will be right in my afterlife.

The psychic concern about salvation has several components.

First, if we are born in sin due to the apple-and-snake scenario of Adam and Eve in the Garden of Eden, it becomes mandatory that Christ in heaven is the only source that can save our soul from burning in hell. Genesis 2-8 is still considered historically true by many. The concept of sin (discussed elsewhere) is a metaphor for evil animal-gene activity in our souls.

The other component of the drive for salvation is fear of the future. We have inherited this fear from our animal ancestors. It is universal, a continuation of the struggle in Nature for each species to perpetuate itself, to the point that people think survival involves hate and killing. We are still fearful about the fate of our existence and destiny.

Such a fear becomes nonexistent when we accept the fact that our life is a gift from the God of the first cause of all creation through the genetic process. By that culture creation process, we are given the opportunity to carry our genetic heritage from our parents to our offspring, our children. During that interval we are given the opportunity to enhance the Jesus-spirit in the genome that we pass on by our behavior in that time period, through genotype-phenotype environmental interaction (culture evolution). We thank God the first cause of all creation and God's gene that they have given us one moment in this creation process to savor the Jesus-spirit of love, mercy and forgiveness in bringing about "thy kingdom come...on earth." We have become immortal to the extent that our behavior has presented an environment of the Jesus-spirit that can be added to the gene for posterity, for all generations to come, to eternity.

The Bible tells us we are born in sin due to the snake-and- apple story in the Garden of Eden, but the theology of genetics tells us that we were born in an animal body about three million years ago. That animal body carries forever the genes in our genome of the animal traits of evil—hate to the point of killing. Thanks be to God the first cause of all creation because God gave us the genes of the psyche, and these God-Christ genes still increase the Jesus-spirit in our soul to overcome all those "sins" of the animal genes in our soul. These genes of the Jesus-spirit will give life to us only if we of our free will pray (meditate) to the Jesus-spirit that lives within us. We are totally responsible for being able to reach the divine. Such is the theology that Zoroastrianism thousands of years ago and Socrates 400 B.C. taught us, namely, that we have inherited all the tools to enable us to reach the divine in heaven here on earth. The fear of hell is gone in genetic theology because hell has disappeared.

Jesus is our savior, not because he can forgive sin through a resurrected Christ on a throne in heaven—a Christ who has never come beyond the imagination of believers. Jesus is our savior because he was born in Nazareth, taught loving relationships and lived a perfect life to the extent of a final crucifixion. He saved us not from the fire of hell but from the probability of humanity becoming extinct on this planet. Extinctions of species have occurred every day for millions of years.

By his life of love, mercy, forgiveness and a simple lifestyle, Jesus showed us how to live, to save us from "hell" here on earth. He told us how to have heaven on this planet. He showed us how to save both ourselves and planet Earth—by meditation on his spirit.

IV. GOD IN DNA

Evolution—God's Process of Creation

DNA—God-Christ Molecule

Gene—Engine of Evolution

Life—Essence of Human Existence

We—Who Are We? We Are What We Are

EVOLUTION—GOD'S PROCESS OF CREATION

Throughout all of human history, man has been interested in his own origin. This interest is reflected in literature and creeds. It is also revealed in creation legends in all religions of antiquity.

The Old Testament of the Bible has two accounts of God's creation and God's power as a ruler. The stories were written by several authors many centuries later than the actual stories. Basically most commentators agree on two major sources, one from southern Canaan, the kingdom of Judah, where God was called Jehovah (Yahweh), and one from northern Canaan, the kingdom of Israel, where God was called Elohim. The northern God, Elohim, seemed to be a more friendly God who had a congenial lunch with Abraham.

Added to these two God descriptions were other accounts in the first five books (Pentateuch) such as Deuteronomist, or D, and Priestly, or P, that also tell about the early Hebrew people. In these accounts, God was never personally seen or contacted and did not write anything.

What is important is that many people recorded and edited the stories in the Bible, and mythical concepts varied, yet all were purportedly recorded by divine inspiration. Such fuzzy variations of different accounts put the credibility of the whole recording of the Old Testament in question. The details of these records vary enough that they cancel out their veracity in many cases.

Later, during the last millenium B.C., a collection of wise sayings was written, attributed to King Solomon because of his legendary wisdom. Wisdom is personified as a woman who says in Proverbs 8 that she was as playful and happy as a child to be working side by side with God in ages past to create everything. Long before the earth was formed, Wisdom and God drew the "blueprint" (*The Living Bible*) to create everything that is. This concept establishes some basics of this book: God, with Wisdom, or God in one with Christ according to John 1:1-5 and Colossians 1:15-19, created everything. If God-Wisdom-Christ is the creator of all, it then follows that the entire creation process *is* God-Christ. This creation process of evolution could be given any other exalted name but I prefer to say the evolutionary creation process *is* God and Christ in one as indicated in the New Testament.

Christians are well acquainted with the names God and Christ. Those names have meaning for us as being concepts we want to continue to worship as we always have, albeit they are presented in a different mantle. In this case they represent a power and potential big enough to start and continue the ongoing creation process. What better name could we give this first cause, which probably no one will ever fully understand, than God-Christ in one, as John says they are. I feel such a concept can fit well into the Christology that we have had for so long, and it can contain all the scientific and archeological evidence that would otherwise soon wipe out all the old concepts in the Bible.

We will repeat many times that there is a credibility gap between the knowledge of science as a reality and assumptions of Christology that have no proof of reality and that dualism exists: body versus soul, realism versus mythology, anthropomorphism versus God-Christ as a spirit, an active personal God-Christ versus the spirit of God-Christ in every human soul.

The omnipotence that primitive people ascribed to their deity made belief inevitable that everything was created *ex nihilo*, out of nothing. Old dogmas of the origin of heaven, earth and living beings, although increasingly coming into question because of scientific and archeological revelations to the contrary in greater quantities, are still accepted by most of today's Christians and Muslims.

The revelation of the real creation process started with Greek philosophers such as Socrates, Plato and Aristotle. Their ideas accrued at nearly the same time as the announcement of the action of God and Wisdom in Proverbs 8. Aristotle (presented elsewhere) stated that soul and body were in one and that creation was an ongoing process instead of *ex nihilo*. He said that the cause and mover of creation was God.

After Aristotle many steps in history took us to where we are today. Copernicus was born in Poland on February 19, 1473. A canon of the cathedral of Krakow, he was also a scientist, and in his "Commentariolus" of 1512 he said that Earth and other planets revolve around the sun. Catholics did not pick this up as heresy, probably because they had not yet begun to fight the Reformation.   But seven decades later Galileo, born February 15, 1564 in Pisa, Italy, and educated in a monastery, became a professor of math, physics and astronomy. He verified the calculations of Copernicus and recorded this information in his scientific writings. Thereupon the Roman Catholic Church threatened him with torture for heresy along with Reformation protesters, so he signed a recantation, was given house arrest instead of prison and continued in his research lab until he reached old age. But he knew that his calculations proved the rotation of planets around the sun.

These events took place in the first half of the 1600s. It was not until 1993, more than 350 years later, that the Vatican announced the Pope apologized to Galileo for the Church's having done him wrong so many years ago.

This story depicts a sad and painful event that will be repeated many, many times before people accept the concept of creation as God and Christ in one. Spiritually God-Christ is not a savior but the name we give to the spirit of goodness that resides in the soul of every human being because it has been put there over a time of more than a million years by the God-Christ creator through the DNA molecule of the genetic chain of chromosomes in the ongoing creation process. God as a ruler, doer and determiner of who goes to heaven and who goes to hell never existed. God-Christ is a spirit of goodness, no more, no less. Spirit cannot live anywhere except in the soul of you and me and all other human beings.

Evolution is the basis of all biological creation processes, but it is much more than that. Evolution is the good story of how God-Christ of the New Testament operated the creation process. That includes evolution of our planet, evolution of the species and evolution of the psyche and soul in our animal body. The Washington Post and Los Angeles Times reported on October 25, 1996 that Pope John Paul II said new research shows that physical evolution is "more than a hypothesis."

As mentioned, John 1:1-5 and Colossians 1:15-19 present Christ and God as one. In more than 40 instances in the New Testament where the authors write about the interaction of God and Christ and humans, they refer to the spirit (of God-Christ) to be reactivated. We know that Jesus was created by God-Christ the Creator through DNA molecules that supplied enough good genes in Joseph and Mary to create a complete God-spirit in a human body. We worship the spirit of Jesus because he was a perfect "Christian," demonstrated by his teaching us to love even our enemies and by his simple lifestyle through which this planet can support its already too-big population.

If we follow New Testament writers literally, Christ and Jesus are conceptually two different beings. One is the Creator written about by John and Paul, going back in time forever. The other is the human Jesus of Nazareth who was born 2000 years ago and whose spirit we have worshiped for 2000 years. We can say with confidence that we do not worship Jesus as a being but worship only his spirit. *Numen summum bonum* (NSB) is our deity.

Before Charles Darwin, biology was in a state of chaos. There were no answers to puzzles that presented themselves, such as why species differ from one another, what the relation is between living forms and fossils found in the earth's crust, why some organisms are found only in certain regions, and many other questions. Organisms are found only as species—groups of individuals that resemble one another more than they resemble any others and that breed only among themselves, a concept that first became precise in the 16th century when, however, each species was regarded as a product of the original Old Testament creation as described in Genesis. No explanation was provided or sought to answer the biological circumstances that forever presented themselves.

Evolution provided the first unifying general principle applicable to all living beings, which are as they now are because they underwent modification during their descent from other species before them. Another signifiant aspect of evolution was that any fact discovered about one species might be applicable to other species as the study of biology progressed and diversified into many branches. These specialties today are biology, comparative anatomy, embryology, paleontology, genetics, biochemistry, physiology and especially the methods of specialization of God's creation process of all organic matter of plants, animals and humans. The understanding of any biological phenomenon is helped by the knowledge of evolutionary principles and mechanisms; many phenomena are inexplicable without the information that Darwin's evolution gives us.

Evolution is also of great significance to the daily lives of human beings. In medicine we could not make real progress in treating human illnesses without realizing the evolutionary changes that are going on in bacteria and viruses. In animal and plant production for food, we have seen advances through selective and genetic engineering according to the evolutionary creation process.

Very soon (as stated in the 1993 *Encyclopedia Americana*) humans will face an even more promising but also fearfully responsible task: taking into their own hands the direction of the evolution of their own species, humankind.

Two recent examples of this potential are:

1. The insertion of immune genes into two children who had lived in a sterile bubble environment for several years because they lacked the genes of immunity to resist infection. After the immunity gene was added to their genome, they were able to attend school as normal students.

2. The 1993 event when Dr. Hall and his associates cloned (created) a human embryo in a Petri dish at George Washington University, using a defective ovum which Dr. Hall was sure would not survive. His main accomplishment was proving that cloning will work in humans as it has in domestic animals.

Thus Darwinian evolution by selection has advanced to the level of genetic engineering to evolve quality plants, animals and humans on demand. This goes on daily in the U.S. So heavy is this responsibility that many people would prefer to ward it off altogether. However it is doubtful that mankind will be able to dodge this task much longer.

One of the theories advanced by cosmologists sets the beginning of cosmic evolution between five and 10 billion years ago. The origin of life that started biological entities, also known as the organic creation process, started about 3.5 billion years ago. At present the three kinds of evolution—cosmic (inorganic), biological (organic) and culture (the psyche containing soul, mind and intelligence)—are all proceeding.

Ethnology, the study of behavior, has yet to find the evolutionary basis for humans' aberrant conduct that allows them to kill their own species wholesale and legally. Even our ancestors the animals do not kill their own species *en masse*. The social importance of evolution in understanding human conduct in the past and providing guidelines for the future is enormous.

The human animal is the only animal in the genetic evolution process that legally kills its own species all over this planet. It is a sad story related to the Bible and the Koran even today. Jesus (on the front cover of this book), the only non-metaphoric Bible character of divinity, has the answer to this tragedy: "Love your enemies" (Matthew 5: 44). The psychic enhancement of love in Jesus' soul through the genetic evolution process has to happen to the souls of all human beings to establish peace on earth. (When in the Bible Jesus was said to become Christ through resurrection and ascension, he joined the killing process, assigning nonbelievers to hell—a fear phenomenon.)

The Gulf War may be a case in point. We cannot condemn President Bush or the soldiers for killing multiple Arabs; we condemn the culture of the Bible and the Koran. They teach that if we kill satan (in this scenario, Sadam Hussein), we have removed evil. Jesus teaches that we can't get rid of satan by killing the evil soul in somebody else—it is in ourselves that we have to meditate. Overpopulation and our extravagant lifestyle must be corrected before an anti-crime gene can be effective.

I hope we are approaching an age in which members of the human species can live a meaningful life. Such an age will come from two sources. One is living and worshiping the life and spirit of Jesus that is in our soul. This can occur instantly as soon as, of free will, we take personal responsibility to act on the genetic makeup of our own soul in love, forgiveness and mercy. Long-term access to a meaningful life is through the creation process of genetic change in our behavior pattern.

We have learned more about this through genetic engineering in the fruit fly drosophila. Geneticists have, by manipulating genes, produced drosophila that will have various behavior patterns. They have genetically created a fly that is hyperactive and a fly that is sluggish, flies that are sexually overactive and flies that are entirely sexually inactive. With humans, the problem is time. The life cycle of a drosophila is about 10 days while the life cycle of a human is 25 years. Therefore what you can change genetically in one year in a fly would take more than 1000 years to change in a human.

Here is another aspect. I remember that on the farm, as soon as a calf or colt passed through the birth canal and fell on the ground, almost immediately it would get up and walk because it needed only the biological creation process. However, a human newborn is completely helpless. It has to go through the culture creation process, which is much more complex and time-consuming. Thus the stage of culture creation will take much longer to reach the heavenly perfection of being.

Another observation is in the area of development. In biology we learned the axiom "Ontogeny recapitulates phylogeny," which means that the fertilized human egg as it develops from a one-celled animal follows in form all the stages of the evolutionary creation process of the human being over a billion years: from one-celled organisms to primitive worm-like animals to fish-like animals to bird-like animals to quadrupeds and finally to human bipeds.

But at this stage the psyche has not yet been activated. I have experienced firsthand as a doctor the stages and form appearances of ontological development. In the early stages of ontology, i.e., the developing fetus, the forms of fish, turtle, chicken, cow and the human are anatomically alike. For example, at six weeks, all intrauterine fetuses reveal the fish slits of our ancient ancestors because the DNA molecule instruction of the creation process has not yet reached the stage of differentiation. If all the foregoing does not make the creation process of evolution clear, we are still stuck with our heads in the sand.

Interesting facts and events can be observed as a part of the evolutionary creation process, e.g., the appendix. Every human that I have operated on had an appendix. It was usually on the right side of the abdominal cavity although in rare cases the DNA's directives switch the appendix to the left side. Sixty years ago when I started my medical practice the appendix was a daily problem to be considered. A ruptured appendix with general peritonitis was serious without antibiotics; death was not a rarity and took both my brother and my uncle.

Yet scientifically and anatomically the appendix is a remnant of the herbivorous mammals of our common distant ancestry. The appendix represents a sac in which bacteria digested the cellulose of hay that was their main food. Since we quit eating alfalfa hay, the sac came into disuse, and the phenotype, interacting with environmental change, changed the genotype to gradually do away with the sac. In the current stage of the creation process, what is left of the sac is a tube-like organ that serves no purpose. But when it becomes inflamed and obstructed with edema it can form an abcess and cause trouble.

One of my own surgical experiences testifies to that problem. In 1980 in the Chaco, the jungle area of Paraguay, South America, it had been raining all day and night. Water and mud was everywhere. At 2 A.M. came a knock on the front door of the little house that my wife Mariam and I had built for ourselves. It was the driver for Peter Duerksen, manager of a 50,000-acre cattle ranch owned by a consortium of German doctors. Peter was a large, muscular young man doubled up with much pain on the floor of a four-wheel-drive van that had plowed its way through 75 miles of mud and water.

I palpitated his abdomen, which was hard as a board. Within an hour I had opened his abdominal cavity and thoroughly irrigated the general peritonitis pus there with sterile saline. The appendix had already sloughed off. Drains were inserted, and he responded well to a common antibiotic because in our genetic creation process of evolution the colon bacilli have a very short life cycle, and these bacilli had not yet developed a genetic resistance to anything in the Chaco. He did all right. Today we can alter genetic evolutionary defects.

The anatomy of the bones of the forearm also demonstrates evolution in the creation process. The humerus, radius, ulna, carpels and metacarpels are all similarly identifiable in salamanders, crocodiles, birds, bats, porpoises, moles and humans. Variations of their functions due to their environment and survival processes have changed the details of the anatomical forms somewhat, but in spite of this evolutionary creation process the hereditary characteristics dating to their early ancestry are recognizable. For instance the greater trochanter of the humerus has left its identifiable mark in each species, although in some cases it has become of no use to their survival.

Traveling through the animal reserve of Kenya near Nairobi, I noticed that all the tall trees looked like a huge umbrella. Upon inquiry I learned that they show what the creation process has done to the giraffe. Because of competition for food with the zebra and the ostrich, giraffes that could reach higher leaves survived, and the DNA genotype in cooperation with the phenotype gradually gave instructions to create a longer neck for the giraffe. As a result the giraffe eats all the leaves on branches up to about a 20-foot level, giving the trees their shape.

The history of evolution is a long and agonizing one. Augustine, considered a conservative old-line theologian of the fourth century, suggested that the Bible story of creation was symbolic and that what we see now has evolved from the original creation. Then Goethe, a German naturalist and poet, envisioned all existing plants as variants of a single underlying prototype or ground plan (*Grund*). He even made a drawing of the primary plan, which he called *Urpflanze*. He came very close to thinking like an evolutionist.

Darwin and his associates presented a good picture of what evolution does and how it operates. Since Darwin knew nothing about genetics he theorized that heredity was transferred to succeeding generations by the blood. The present gene process was discovered in the late 1800s by Mendel, a Bohemian monk and botanist. He held that characteristics were transmitted by independent segregating items of heredity that are now called genes.

Aristotle, the Greek philosopher of 300 B.C., wrote of the unmoved mover that he called God and of movement in constant motion in the universe. He as well as his teacher Socrates wrote about a succession of souls from generation to generation. Aristotle taught that man was the whole microcosm of the universe. He suggested that man represents a product of the evolution of everything that has been created.

Presenting the evolutionary creation process gives us some direction on how we can assist in leading humankind to a more meaningful life on planet Earth, so we will review the evolution of plants and animals in recent years. Enormous changes have taken place in the last human generation in the shape, size, taste and quantity of plant and animal species. Genetic engineering has brought us larger or seedless fruits and vegetables, milder-tasting onions, grains with huge increases in production, cattle without horns, cows with doubled milk production and an Angus breed with more meat.

We may assume that the next genetic change in animals is in behavior, or what we might call the psyche of animals. Modification of behavior has already been achieved in the drosophila fruit fly. Its short, 10-day generation cycle makes it possible for it to go through enough cycles to finally make genetic characteristics of behavior patterns stick (although the genetic process is subject to a certain percentage of failures). Science can do to drosophila in one year what would take more than 1000 years to do to human beings. Changes in human behavior come slowly; however, in the three million years that the God-Christ DNA molecule has been sending into human beings the genes to build the soul of our psyche, including all of God's spirit of goodness, love and mercy, we have been very fortunate when we compare our psyche with our animal ancestors.

According to the New Testament the creation process was started by God-Christ, going back in time forever in the inorganic universe of galaxies, stars, planets and satellites. The organic creation process was originated upon our earth, which is a satellite of our sun, by the God-Christ DNA molecule about 3.5 billion year ago. The third system of creation, culture, identified as the psyche, started about two million years ago. (This is treated in more detail elsewhere.)   This discussion of the process of evolution and creation by genetic engineering demonstrates the enormous responsibilities that rest upon us with potential that we have always accepted as belonging to God and to God alone. All the possibilities make God in our soul so important. God does not have an 800 number in heaven, which does not exist. Prayer is a communion and communication of spirit in the soul of every human being through meditation.

Two million years ago God-Christ with the DNA molecule started inserting soul, mind and intelligence into the psyche of all humans. We have now come to the time when everyone needs to learn who he or she is. We can no longer call on God on high because he is not there anymore. God's spirit of goodness can be only in your and my soul and nowhere else. The spirit can survive only in our souls. We have to take responsibility for what happens to us and the rest of the world, using our reason.

In short, the theory of evolution was presented by Charles Darwin in the middle 1800s. It was an imagined plan about the existence of a process. Then in the late 1800s the Austrian monk and botanist Mendel converted that theory into a hypothesis that was unproved but furnished a basis for further investigation of evolution. Next, in 1953 Dr. Francis Crick, a molecular biologist, added another fact among many others to prove that the hypothesis of evolution is a verifiable fact and the true reality of every human being. At Cambridge University northeast of London he identified the DNA chromosome that carries millions of nucleotides to form the gene that controls all life.

Now Pope John Paul II says DNA evolution is a fact. Another recently established fact is that the coding system of DNA molecules in the cells of all plants, animals and humans is the same. This discovery makes evolution an inarguable fact. (How the genes act will be detailed elsewhere; see chart.)

DNA—GOD-CHRIST MOLECULE OF CREATION

DNA (deoxyribonucleic acid) is a large molecule that directs every-thing that is alive—all plants, all animals and all humans.

The DNA molecule started to create living organisms 3.5 billion years ago,according to morsels of bacteria that have been found in rock crevices in Greenland. In Australia, fossils were found of algae that appeared one billion years later. Oxygen-producing photo-synthetic organisms were identified by fossils dated 2.5 billion years ago. These were followed by an oxygen-rich atmosphere, one-celled sexual organisms, one-celled seaweed and the first animal fossils, dated as less than one billion years ago.

With oxygen in the air and weeds on the earth's surface, the animal creation process during the last 500 million years came along more rapid-ly, from crawling animals and sea animals to dinosaurs to mammals and quadrupeds to bipeds. Then, three million years ago Australopithecus, our first ancestor with human characteristics, appeared. The first Australopithecus fossil was found by Raymond Dart in South Africa.

The above findings are confirmed by all recognized encyclopedias, textbooks and scientific literature available for everyone to read.

Fundamentalist believers in all three religions that worship God through Abraham, namely Jews, Christians and Muslims, still negate all the scientific findings that make their theology obsolete. How long can religion based only on beliefs that go all the way back to Moses' story of God creating the Garden of Eden, deny scientific evidence that we see in fossil remains of all past times, plus the DNA creative activity that we can see under an electron microscope? This polarizing struggle between reli-gious belief in an intervening God who does everything for us versus belief in a divinity that rests in the soul of every human being, started long before Moses was born and is our problem.

Persian ancestors 20,000 years ago had a faith that was a predecessor to Zoroaster's teaching that God, the spirit of goodness, could live only in the souls of all human beings to control their evil.

During the time of the Old Testament prophets, Socrates, a Greek philosopher, took up the teaching of God in the soul of us all. He was followed by Plato, who started the Academy in Athens in 387 B.C. Here Aristotle taught not only that the God-spirit in everyone's soul could elevate that person to the divine without an intercessor but also that culture creation was an evolutionary process. This Greek theology survived with the Academy for nearly 1000 years. The Roman emperor Constantine declared Christianity the national religion, and the Roman emperor Justinian tried to kill Greek theology by closing the Academy in 529 A.D. (The Greek Academy, however, is considered the ancestor of all present colleges and universities in the world.)

So we again see the controversy between fundamentalist theology versus the theology of God in the soul of humankind and creation as an ongoing process of evolution. While I expect this controversy to continue, I feel it my duty to put all the cards on the table for everyone to see as I try to present a picture of the DNA molecule.

The DNA molecule funtions in the nucleus of each cell, which is the starting unit of all plant, animal and human reproduction. All these cells have a nucleus, cytoplasm and cell membrane. Reproduction of all organisms as it takes place in the cell is directed (coded) by DNA. Beginning with the genotype (blueprint), this reproductive coding goes to the phenotype and to the ribosome of the cytoplasm to synthesize the amino acids (of which 20 have been identified) into proteins at the cell membrane, to form body parts. This intracellular coding system in reproduction is essentially the same in plants, animals and humans.

DNA bears all the primary direction for the numerous processes that enter into the development and function of all organic life. In the case of the human being, the DNA molecule contains the genes in the father's gamete (mature sperm ready for fertilization), and it joins the DNA molecule in the mother's gamete (ovum, or egg) to form a fertilized egg cell carrying all the specifications in the molecular code of the nucleotides to determine all the details of the character and form of the offspring (see chart).

The nucleotides are the sugar and phosphate units that structure the strands of the chromosomes holding the base nucleotide units that carry the genes of the genetic code. The sugar and phosphate are what might be called the spine of the chromosomal strands that take the form of a helix. The base of the nucleotides that carry the genetic code is attached to the strands of the helix of the chromosome in a perpendicular fashion. The base of the nucleotides that make the genetic code is ademine-thymine-guanine-cytosine. (The coding mechanism will be discussed in "Gene.")

In this discussion of the DNA molecule that is frequently talked about in the media, I must ask: Can we accept the working of this molecule as our God at work? I know the Bible God. I have tried to live by him for 90 years. But having been in science 75 years, I cannot make myself believe that science is a fake.

During all those years I have been trying to apply the face of my God to all the scientific findings of the ongoing creation process. I cannot deny the God that I have known for 90 years; at the same time I cannot wish away all the scientific facts that have become part of my knowledge for 75 years. How can I wish away scientific realities that I can see with my own eyes, like the DNA molecule's chromosomes under an electron microscope, in favor of a God based entirely on beliefs as stated in the Bible, a God that no one has ever seen according to the New Testament?

There has to be a middle ground where the two concepts meet. There has to be an amalgamation of two concepts that have been fighting each other for thousands of years; for example, Aristotle's concept versus Jewish ideas.

Humans as a species, like all other mammals (animals with mammary glands), come in two sexes. The male (with an undeveloped mammary gland) has a gamete in his sperm of 22 plus Y single-helix chromosomes containing DNA molecules. The female (with a womb) has 22 plus X single-helix chromosomes in her ovarian gamete. After copulation these two gametes meet in a new cell nucleus, and a process of miosis (or myosis) takes place to form a zygote (union of the two gametes). In the fertilization process in the zygote's DNA molecules, millions of unpaired nucleotides try to attach themselves to complementary nucleotides on the empty side of the chromosomes' single helixes. The resulting zygote is a new fetus, with a new combination of chromosomes, that grows by division, duplicating its first cells.

In 1993, Doctors Hall and Stillman of George Washington University in Washington, D.C., after the first duplication of a zygote, split that first duplicate to form a new human embryo (see chart).

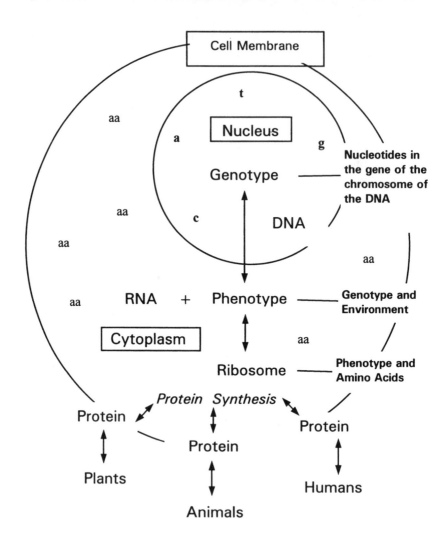

DNA   - Deoxyribonucleic acid

RNA   - ribonucleic acid

Nucleus - nucleotide of the gene (a-c-g-t)

Chr   - chromosome of millions of paired nucleotides attached to form a double helix

Gene   - section of the chromosome that carries all the directives for evolution creation

aa   - amino acids

The cell starts all life. The cell has the same structure in plants, animals and humans. It has a nucleus, cytoplasm and outer cell membrane. In the nucleus are all the components of organic evolution. They are the nucleotides of the chromosomes in the DNA molecule. They form the genotype (blueprint) for creation. That is transfered to the phenotype (carpenter) who forms the ribosome (construction) of amino acids into protein (body parts) by synthesis. This is a coding process in all plants, animals and human beings. This process starts with the smallest entity in nature—the atom. They are: C-Carbon; N-Nitrogen; O-Oxygen; and H-Hydrogen. They form the nucleotides (a-c-g-t) in a series of the chromosomes of the DNA molecule. The gene is formed by a section of nucleotides in the chromosome.

The intracellular coding system of creation starts with the genotype (blueprint) of DNA. It has the nucleotides (a-c-g-t) of the gene, a section of the chromosome to advance the code to the phenotype of the RNA in the cytoplasm of the cell.

The phenotype (carpenter) adds the influence of the environment to the genotype to code the ribosome which has the amino acids (building blocks) for the synthesis (construction) to create the body parts.

Thus the genotype-phenotype-environment-interaction is only the evolution factor of the synthesis of amino acids into protein routine to create human parts—psychic and physical.

NATURAL FERTILIZATION

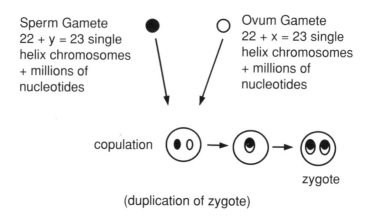

Sperm Gamete
22 + y = 23 single
helix chromosomes
+ millions of
nucleotides

Ovum Gamete
22 + x = 23 single
helix chromosomes
+ millions of
nucleotides

copulation

zygote

(duplication of zygote)

IN VITRO FERTILIZATION - IN PETRI DISH

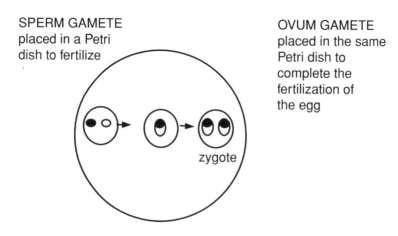

SPERM GAMETE
placed in a Petri
dish to fertilize

OVUM GAMETE
placed in the same
Petri dish to
complete the
fertilization of
the egg

zygote

The in vitro manipulation of the reproducing entities—in Petri dish or test tube—has been done for almost 50 years. It is done to produce various commercially profitable living end products. In 1953, science cloned the first frog from a cell of the tadpole—a scientific achievement. In 1980, the first cattle embryos were cloned—a profitable commercial achievement. In 1993, Dr. Hall cloned the first human embryo—an achievement that portends the future.

CLONING

CLONING - *single helix* - meiotic level - in vitro

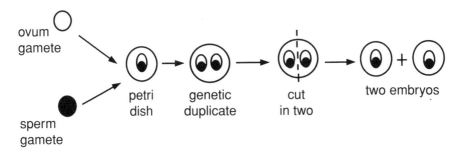

ovum
gamete

petri
dish

genetic
duplicate

cut
in two

two embryos

sperm
gamete

This cloning process has been done commercially for over 10 years—as related elsewhere of the Santa Gertrudis cattle in Paraguay. Also Dr. Hall did it on human embryos.

CLONING - *double helix* - mitotic level method by Dr. Wilmuth of Scotland - 1997

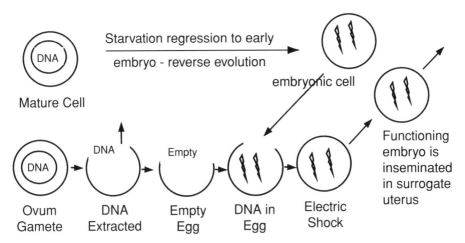

Starvation regression to early
embryo - reverse evolution

embryonic cell

Mature Cell

Functioning
embryo is
inseminated
in surrogate
uterus

Ovum Gamete	DNA Extracted	Empty Egg	DNA in Egg	Electric Shock

The Wilmuth breakthrough is the gene response to environment—starvation—with the God-spirit intellect to survive its early psyche. It could regress itself to its early embryonic state to again replicate itself. This event corroborates the genotype-phenotype-environment interaction as a mode of gnetic evolution.

Gene DNA, anatomy and operation

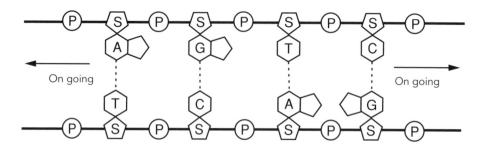

A simple diagram of a chromosome with the bars of either A-C-G-T attached to structure of the helix. The structure for the nucleotides is P-Phosphate and S-Sugar as the spine of the helix.

Helix loop of the chromosome double helix, one of millions in the DNA molecule.

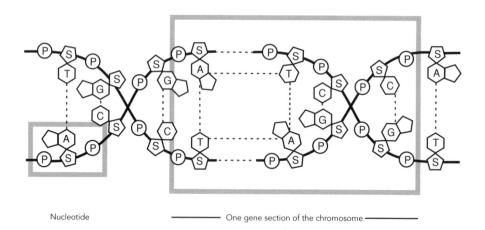

Nucleotide   ——— One gene section of the chromosome ———

Chromosome is a chain of attached nucleotides in the form of a double helix as above, or they appear in a single helix as in the gamete of the sperm and the gamete of the ovum that meet after copulation to form the zygote as the first step in human fertilization.

Here are four nucleotides paired and attached to the "P" and "S" frame structure, and each nucleotide presents one of four bar letters of the entire gene alphabet, i.e., A–Adenine, C–Cytosine, G–Guanine and T–thymine. These genetic bars are made of atoms, C–Carbon, N–Nitrogen, H–Hydrogen, and O–Oxygen.

This diagram illustrates the smallest molecule–a part of the chromasome–a part of D.N.A., containing many smaller molecules in the form of a double helix called chromosomes. The chromosomes contain millions of nucleotides bonded in pairs to form the double helix. The nucleotides carry the gene letters. These letters are shown here as construction formulas. They are constructed of atoms (the smallest organic entities as C–Carbon, N–Nitrogen, H–Hydrogen, and O–Oxygen). The chromosome was first recognized by Dr. Crick in 1953 under the electron microscope.

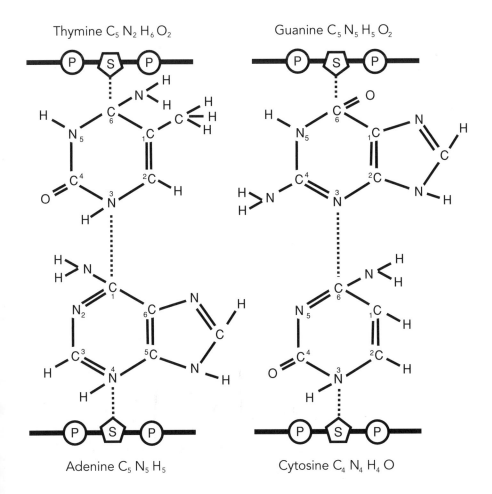

Thymine $C_5 N_2 H_6 O_2$

Guanine $C_5 N_5 H_5 O_2$

Adenine $C_5 N_5 H_5$

Cytosine $C_4 N_4 H_4 O$

A second manner of reproduction in nature is called mitosis. In this process the DNA molecule that carries all the directives of the X and Y chromosomes replicates itself by division instead of by joined gametes (miosis). This means that the new cells all have the same chromosomes as the original. By mitosis in a process of nuclear transfer, Dr. Ian Wilmut, of Roslim Research Institute near Edinburgh, Scotland, cloned a sheep from an adult DNA molecule that he excised from the tissue cells of an adult sheep (a mammary animal). In a culture medium he conditioned that DNA by starvation and electric stimuli so that it would not be rejected by an empty egg in another sheep's ovary. He emptied the other sheep's ovary egg by sucking out its own DNA. The cultured DNA placed in the empty egg replicated into an embryo, which when placed into the uterus, gestated into a duplicate live sheep. This event, related in *Science* magazine in 1997, was heralded in the press everywhere overnight (see chart).

Following are reasons why there must be an amalgamation between the Bible God and the scientific creation process of evolution (that the same Bible God created as the first cause) because the two world views have existed side by side for thousands of years:

1. We can no longer wish away what science has discovered all over the world. The longer we attempt such a move, the more will young science students drift away from the Bible's divinity. That is tragic. They will not accept the old-time religion. We all need to accept the beauty of the Bible for what it is, as metaphors.

2. Two billion followers of Judeo-Christian and Muslim beliefs adhere to the God of Abraham. Such a large number will decide our destiny for some time to come. To stop the conflict of faith versus knowledge—knowledge as a reality and the truth of nature—is long overdue.

3. Most important, an amalgam of science and the God of the Bible and the Koran must take place because present theologies have given us nothing but crime and killings. There has been no peaceful and meaningful living. Crime on the street is getting worse with nearly two million Americans in prisons, and God has not answered our prayers and come down from heaven to restore peace.

It is time for each one of us to pray to the God in our soul to make us serve our responsibility to make things happen. While the Bible has done nothing to ease street violence, the DNA molecule has enhanced the Jesus-spirit in the international arena considerably. We have come from a God that killed almost all living beings in the Noah flood to a time when we have a world court, a United Nations that recently affected a resolution in Haiti and Jerusalem and an election in Bosnia.

The most basic consideration in this book is the three-phase creation process of which God is the first cause. This is verified by the Bible and by Thomas Aquinas in the 13th century. Therefore the concept of a hands-on operating God changes to a God representing all our incomprehensibles. God is entirely foreign to our senses, and we cannot comprehend time and space.

Finally we come to the DNA molecule. We know much about how the DNA molecule and its smaller component, the gene, works, but we know nothing about the can-do *Lebenkraft* (life force) of the gene. When we equate all these incomprehensibles, we must conclude that they belong to God. They are God's secrets.

This book's scenario presents God the first cause working inside the gene for three million years, infusing his Jesus-spirit into our animal bodies in the culture creation process in the form of the psyche with our soul, which has the capacity to host his spirit and bring it to fruition by meditation.

Mother Teresa made history by being worshiped as a saint for her unselfish service to unwanted children. Science condemns her church for teaching that birth control, tubal ligation and abortion are sin. Mennonite doctors in India do tubal ligations to avoid unwanted children. During Mother Teresa's lifetime the population of India increased from 300 to 900 million. Her constituency is now hoping for her sainthood from God in heaven.

Princess Diana made history because a woman of high status let a beautiful soul full of goodness and compassion lead her life. At her funeral were two "sermons." Earl Spencer, her brother, related how a traditional Christian monarchy destroyed that soul, and Elton John sang a eulogy to that soul. In those two funeral "sermons" there was not mentioned a hint of heaven, God, Christ or being saved from sin to spend eternity in heaven forever.

It was repeatedly documented that the public response to Diana's death was so enormous that London had lengthened the funeral procession tour several times to allow the many thousands of followers of the "Diana God in her soul" to view the hearse that carried her corpse because she had formerly been activated by the God gene in her spirit into acts of goodness all over the world.

Outside of the religious community there was very little public response documenting the death of Mother Theresa.

By comparision these two episodes tell me knowledgeable humans have decided that every human being has to be personally responsible to activate God in their spirit instead of trying to satisfy an imaginary God in heaven somewhere.

The enormity of these episodes was demonstrated by sales of the Elton John tapes. On October 22, 1997 television news reported that he had sold *thirty-one million, five hundred thousand*—31,500,000 copies—of his song of eulogy at Westminster Abbey in memory of the God-spirit in the soul of Princess Diana, which she meditated into action in her life. Such response all over the world had never happened before. Even in my little town of Newton, Kansas the few Elton John tapes allotted here were sold on the spot.

People responded by the millions entirely of their free will, not by urging of the clergy, exemplifying what this book is all about better than anything I have written. I predict that this phenomenon will never die.

GENE—ENGINE
OF EVOLUTION

The gene is defined as one of the complex protein molecules associated with chromosomes of reproductive cells. A gene may act as a unit or in various biochemically determined combinations in the transmission of specific hereditary characteristics from parent to offspring.

During the last 100 years we have learned through scientific discoveries that God, the first cause of all creation, controls the evolution of life with the DNA (deoxyribonucleic acid) molecule, of which the gene is the active component. The gene is the life of everything that grows. The gene is life. There never was any life on this planet without the gene.

A gene of the DNA molecule started all of life here billions of years ago. Such a gene start is verified by a morsel of bacteria found as a fossil with DNA in it in rock strata in Greenland, dating the beginning of life as existing 3.5 billion years ago. How the God-DNA gene created the start of the organic creation process upon an inorganic universe is the most challenging research project today in molecular biology. It may remain an incomprehensible secret of God's mystery.

Sooner or later science will learn how God-DNA genes started life in stone crevices, but how the gene can do what it is doing will always remain God's secret. The can-do of the gene equates with the incomprehensibles of God himself. (Other incomprehensibles are time and space.)

Of all the incomprehensible secrets of God, the gene is the most exciting and relevant secret of life as we live it. Every day science comes up with breakthroughs in how the gene creates life. On November 24, 1994 the New York Times News Service reported a technique of altering genes in sperm, passing on changes to animal progeny in work done at the University of Pennsylvania.

But God, the first cause of creation and evolution, will very likely always keep his secret of how the gene can do what it has done and will continue to do forever. The German language has a more descriptive word for the can-do of God's gene drive, *Lebenkraft* (life force). The Bible teaches us that God is life and that without God there is no life everlasting. Therefore it is incumbent upon us to equate the incomprehensible God with the incomprehensible gene as both representing the *Lebenkraft* of all life.

This concept of life calls for an evaluation of the credibility of concepts in the Bible. When the Bible was written, nobody even suspected the existence of a DNA molecule, much less gene control over all life. But these writers felt the enormous importance of their existence and of the first cause of all creation. They felt there had to be a God who created everything.

Beyond creation, the Bible concluded falsely that God controlled everything in day-to-day happenings, but Bible writers did a noble job in describing a system that made sense for that time of scientific ignorance. Today we can scientifically verify the gene infused by God into the psyche in our animal body, starting with Australopithecus in Africa three million years ago. We used that psyche of soul, mind and intelligence to learn in science the details of the creation process and how they happened. Thus we would be derelict if we neglected to use that mind and intelligence to learn who God is. We cannot fault Bible writers for failing to give us details of the creation process because they did not know any better. But by the same reasoning, we cannot give them credit for being able to negate our creation facts based on scientific findings that we know today.

Four components cause the controversy regarding acceptance of the genetic process as controlling all life and our science theology versus the prevailing concept that God the Creator is also an intervening God who is a hands-on operator in response to all our prayers to him out there somewhere.

1. The first component is emotion. It is so "heartwarming" to reach an emotional high when you hear about Jesus being nailed to the cross and blood running down his body. For the short term, such an emotional high satisfies the urge that exists in the soul that was infused into our body over a period of three million years. The long- term quality of the

crucified Jesus is his spirit that he surrendered to the souls of humankind when he was dying. The Jesus-spirit is our salvation because his love, mercy, forgiveness and a simple lifestyle show us how we are to live our lives and enhance our soul quality for our offspring. In traditional Christology it is the resurrected Christ who manipulates all the good from heaven. The urge to practice the Jesus-spirit rings a bell in every human being if and when he or she asks for it. The emotional good feeling after "making everything right with the Lord" does nothing to enhance the ability within us to practice the Jesus-spirit in concert with others as we communicate one with another in meditation in association with all humankind.

2. The second component involved in trading gene control of life for the eschatology of the Bible is responsibility. In the gene- control concept, we are entirely responsible for who we are. We can't pray to a God out yonder somewhere to do the work for us. We can only pray to the God within our soul to do our bidding. Submission of believers to another deity tends to ease the pressure on their responsibility to activate the God-spirit within them. According to biblical eschatology we can reach heaven only through Christ, who will open the door only after we have confessed our sins and made everything right with a God out yonder somewhere. In the genetic creation concept, God the first cause of all creation has already acted by infusing his Holy Spirit in a gene into our animal body, and it is entirely our responsibility, using our own free will to attain heaven right here on earth. If we don't strive to reach God's will today we will never make it to any heaven. Faith in a resurrected Christ caused the Heaven's Gate group to commit suicide in 1997 to reach heaven. These persons believed the same faith of all Christology; they worshiped and obeyed the same Christ of the Bible, so they thought they would arrive early to Christ in a heaven that never existed.

3. The third component of the Bible-gene controversy is reality. The question is always: Do we worship something real such as a spirit, or do we have to incarnate that spirit into an active God to be worshiped? The prophets and Gospel writers were forced to incarnate all spirits so that they could present them as pieces of merchandise acceptable to people of those times. Actually, the believers and the geneticists are praying for the same end point—the meaning of life. To achieve such a goal we must see that the control of all life has changed from an imaginary intervening

God to the God of the gene, which according to all scientific findings directs all life.

4. The fourth component is fear. We fear that the biblical God will not accept us in heaven. That fear is *out* when we realize that "heaven" is here with us now if we of our free will make it so with the Jesus-spirit that is in our soul, through meditation. Therefore to bring to us the reality of this gene as the giver of all life we must identify this God gene to which we have given such high duty. This will not be a scientific presentation of genetics but a general overview of the genetic functions. (I am not a geneticist.)

The DNA molecule directs all the characteristics and behavior patterns of humans from one generation to the next. Yet it is smaller than a speck of dust, too small to see under an ordinary microscope. Scientists agree that a human being has so many DNA molecules that if all the strands of the chromosome helix in these molecules were attached end to end, that continuous strand would reach from here to the moon thousands of times.

The gene is a complex protein molecule that is part of the larger DNA molecule. This DNA molecule is made up of smaller molecules called nucleotides. In the genetic laboratory scientists can demonstrate the gene riding on nucleotides, which can be considered as free-floating segments of one of the chromosome strands. Nucleotides look for a matching nucleotide in the opposite strand of the double helix of the chromosome, with which to join.

A nucleotide has three smaller molecules of sugar and phosphate that furnish the structure and strength, the spine of the double strands of the chromosome helix. The smaller molecules are attracted to the nucleotide section of the chromosome strand in a random sequence, floating in the DNA in the cell nucleus, trying to find a matching mate that will bond to form the chromosome chain. The double helix of the chromosome is held together by hydrogen bonds between adenine and thymine, guanine and cytosine, the base of A—T and G—C, the gene alphabet (see chart). The bonding of such nucleotide base molecules can occur only if the sequence of the letters of opposing nucleotides can match A to T and G to C. Nothing else will work. Thus there are probably millions of nucleotides with variable sequences of the gene, seeking to find a mate in the nucleus of the body cell. It is the position and sequence of these little base molecules that contain all the directives of the creation process from generation to generation, a process that God the first cause of creation originated 3.5 billion years ago. Our destiny was actually started by God at that far-away time.

The complete gene setup of human DNA is usually known as the genome. The genome of a new individual is formed when the male gamete with 22 plus X chromosomes and the female gamete with 22 plus Y chromosomes unite in the nucleus to form a zygote (a cell that has doubled its chromosomes, i.e., a just-fertilized egg). In the nucleus of this zygote are millions of nucleotides of both the male and female gametes that have just joined. All are attracted to the matching nucleotides of the 46 single-helix chromosomes. The matching has to be A to T, G to C. When the matching and hydrogen bonding are completed, 46 double-helix chromosomes contain a full complement of hereditary characteristics. As we visualize this scenario we can understand the great variation in traits of siblings in all families.

We learn more every day about the "how" of the genetic process but nothing about what made the gene tick in the beginning,

We do not need to accept that *Lebenkraft* secret of God on faith because we know it is there. We can perceive with our senses the result of that *Lebenkraft* of the God gene every day. New genes that have been identified or modified are frequently reported by the press.

The most exciting and challenging research is to learn how the God gene could come from the entirely inorganic earth substance that was entirely absent of any life (no gene) 3.5 billion years ago. One clue to how the first gene was formed was reported in the October 11, 1993 issue of *Time*. At the Scripps Research Institute in La Jolla, California, in April 1993 a snippet of synthetic RNA, which is a sidekick of DNA, started to replicate itself in a test tube. It performed new and unexpected chemical tricks. With great excitement Scripps research scientists asked: Is this how life began? Never before had scientists come so close to the line that separates the living from the dead. This genetic research was followed later by a research conference on the origin of life in Barcelona, Spain, that resolved nothing. The beginning of life remains one of God's mysteries.

Science writers all over the world are telling us today the story of how the gene directs all life and has been doing so for more than three billion years. Science has established beyond a shadow of a doubt that the gene has always directed the creation of all organic matter—all plants, animals and humans. Therefore if we accept God as the first cause of all creation (as the Bible and I do) then the only conclusion we can draw is the concept that the gene and God are as one and the cause of creation.

We have just established one handle on who God is. Furthermore we agree that God creates all life as the Bible states, but the how of God's control over us has drastically changed because of scientific findings. We no longer have to believe in something that never existed. God does not control us by intervening as a gift of prayer to change our circumstances of the moment. At the same time, God with the gene completely determined who we are through the genetic process. An intervening God very likely never existed in reality ever.

Science has crossed the threshold where man "plays God" to the territory where God the first cause has shown how we can help God the Creator to create better human beings through genetic engineering. The God gene that is the first cause of all creation started the culture creation of humans three million years ago by infusing the gene of the psyche. The psyche included a soul that could host the Jesus-spirit of love, mercy, forgiveness and a simple lifestyle. (The importance of the divine Jesus-spirit of the New Testament is discussed elsewhere.)

The God-gene has genetically engineered us from the status of Australopithecus of Africa three million years ago to us as Homo Sapiens today. Fossil specimens by the thousands give us an incomplete but adequate step-by-step history of the genetic evolution of humankind from our ancestors the animals to our present being with a psyche of soul, mind and intelligence. (This parade of fossils of our lineage is detailed elsewhere.) Fossil specimens need not be accepted by faith because they are on display in museums for everyone to perceive with their senses. Therefore it's all right to accept evidence of the genetic evolution of existing human beings; it is not belief in something that does not exist.

But the best is yet to come. Science is rapidly approaching the time that it can decide what genes to propagate. It will soon be able to decide what kind of human beings we want our offspring to be. It will soon be able to give our great-grandchildren better lives. All this potential-behavior genetics makes more responsibility in our psyche crucial. We need to pray to the God within us because the God of Moses' heaven does not understand the behavior genetics that now appears in genetic textbooks.

The question now becomes: What is a better life? To answer that we have to go back to 400 B.C. When Old Testament writers were dreaming of the Garden of Eden and Paradise, Socrates taught that everyone could reach heaven here on earth on his own by praying to the God in his own soul. That leads to happiness, answering the prayer "thy kingdom come...on earth."

How does science do this genetic engineering? Details of this are not pertinent to our discussion. We have known for many years that genetic engineering is alive and growing by leaps and bounds. At the breakfast table, we have been eating genetically cloned cereal for many years. On the farm, genetically cloned cattle have appeared in quantity for more than 10 years. In August 1995 while spending the summer in South America, I attended a "county fair" in Fernheim Colony, Paraguay. Thoroughbred registered cattle were paraded for our inspection. The last item in the long parade was a cow with six of her identical calf offspring.

Such a cloning process consists of extracting one ovum trans-abdominally and in a test tube fertilizing it with the sperm of a thoroughbred registered bull. This zygote, or fertilized egg with 23 chromosomes from each parent, was placed in a petri dish. After the first division forming two pairs of chromosomes, the dish was opened and the two pairs were separated to form two separate zygotes, or fertilized eggs. After repeated separations, these six fertilized eggs were inseminated into six surrogate-mother cows. So here paraded a big, beautiful red Santa Gertrudis cow with six little Santas dribbling along beside her. This is reproduction of a quality mammal in quantity on demand by genetic engineering. This kind of procedure that creates extra animals in the jungle of the Chaco can be performed with any human male and female reproductive system anywhere today.

The involvement of human beings in genetic engineering of some type are frequently reported by major universities and laboratories all over the world. One example is the two "bubble-baby" girls who lacked a gene in their genome that produces an immune response to infections so they had to live in a bubble with sterile atmosphere to survive against a potential infection. The proper genes were inserted, and now these two girls are going to school somewhere in Ohio like all other children.

Another event that is not strictly genetic engineering but that threatens the conventional believer more than genetic engineering is human cloning, which took place for the first time in 1993 at George

Washington University and was reported in the November 6, 1993 *Time*. The cloning of a human embryo by Dr. Stillman and Dr. Hall was really a mechanical separation of embryo cells of a fertilized ovum (zygote) after their first division. The real secret that made such separation possible was the intelligence of the gene to keep everything in balance going from one cell to two cells, ending up with two equal, functional genetic systems.

The above two events will soon become routine occurrences, and believers in the teleology of instant creation can in no way wish away routine happenings today. When will we have courage enough to pray to the Jesus-spirit in our soul to solve our problems? Today?

A few basic generalities are involved in genetic engineering that we can consider without stretching our intelligence beyond retrieving:

1. The first item is the virus, a pesky little jerk. Nobody knows whether or not it is alive. It is not a cell. It has no nucleus; therefore its life is in question. But it does have a DNA molecule covered with a thin membrane. Scientists have labeled the virus as a free-floating DNA molecule looking frantically for a host cell to suck for a living because the viruses are parasites. They have to beg for a life system, a cell to attach to in order to make a living. In so doing the virus causes all our colds and flu (influenza) and even AIDS (acquired immune-deficiency syndrome). As every doctor knows, the virus does not respond to antibiotics. But it can carry a gene into any cell that it enters, and in that cell it not only lives but replicates both itself and its attached genes by the millions in a minute. By this behavior, the virus becomes a major actor in the process of genetic transference.

2. The second item necessary for genetic manipulation is the cell. The cell is the working unit of all life, whether plant, animal or human. All cells have a nucleus and cytoplasm. In a human the nucleus contains most of the genes of the chromosome in the DNA molecule of that cell. Those genes have millions of directives that determine what kind of offspring will come forth, and the genes have done exactly that for 3.5 billion years, first in plants, later in animals, and in the last three million years in humans (see charts). The cytoplasm of the cell of all life is a viscous substance that occupies most of the space in that cell. Encapsulated by a thin membrane the cytoplasm houses the nucleus in its center. The cytoplasm houses many other minor items for its operation such as free-floating nucleotides and mitochondria. The mitochondria also assist in cell metabolism and in producing enzymes.

3. The third item that enables genetic engineering is the bacterium, a living cell outside our body cells. It is freely available to carry a gene to our body cells to accomplish the gene therapy we wish to achieve. Hence by being invaded by a virus that has a specific gene laid on it, the bacterium carries the viral DNA with the gene attached into the human cell system. Bacteria are the carriers by way of the virus in this transfer process of a specific gene into our genome to make our life better. Bacteria carry these genes into our hereditary apparatus in many ways, such as conjugation (joining), injection, or splicing. But it must be said that gene activity that alters our life has barely begun, and its future is enormous beyond all comprehension.

4. The fourth item to enter this genetic process is the enzyme, a protein. An enzyme is to organic chemistry what a catalyst is to inorganic chemistry—both alter the reaction toward the end product. Some writers have likened the enzyme interferon to a pair of scissors that cuts the nucleotide base bond between the "alphabet" of the gene letters in the chromosome, thus killing the gene activity. Interferon has an important role, as will be explained. When a virus finds a cell to bunk in, it discharges all its innards into the cell's protoplasm, including its own DNA plus the gene that the research laboratory has laid upon it. In the cytoplasm of the cell, the gene replicates rapidly, millions per minute. This replicating gene in the cytoplasm is a specific type chosen to produce a specific genetic result in offspring. A practical application of all these entities and their activities relates to a cancer cure. Virus-infected cells will produce the protein interferon to halt the multiplication of the virus.

Imagine that a cell is attacked by a virus that carries with it a cancer gene. The virus has injected the innards of its DNA plus the cancer gene into the human blood cell. The cell then by a roundabout way produces the enzyme that cuts the bonds of the cancer gene letters and thus kills the invading cancer-producing gene. For this specific cancer, this cell activity has been a cure. But this gene has not had a chance to cure any other type or form of cancer, of which there are an unknown number.

In 1930 Dean Wahl, chief executive officer of the University of Kansas School of Medicine and head of the Pathology Department, told us medical students that a cure for cancer will not come until we discover what and how the growth of body cells is controlled. In 1953 Crick and Watson of Cambridge University, England, showed and identified the control factor under the electron microscope—the gene of the chromosome in the nucleus of every human cell.

Cancer is an overgrowth of too many cells from one cell. Too many cells in one place form an enlargement, or tumor. The reason for that cell overgrowth is a gene that is out of whack. That gene is picked up by a virus, which then attaches itself to a blood cell and travels to the liver, lung, brain, wherever, activating metastasis (spread of the cancer to other places in the body). One genetic cancer cure is interferon, an enzyme that promotes chemical reaction without being an ingredient in the process. In molecular biology the enzyme functions as a scissors, cutting the weak hydrogen bonds that hold together the hundreds of paired nucleotides that form the gene causing the cancer. When the gene's nucleotide bond is cut, the "rogue" gene disappears and that particular cancer is cured.

This action works for only one type of leukemia cancer. In the thousands of variations of modes and grades of cancer, we have so far only one genetic cure through interferon. As amateurs in this whole scenario, we will need hundreds of years to find genetic cures for all the cancers in the human body. The interferon program is worth continuing.

In human life, medical and behavioral genetics can be divided into four areas:

1. Correcting or inserting a faulty or missing gene. This was carried out in the case of the bubble babies.

2. Attempting to insert a gene that would correct a defect from appearing in subsequent generations.

3. Inserting a gene that would add certain characteristics, for example, a gene to increase the growth hormone.

4. Inserting a gene that would enhance the quality of the psyche (soul, mind, intelligence)—the gene of behavior.

Such research has a high priority and has produced several books on behavior genetics. This process is also the most controversial for religious Fundamentalists who label it "playing God."

In conclusion, four concepts related to the gene are involved:

1. The gene is the only item that is alive on our planet. Life is not only existence of the gene but also a process.

2. The ability of the gene to do what it does is and always will be an incomprehensible. When we equate all the incomprehensibles we have to conclude that the gene is God at work.

3. The gene gives us our immortality. The same gene directives that created me will create my offspring. We live in the genes of our progeny forever.

4. Since the gene is God working within us human beings, maybe that process forms a bond between us and the prevailing God concept.

LIFE—ESSENCE OF HUMAN EXISTENCE

W hat is life? It can be said that life is the essence of the quality of human existence, a quality beyond inorganic substance in human affairs.

The Bible says that only God in heaven above gives and controls all life. Science says that the gene of the DNA molecule is the only entity that is alive on this earth. The gene has been, is and will be alive and active to determine life to eternity. We can verify that the gene controls all organic and culture evolution. This evolution tells us where we come from, who we are and where we are going in the creation process. Science says that no other life has ever existed.

The churchman Father Thomas Keating was asked on public television June 14, 1997 if we would see each other in heaven. He suggested that he was not interested in that God. The God we created should go because he never existed. Keating worshiped the spirit of that God as it reveals itself in human life.

His words indicate that some compromises must be made if the Bible and science are to live together. Such compatibility requires that we accept God-Christ as one and as the first cause of all creation according to New Testament writers John and Paul. But we must also accept the proven fact that God-Christ created the culture of the psyche—soul, mind and intelligence—with the action of the gene of the DNA molecule. Such God-Christ gene activity is today a most serious scientific challenge known as behavior genetics. Ample scientific literature and textbooks are now appearing on the subject of genetic control of human behavior variations. Compromises by Bible believers are appropriate because:

1. Compromise is necessary for us to save the beautiful spiritual literature that the Bible presents to us.

2. Moses and the Bible writers knew nothing about the DNA molecule and its genes in relation to the creation process. They did very well in presenting the *NSB* in perceptible form to the senses 2000 years ago as God, heaven and hell. They did not have the knowledge to do otherwise. Also the Bible writers followed the form of the divine that was presented to the world by many other cosmologies of antiquity.

3. John 1 and Colossians 1 state very specifically that God-Christ as one created everything. The Bible by its own rhetoric calls for such consideration.

4. Science can show us that God used the gene in the culture creation process to develop in us the psyche containing the soul, mind and intelligence. That process made human beings out of our animal ancestors.

We can trace step by step scientifically the evolution of culture that the gene started in us in the form of the psyche, beginning with Australopithecus in Africa more than three milion years ago. That evolutionary process is enhancing our soul quality continuously today.

The essence of that process is the life of the gene. The Apostle Paul calls that life the power that holds everything together— in German, *Lebenkraft*. The "Miss" Wisdom presented in Proverbs 8 as working with God to form the "blueprint" of Nature is actually the DNA molecule that powers evolution. The drive that enables the gene to do what it does very likely belongs to the secrets of God—one of the incomprehensibles that make up our God.

The reality in life is gene activity in the culture creation process. The gene is a combination of nucleotides in pairs presenting the chromosome helix that directs the hereditary process. The genes in the chromosome are so small that they have to be enlarged several thousand times through the electron microscope to be perceptible to the human eye. Visual perception of the nucleotides in their various positions and sequences make it possible for a group of geneticists from all over the world to work for the next several years on the Genome Project, mapping genes in the cells of our human body. The geneticists are, so to speak, putting a "street number" on genes as they appear under the microscope. Francis Collins of the National Institutes of Health, among others, is directing the mapping of some three billion pairs of nucleotides that form the genes. (The anatomy of this process is related elsewhere.)

The gene is incomprehensible. It is measured in size by the linear unit used to measure the wavelength of light. This unit, called an angstrom, is one centimeter times a fraction of 1 over 10 to the 8th power (1 cm. x 1/10 squared eight times) or one-hundred-millionth of a centimeter. In addition to the incomprehensibleness of the minuscule size of the gene is another incomprehensibility: This gene carries millions of directives that it has acquired during the millions of years of genotype-phenotype environmental interaction in the organic and culture creation processes.

All the above incomprehensibles form a concept equating them with the incomprehensible being of God and Christ as one. Such a concept would give substance to God-Christ as the first cause of all creation and as a being in our image that can carry a burden that is beyond scientists to articulate and define.

It is the incomprehensible God-Christ gene that has given us life with soul, mind and intelligence. These qualities of life raised us from our ancestors the animals to where we are today. That same God-Christ gene is enhancing the quality of our humanness every day now and forever, and that gene will appear in our offspring forever, thus giving us everlasting life. We will live in those genes forever as our immortality.

WE—WHO ARE WE?
WE ARE WHAT WE ARE

W e have discussed the God of Israel, the God of Jesus and the God with Christ as creator of everything. We must now ask about ourselves: Who are we? Where did we come from? How did we get here? Where are we going?

We are an extremely minute section of a creation process that has been in operation forever. Mineral, or inorganic, substance and its activity probably go back forever. The concept of the big bang and other explanations of inorganic substance are still very fuzzy. The formation of galaxies, stars, planets, liquids and gases out of inorganic substances is not within the realm of our discussion. We must confine this discussion to the organic substance that creates all living organisms on this planet.

Earth is one of nine planets orbiting around our star, the sun. That fact conjures up many possible scenarios such as the probability that there are many civilizations like ours on planets of the other millions of stars in the universe. It is also very probable that civilizations, either our own or civilizations on other planets, may be completely destroyed by collisions with large meteors hitting planets.

We are concerned as we analyze the meaning of life for us. Science tells us that the organic substance from which we came started about four billion years ago in the creation process. It is probable that this process had cataclysmic interruptions several times as when dinosaurs totally disappeared. Scientific findings indicate a schedule of creation process as follows, with "B" representing billion of years B.C., and "M" signifying million:

4.5 B—Earth and moon show their presence.

4 B—Heavy bombardment of the earth by meteors possibly kills early life several times over, but life survives and continues its creation process.

3.8 B—Evidence of organic life: A morsel of bacteria with DNA in it in rock sediment in Greenland dates from this period.

3.5 B—Fossils in Australia having the appearance of algae are of this time.

2.8 B—Oxygen-producing photosynthetic organisms come into being.

2 B—Oxygen-rich atmosphere exists.

1.8 B—One-celled organisms with a nucleus develop..

1.2 B—First one-celled sexual organisms are present.

.8 B—First multi-celled seaweed appears.

.6 B—First animals of low-level form appear.

100 M—Dinosaurs roam the earth.

3 M—Early human beings appear.

According to late scientific discoveries, deoxyribonucleic acid, or DNA, is the controlling and directing molecule of all organic matter—plants, animals and humans. This molecule has started and directed the creation process of human beings from the beginning. This was indicated in the Bible more than 2000 years ago. John and Paul in the New Testament tell us that Christ with God created everything that was made, starting before anything else existed. In Proverbs 8, "Miss" Wisdom works side by side with God to plan the "blueprint" for the creation of everything that is. Those writers could not tell us how God-Christ created us in God's and Christ's image. John says Christ and God in this creative act were one. Bible writers did not know the method of creation and its mechanisms because then people still thought the earth was flat. I think we have now reached the top of the mountain, and the mountaintop tells us the DNA is God-Christ in the creation process. God-Christ and DNA are the same being with different names. How can we say that?

1. All believers in God and Christ would not dare to say that God-Christ is not big enough to create and direct this molecule in the ever-ongoing process of creation that has finally developed us as we are today.

2. I am very comfortable with calling this molecular activity our God-Christ concept. Christians know Christ well, having worshiped him for 2000 years. We are only lately discovering *how* he is creating us.

3. The Bible is very specific that God and Christ created everything. Science is becoming more specific concerning what, how and when we were created. Since God-Christ and the DNA molecule cover the same process in every detail as far as we can determine, it follows that they are the same.

4. The only thing that has changed is that we can now see, partially under the electron microscope, some of the methods used to create us.

From here on I will talk at random about some facts, events and concepts that helped me into this mountaintop experience. Our physical heritage is important. Sixty-five years ago my lab partner Emory and I lifted a human body called a cadaver out of a huge tank of phenol solution. We dissected and demonstrated in detail every bone, muscle, blood vessel, nerve and organ in the thoracic and abdominal cavity. For a whole year we worked on that project. Then I spent Christmas vacation with my folks on the farm. As was the custom we butchered. I chose to dissect out the viscera of the hog from the thoracic and abdominal cavity. With that experience and with study of comparative anatomy, physiology of humans and animals and biochemical studies of humans and animals, there is no way we can deny that we have a common ancestry with all animals.

We can even accept that our souls started in animals. Soul in a dog! Recently I visited my granddaughter in Fresno, California. She and her roommate have a dog in their apartment. The dog is well-trained, and that night during dinner he walked back and forth behind the coffee table salivating from the smell of the food. He wasn't too sure of me and did not stand close to me. I dipped my finger into the chili bowl and offered it to the dog. We became fast friends. That night he slept outside my door. There was something in the soul of his pysche that wanted to express appreciation and hope. Another grandchild was working at the National Institutes of Health in Bethesda, Maryland. His research team was working on pig heart valves as a replacement for human valves that wear out. We must be related to the animals if body parts can be interchanged between animals and human beings. Pig valves have been replacing human heart valves by the thousands in recent years.

However we also carry in our psyches the animal genes of evil desires from our ancestors and the will to kill our neighbor animals to survive as a species. But the God-gene has most generously added to our genome the genes of supreme goodness, which we may call God or, more appropriately, the Jesus-spirit. This Jesus-spirit that lives within us can overcome all the evil animal genes (called "sin" and "Satan" in the Bible) if we choose to have it do so. The genetics of behavior within us is slowly changing our life to a spirit of supreme goodness—*numen summum bonum*, or NSB.

Therefore it becomes adamant that today in all our churches and religious activities we concentrate on enhancing the Jesus-spirit in our souls. Such growth of the Jesus-spirit of love, mercy, forgiveness and simple lifestyle can conceivably be continued in our present church services through meditation to that spirit in our souls. Worship services can enable all members to enhance that spirit within them by communicating with each other in that spirit in an organized service of the church fellowship.

The difficult and significant concept about ourselves is the fact of nature that we humans have two beings within us working side by side forever. We share common ancestry with all animals and therefore we carry in our genome all the animal genes that must be regulated for us to rise above the level of the quality of life of our animal ancestors. The regulator is the second essence of our being—a power or quality that has been incarnated in the world of the Bible and the Koran as God, Christ or Allah—the psyche containing soul, mind and intelligence. The essence that those metaphors for God dramatize from every church pulpit is the quality we enjoy that our animal siblings have not received. That essence of the human psyche needs no proof. We can all recognize the human quality that our animal ancestors do not have simply by critically looking at ourselves and our behavior compared to that of animals around us.

The next question is: How do the animal genes and the opposing good genes function in human affairs of life today?

Throughout the organic creation process on up through animals, physical life is interested in only one thing—survival of the species. That goal has for billions of years generated the genes of pride, egoism, lust, suspicion, distrust, aggression, combativeness, hate, destruction and the death of the competition.

We have known that the anatomy and physiology of all mammals point to the fact that humans have a common ancestry with all other animals. But we now have additional proof in that the coding commonality in intracellular genetic reproduction processes shows that half of our being is animal in common with all animals. Science has discovered and learned that intracellular molecular reproduction coding is basically the same in the cells of plants, animals and humans (see chart of cells).

Every one of the above organisms is composed of cells, wholly and completely. The cell is the only physical entity of anything that is alive. In plants, animals and humans, cells have a nucleus, cytoplasm and cell membrane as their anatomy, with which they function in reproduction. In the nucleus is located the genotype that carries the complete "blueprint" or characteristics that it has accumulated for millions of years. This blueprint may have the label of grass or pig or human as determined by the genes of its parents. The genotype in the nucleus of the cell of that grass or pig or human sends its blueprint message to the phenotype of the ribonucleic acid (RNA) to the amino acid of the ribosome of the cell in the cytoplasm to synthesize the leaf or the pig nose or the human brain. That system of the process is essentially identical in all three organisms. The difference is one of time, i.e., the time in the four billion years of creation that the gene dates back to as a stage of plant, animal or human.

All life began in the organic creation process about four billion years ago with a morsel of a bacteria cell that had a DNA molecule in its nucleus. That DNA molecule started replicating organic creations. About two billion years later these coding products could be identified as species such as grass. The gene, adding new characteristics to its coding details through genotype-phenotype environmental interaction, had advanced enough in another billion years to code for the synthesizing of animals. In this creation of God-Christ the first cause, the gene coded an animal called Australopithecus, whose fossil remains of three million years ago were found in Africa (related elsewhere). This specimen showed the beginning of the genotype that would code the evolution of the human being.

This coding system that has come to us in four billion years through plants and animals to our own human animal bodies can be explained in more specific form and terminology. As mentioned earlier, all life is based on one cell entity. Each cell has a central spherical nucleus floating in a larger cytoplasm encased in a cell membrane. Each nucleus contains millions of nucleotides that form the chromosomes and the genotypes. The chromosomes can be identified under the electron microscope. The genotoype, which carries all the directives for the creation of plants, animals and humans, sends its creation instructions to the phenotype of the RNA to engineer the amino acids in the cell cytoplasm, thus creating by protein synthesis the size, shape and behavior of the plant or animal or human being.

The organ transplant consortium that keeps thousands of human beings alive and functioning by transplanting donor human organs to replace organs in us that are worn out tells us that our body is just another animal. For several years, thousands of human beings have lived with a pig heart valve to recirculate all the blood in their body to keep them alive. With that fact in mind, the New York Times News Service featured an article in January 1996 stating that four small biotechnology companies and their academic collaborators are racing to develop a pig that could serve as a donor of its functioning organs to replace a wornout human heart, lungs, kidneys and-or liver. This solution involves genetic engineering of the pig's immune system to make its organs acceptable to the immune system of humans to prevent rejection of the transplanted pig organ.

We doctors have for 100 years recognized the axiom "Ontogony recapitulates phylogony." That axiom says that the fetus of all animals including the human animal has the same configurations within their uteri in the early weeks of gestation. These early-gestation fetuses show the fin indentations of the fish, our ancestor of more than one billion years ago. This physical mark is present in the early gestational fetuses of the fish, turtle, chicken and cow, and it is equally distinctly present in the early fetus in the uterus of every human mother.

We have just proved to the thinking mind that our physical body is just another animal. The psyche with the soul quality of the Jesus-spirit is beautifully dramatized in the New Testament of the Bible as it portrays Jesus. Here we try to relate the character of these two entities living together and interacting in us to achieve a good or bad quality in our life. The animal genes and the psyche often oppose each other. Socrates taught in 350 B.C. that the God connotation is present in every human soul born on earth. Every human must live the Jesus-spirit in his soul to reach heaven on earth.

An animal can be defined as a conscious living organism capable of voluntary motion and sensation, and distinguished from plants, which lack that quality; or, any creature as distinguished from man; a beast or brute; a bestial human. The dictionary infers that, besides behaviorial differences, the molecular biology of all these organisms of plants, animals and humans is the same. We have verified this similarity by presenting the intracellular coding process, systematically identical in plant, animal and human cells. The cell with a nucleus ontaining the DNA creationary evolution process is the foundation of all life and is the creation process (see chart).

I define the psyche of the gene "blueprint" in human beings as the human soul, mind and intelligence. The interaction of psyche genes and animal genes in our soul determines who we are and how we behave. The discipline of our animal genes by the genes of our psyche always determines how much we are human and how much we are still animal or choose to be animal.

To come to any sort of consensus on the reality of the interaction in our soul of animal genetic traits and psyche genetic traits that the gene has put into our animal bodies, we need to quantify these two adversaries in our souls and in every soul on earth—four billion souls.

The quality of the psyche seems to be very simple. It is the Jesus-spirit that is our God. This spirit includes love, mercy, humility, forgiveness and a simple lifestyle. Such behavior will be our salvation, bringing us "thy kingdom come...on earth."

To quantify the quality of the animal-trait genes in our soul is more difficult because they are an accumulation of the efforts of our animal species to survive for more than a billion years. Traits for survival were behaviors of cruelty and the destruction of competing species to avoid extinction. Science tells us that millions of species became extinct on a regular basis throughout this creation process, those being the ones that were less aggressive. To sustain survival we practiced hate, distrust, combativeness, crime and killing. Genetically, with such genes within our soul we were "born in sin" as the Bible states. But Bible writers did not know that the DNA gene (the spirit of supreme goodness that can overcome all these evils) had been added over the last million years. Even as I wrote this in August 1996, a television report said a three-year-old child in Chicago fell 18 feet into an ape pit in the zoo. The severely injured body was picked up and carried to the zoo attendant by a female ape. She has acquired a small bit of the goodness gene.

In human affairs the characteristics of the evil animal genes in us appear unrecognized in many circumstances. In professional sports today on the line of scrimmage in football and "in the paint" in basketball the Jesus-spirit of love, mercy, humility and forgiveness has gotten lost. The loss of that spirit lies not only in the players. Pleasure in the animal gene of fighting lies in us as spectators in the stadium or as we act out our animal genes in front of the tube (TV).

That same animal gene within us has devastated human life for 10,000 years. We declare war to legalize murder. These declarations of war come in many forms—gang wars, drive-by shootings, and religious, political and ethnic wars (Palestine, Bosnia, Northern Ireland). But more seriously they come as economic greed. The U.S. killed 100,000 Arabs to gain the security of Kuwait oil for its extravagant living.

The animal gene within us is also devastating to human existence in sexual behavior. Such behavior of our genetic sex drive reveals itself in several areas as follows: Every one of the four billion humans on this planet has the sexual urge presented to it by the animal gene that generates procreation. That animal gene has done so for more than 500 million years and will continue to do so forever with some reduction modification through genotype-phenotype environmental interaction.

For a short-term solution we must attack the existing daily motivation. The instant pleasure that comes with a sexual orgasm is high on the list of motivations to copulate. Copulation is the most beautiful of human activities when it leads to an offspring who is wanted and loved and who can and will be nurtured into a being hosting the Jesus-spirit. Copulation is necessary to satisfy our inherited animal-urge gene that ensures survival of the species, and it can be beautiful when it is accompanied with the birth-control process to avoid unwanted babies.

Beyond that, the problems that are caused by sexual overdrive have to be attacked as the biological fact that we are half animal. The solution lies in the animal genes and not in the whole human person. It means the psychic control of our animal genes. The gene of sexual overdrive, by the deterrent of the soul quality, can be and usually is kept in perfect harmony with our psychic nature.

When this harmony is not operating, we are in trouble that presents serious problems in life. Sex-related evils of overpopulation, abortion, harassment, abuse, divorce, rape and killing can be solved by neutralizing or eliminating a sex drive that is severe enough to cause such evils. Medical science is able to neutralize male sex overdrive temporarily by injecting a female hormone, Provera. Such chemical castration is now legislated in California. It is an uncertain and temporary castration. Science has been able to stop all sex urge by genetic engineering or by surgical castration. Genetic changes in the genome to affect sexuality have so far been done only in the fruit fly drosophila.

When I say surgical castration is a satisfactory option, friends who value testosterone think I am a fool. But such male animal testosterone domestication has been routine for horses and oxen on the farm for 1000 years with good results, turning bulls into useful oxen and stallions into domesticated horses. About 20 years ago I was surgically castrated for cancer of the prostate gland, and I have to testify to you that, for me, castration improved the quality of my life. I have no desire to bring back the instant pleasure of a sexual orgasm. I don't have to get even with my body. The surgery made me more tranquil and less combative.

From all that experience it can be postulated that many prison cells could be emptied by the simple surgical procedure of castration. We have today 1,580,000 prisoners in jail, mostly male. Many of the females there were imprisoned because they killed their mates to protect themselves. Sexual harassment, child abuse and wife abuse are the more benign crimes perpetuated by our animal genes that could often be solved by the restraining order of our behavior gene. In more severe and persistent cases, gene therapy or surgical castration might be indicated.

Pride and greed in the human animal are only marginal involvements of the sex gene. They need to be attacked only when they lead to more serious crimes. Prostitution is a natural-animal-gene sex activity. It is forced upon us by our genetic history because three million years ago uninhibited sex was necessary for survival of the species. Since then, through genotype-phenotype environmental interaction this institution is diminishing every day as long as we present the proper environment to direct the gene for the next generation.

Crime and murder seem to originate mostly with the animal genes of the male. Most criminals are male. The solution could be found in several options:

1. Domesticate the animal genes of crime in humanity.

2. Use genetic engineering to treat the genes of the criminal instead of the whole human being. Even as I write this, many textbooks reveal the change that genetic engineering can make in our behavior as science has done in animals.

3. Perhaps use our prisons only to protect us from dangerous human animals and not from persons with defects that can be corrected by scientific means.

Overpopulation caused by sexual activity is the greatest threat to survival of the human species. Three humans are added to this planet every second of the day and night. (When I was practicing medicine, it seemed to me that most of them came during the nighttime.) Two factors can solve that problem: First, the gene gave us the mind and intelligence to do so. Second, the gene has for millions of years been able to maintain a balance between numbers of a species and the resources that can sustain those numbers.

Divorce occurs in 50 percent of all marriages in the U.S. today. Sexual incompatibilities usually bring misery and many resulting problems, all needing solutions of personal responsibility. Divorce is usually related to sex and animal-gene action. That animal sex gene within us is still striving to survive extinction because of a billion years of experience. The strife within us calls for uninhibited copulation, often with new partners. We will have to deal with that genetic force within us forever. However for survival of our soul and enhancement to raise the quality of our life above that of our animal ancestors, God-Christ the first cause of all creation has directed the DNA molecule to grow the Jesus-spirit in our souls.

Abortion is another sex-related issue. Abortion is a terrible solution to a serious sex problem. But to force unwanted human beings to be born is infinitely worse. Our jails are full of them. If the Christian Coalition can't solve excessive sexual behavior we will of necessity have many more abortions. Abortion kills only the animal body. As Dr. Albert Schweitzer told me, we are not human until the Jesus-spirit appears actively in our consciousness. Souls containing the Jesus-spirit can solve our animal problems forever. The end result will show how much we are human or animal.

V. DEISM

Atheism—Denying the Heaven God

Spirit—The Jesus-Spirit is God

Prayer—Meditating on the God-Spirit Within

Eastern Religion—Deism as God in Soul

Theology—Theologians' Concepts of God

Credibility—Science Exposes God Myth

Schweitzer—Life is to Serve

Change—Science Changes the Concept of God

Epilogue

ATHEISM—DENYING
THE HEAVEN GOD

Atheist! Am I an atheist? That depends upon what is generally accepted as atheism. If God is the God of fundamentalist Jews, Christians or Muslims, then I am an atheist.

The fundamentalist Muslim has to kneel on the floor and bow his forehead to the floor, often on a prayer rug. Prayer is required five times a day facing Mecca.

This ritual brings to my mind a specific event. When my dear wife Mariam and I were traveling on a freighter from New York to Bombay, Mariam's childhood home, our ship anchored on Great Bitter Lake, waiting its turn to pass through the Suez Canal. Mariam and I were lounging on deck chairs, enjoying the fresh cool air of a breeze blowing gently from the west. Mariam was writing letters and I was watching two Muslims fishing out of a small boat. Whatever they had been drinking had filled the urinary bladder of one man to over-full. He stood up at the edge of the boat to relieve himself. But he had a problem. He should not do it to the east— toward Allah in Mecca—and to the west, the wind was against him. I tapped Mariam on her shoulder and pointed to the boat, saying, "That guy has a problem." He wet down his pant leg in deference to the deity of Allah.

The Roman Catholic has to kneel to the cross as he enters the church; he has to cross himself and he may be reciting his beads or even sprinkling with holy water. It seems to have happened that a sinner had to pay money to be released from "purgatory."

The fundamentalist Protestant has to send his children to a Bible school so that they won't be polluted by scientific knowledge, but more important is that in Bible school they will learn to worship the Bible.

A divisive symbol in Christian churches is the mandatory procedure of baptism. Should you be dunked forward or backward or just sprinkled?

I was baptized on the confession of my sins, but as hard as I tried to do the accepted thing as required by the clergy, it never worked out very well with me. I can well remember myself as I went to the rural Alexanderwohl Mennonite Church. I was too small to sit by myself, so I sat with Dad. When the elder announced prayer, we all got up on our feet and turned around to kneel on the floor, facing the bench. With our elbows on the bench, we folded our hands and bowed our head to our hands. I assumed that most participants were sure that God was watching all that symbolism and kept score on each one of them. All this, even at my early age, left me with a terrible guilt feeling about my hypocrisy.

All these rituals are not evil in themselves but they have tragic consequences. The God-DNA molecule has spent three million years infusing the activity of our soul into our animal body. This soul has acquired the Jesus-spirit of love, mercy, forgiveness and a simple lifestyle aimed at survival on this planet for all of us together. That Jesus-spirit asks for a positive response by us. This presents a tragedy because the rituals are the mechanics of a spiritual urge in us that should bring out the spirituality of Jesus instead of the symbolism. The rituals create an emotional high with a handle but do very little to charge up our soul with the Jesus-spirit.

These ritual scenarios have some glaring results today. One is in Jerusalem, which I have observed firsthand. The Jews weep at the Wailing Wall to satisfy their God-spirit. The Muslims kneel and bow their foreheads to the floor in the Mosque of Omar to satisfy the urge in their soul of their God-spirit. Having thus satisfied the spiritual nature, they turn to the genes of their animal ancestors and kill each other, justified by the animal nature that kills other animals for their species to survive—routine in the animal kingdom of nature that began over three billion years ago. Such a nature all human beings carry with them in their genetic makeup. It is this animal nature in our genetic soul that the Jesus-spirit has to overcome. Potential for a Jesus-spirit within us makes us valuable human beings. Our animal body has no value.

There is another God that I have trouble dealing with. That is the God of so-called "patriotism." On the only Sunday morning that half a million American soldiers were carrying out their patriotic duty in Kuwait, television showed President and Mrs. Bush worshiping in their church. George Bush sat next to the aisle on the church bench, so the camera could easily show the world the God of patriotism. When the preacher asked for prayer, Mr. Bush sat with his head bowed and his eyes closed and his forehead shielded with his left hand. The whole country prayed to bless all the patriotic soldiers because they were able to kill 100,000 Iraqi people. No further comment.

I have related some of the present God concepts that make me an atheist in respect to these Gods. I shall now present a God and a Jesus that make me not an atheist. I am not an atheist because I accept God as the first cause of all creation processes. Such a concept was first related specifically by a respected Christian theologian, Thomas Aquinas, in the 13th century. That concept of God is also biblical, as related in Proverbs of the Old Testament and in John and Colossians in the New Testament.

Also, I am not an atheist because I totally accept Jesus as my savior and the savior of all humankind. That salvation has nothing to do with sin. Sin is nothing more nor less than us acting out the animal nature that is within us. (I discuss the sin concept elsewhere.) The salvation by Jesus is through the Jesus-spirit in his soul that he released to the souls of all of us in his last response on the cross, as related in all the Gospels: "I give my spirit" (a paraphrase of his words as he died). He was not interested in what happened to his body. His only concern was that the spirit of his teaching and lifestyle be passed on to us.

I am not an atheist because I know that God's spirit of goodness—his *numen summum bonum*, or NSB—lives within me. It took God with his DNA molecule three million years to bring us from Australopithecus (African ape making the transition to walking on two feet) to where we are today. God the first cause of all creation directed culture creation by infusing the psyche with the soul into our animal body. We consider that God's DNA has conceivably done such an infusion by mutation or by genotype-phenotype environmental interaction. Scientists are actively working out God's secret of such psyche infusion in a science called behavior genetics.

While science works on how the genes do their work, we already know that we human beings are the only organism that can host a God-spirit. I ask the jackass on our farm about the Jesus-spirit and he does not even look at me, he does not even wiggle an ear, he is totally oblivious of the spirit. But when I show him a red corn ear—oh boy! He starts salivating and he cocks both ears straight up.

I am not an atheist because I accept God as the holder and essence of the secrets of all incomprehensibles. Some of these incomprehensibles are: When did time begin? Where does space end in the universe? God is unseen—another mystery. Finally, what is the incomprehensible power or quality or cause that makes the gene "tick"? I equate all these incomprehensibles with "God with his secrets." The connotation in our culture of God as almighty and immortal fits DNA as possessor of these secret incomprehensibles, and fits God, who can deal with them for us. They represent the mystery of God.

During this writing I paradoxically pray that all present church activities keep on prospering because currently the church is the only organized effort leading people to the Jesus-spirit. Also, it is prudent for me to wait many years for my family and friends to accept my divinity concepts. After all, it took three million years to progress from my ancestors to where I am as a human today. This writing is my prayer to my 15 great-grandchildren to keep their options open. I am sure most of them when they become educated will accept my concept of the process of divinity. I pray that they will not abandon the Bible. My plea to them is: Don't give up on the beautiful literature and music that Christianity has created. Keep the Christmas celebration continuing forever. Christmas is not only beautiful but also the universal birthday of Jesus, who showed us how to solve all problems by his teaching and behavior, which is the salvation of our survival. Most important, the gene will make us better and thus bring to pass "thy kingdom come...on earth."

Finally, I can't be an atheist because, by the dictum of Martin Luther, I am praying to the God, or NSB, in my soul. I am worshiping the gene of God the first cause of all creation. I can see God at work under the electron microscope.

Why should I reject all three monotheistic Gods—Yahweh, Christ and Allah? Because they are all incarnations of a spirit that lives in my soul every day. Maybe a more important reason for rejection is that they all teach the same eschatology of death, resurrection, and judgment of hell or heaven for eternity. Science tells us that the tenets of all three Gods of incarnation, eschatology, teleology, creation *ex nihilo*, and apocalypse are untenable. Other aspects are:

1. Our young university students are looking for a "different faith," as recorded in a full-page article in the Wichita Eagle of February 25,

1995. Several Wichita State University students were more interested in the quality of their soul than in attending a formal church service.

2. The presently existing monotheisms are, and have for 1000 years, become belligerent for the sake of righteousness, causing killings and wars all over the world.

3. We each need to place responsibility entirely on ourselves for the divinity and sacredness in our soul instead of expecting a God out yonder somewhere to hand it to us on a platter when we ask for it.

4. All churches and religious institutions have to learn somehow how to pray to the only God and Jesus-spirit that resides in our souls individually. We need the organized efforts of present religious institutions to enhance the Jesus-spirit within us to completely overcome the genes of evil desires of our animal ancestors. To cure evil and crime, we need to know that they are caused by the animal genes within us and not by Satan.

The cure comes from within our Jesus-spirit and not from a resurrected Christ in heaven somewhere.

SPIRIT—THE JESUS-
SPIRIT IS GOD

Spirit, the common ground of religion and science in life that solves our problems, is the vital essence or animating force in living organisms, especially man, often considered divine in origin, the part of a human being that is incorporeal, invisible and characterized by intelligence, personality, self-consciousness and will—the mind.

We know that God-Christ's DNA creationary process has genetically created a psyche with a soul in it. That soul makes life meaningful by the quality and activity of the spirits that are found in this soul. What does the New Testament tell us about how God fits into this soul that has taken a million years to develop? New Testament passages (*The Living Bible*) will give us some answers.

Mark 1:12: "Immediately the Holy Spirit urged Jesus into the desert." This verse tells us that the spirit was very important even to the life of Jesus.

Mark 3:28: "'I solemnly declare that any sin of man can be forgiven, even blasphemy against me; but blasphemy against the Holy Spirit can never be forgiven. It is an eternal sin.'" (A similar statement is Matthew 12:32b: "....speaking against the Holy Spirit shall never be forgiven....") Jesus is saying how important the Holy Spirit is to him and us.

Mark 7:15: "'Your souls aren't harmed by what you eat, but by what you think and say.'" Here Jesus tells us we have control of the quality of our souls. Quality of life guided by the soul is ours to have if we so choose by our own free will. We need to find out who we are. Are we able physically and mentally—for what achievement?

Mark 8: 36: "'And how does a man benefit if he gains the whole world and loses his soul in the process? For is anything worth more than his soul?'" On the open market, my soul is not worth much. But to me it is worth more than the entire wealth of the world because if I don't have good soul directives that keep me from destroying myself, I have nothing regardless of what the world is worth.

Mark 15:37: "Then Jesus uttered another loud cry, and dismissed his spirit." That event shows that the spirit of Jesus' soul was his life. When he made this utterance he was not concerned about his physical life. He passed his spirit on to us. All who are followers of Jesus feel a deep responsibility and urge to pick up that spirit of Jesus from the cross and welcome it into our souls. Jesus' spirit includes his teaching of love and mercy. His spirit also presents our souls with a lifestyle of plain living standards that will help our planet to endure. It is very possible that the spirit of Jesus on the cross will be the only legacy that all Christendom will carry into the next millennium for survival forever.

Matthew 4:1: "Then Jesus was led out into the wilderness by the Holy Spirit, to be tempted there by Satan." This verse reminds us that meditating to operate the spirit of goodness for satisfactory results has its problems. It also shows that we have free will in our soul to change evil into this spirit of supreme goodness (*numen summum bonum*, or NSB) through meditation. We may call this change process our serious prayer to our spirit of God's goodness. During Jesus' time people gave a name to evil thought in the soul, calling it Satan or the devil. Since then, however, we have learned that we humans are descendants of our animal ancestors; therefore any disrespect for God's NSB is only a holdover of the behavior of our animal ancestors. We don't need to carry with us the fear of Satan and hell forever. We now have Jesus' spirit of goodness to cover those deficiencies.

Matthew 5:6: "'Happy are those who long to be just and good, for they shall be completely satisfied.'" Again, since the NSB in our soul covers all evil, we are encouraged to be good, and goodness will bring us satisfaction. Jesus stated this in his Sermon on the Mount. Other of his teachings were humility, mourning, meekness, kindness, purity in heart, peacemaking and goodness.

Matthew 12:18: "He is my Beloved, in whom my soul delights. I will put my Spirit upon Him...." This refers to a prophecy in Isaiah 42:1-2.

Matthew 12:28: "'But if I am casting out demons by the Spirit of God, then the Kingdom of God has arrived among you.'" Casting out evil (demons) in our soul by God's NSB tells us that we can clean up our soul of the most evil (Satan). Also note that Jesus did not say it was God but God's spirit that cleaned up the soul.

Luke 1:15b: Zacharias learns that he will have a son who "'will be filled with the Holy Spirit....'" This was the life of the soul.

Luke 4:14.. "Then Jesus returned to Galilee full of the Holy Spirit's power." 4:18: "The Spirit of the Lord is upon me...." Not Jesus but God's spirit in Jesus' soul has the power and does all the work. In all humankind, the presence of God's NSB is life and all that life brings. In these verses God and Jesus represent this NSB as metaphors.

John 1:1-5: "Before anything else existed [literally, in the beginning], there was Christ [the Word], with God. He has always been alive and is himself God. He created everything there is—nothing exists that he didn't make. Eternal life is in him, and this life gives light to all mankind. His life is the light that shines through the darkness—and the darkness can never extinguish it." In this passage God and Christ are presented as one and the same. That sameness makes sense, and we write about them as John did. Christ-God is the cause of the creation process, the cause of everything that exists as Thomas Aquinas said in the 13th century. We know a great deal about the process of creation and the laws that keep the universe going. We know about the creation process of inorganic, organic and culture elements, but we know nothing about the value or force of the cause and the essence of life— an incomprehensibleness, a mystery, one of the secrets of a mythic God. To call this unknown cause God-Christ seems very appropriate. Then God-Christ is not only a spirit but a cause as Thomas Aquinas said. Furthermore if we read the Bible literally when possible, then Christ and Jesus are two different beings. Christ is the creator of everything according to John and Paul. Jesus, who was human-born, serves as a role model for us to live by.

John 3:6: "'Men can only reproduce human life, but the Holy Spirit gives new life from heaven." Since we have discovered that heaven is not a place but a concept of perfection, we are again reminded that God-Christ in creating organic matter through the direction of the DNA molecule has inserted more genes of the Holy Spirit into the souls of all human beings. The behavior aspect of genetic insertion can be demonstrated today in laboratory experiments with the drosophila fruit fly— behavior genetics.

John 4:24: "'For God is a spirit, and we must have his help to worship as we should." This verse is complete and to the point, stating that

God is not a being but a spirit. No more dichotomy of prayer to a God on the firmament but meditation on God's NSB in our soul. It is quite clear in the Bible and especially in the New Testament that God is the *numen summum bonum*.

John 8:58: "'The absolute truth is that I was in existence before Abraham was ever born!'" Jesus is telling us that his spirit entered human consciousness before the biblical heavenly God of Abraham. Scientific findings make us think that Jesus' spirit of goodness started three million years ago with Australopithecus.

John 12:27: "'Now my soul is deeply troubled. Shall I pray, "Father, save me from what lies ahead"?'" Bible writers agree that Jesus still had to pray to God on the firmament. Now we know from scriptures that we carry God's NSB with us in our souls every day and everywhere. We read in the Bible about the Old Testament God's behavior of fear, anger, vengeance and force and about the New Testament God-Christ's spirit of love, truth, peace (loving enemies) and all the blessings of the Sermon on the Mount. Now we refer to passages that place this spirit of the New Testament in our souls. Meditating on God-Christ's spirit of goodness makes that spirit operative on the spot. It is not what we believe that counts because we know that we have the spirit of God-Christ's goodness within us waiting to be put into action.

John 16:13: "'When the Holy Spirit, who is truth, comes, he shall guide you into all truths, for he will not be presenting his own ideas, but will be passing on to you what he has heard. He will tell you about the future.'" This verse assures us that the spirit will show us how we can solve future problems that we have on this planet to give us a meaningful life (heaven) for future generations. The Holy Spirit will tell us how we can control overpopulation that has created a living hell in some places. We will have an Armageddon, but it will not be a battle as pictured in the Bible; it will be mass starvation. Three new human mouths to feed arise every second, day and night, on this planet. We will have to control overpopulation. Our animal ancestors did a better job, but their means of doing it can be improved if we but use the intelligence that God-Christ genes inserted into our psyche. The Holy Spirit will tell us how we can stop the pollution we have perpetrated on this planet that God-Christ created for us. Earth was beautiful when we humans took over; now it smells bad. Overpopulation and extravagant lifestyles are the producers of pollution. That spirit of Jesus of a simple lifestyle can become very important in the process of "thy kingdom come...on earth."

John 20: 22-23: "Then he breathed on them and told them, 'Receive the Holy Spirit. If you forgive anyone's sins, they are forgiven. If you refuse to forgive them, they are unforgiven." According to the Lord's Prayer, my sins are forgiven only as I forgive all other people. The grace and forgiving power of the crucified Jesus cannot help in this process unless you get the spirit of God's goodness in your soul in gear. If you sin against your neighbor, you go to him and settle up instead of putting the burden of your sin on the shoulder of some Christ the Resurrected One out there somewhere.

Romans 5:5b: "...God has given us the Holy Spirit to fill our hearts with his love." This repeats the process of the genetic addition of love to the genome of our soul.

Romans 8:6: "Following after the Holy Spirit leads to life and peace...." 8:9b: "You are controlled by your new nature if you have the Spirit of God living in you." 8:11: "And if the Spirit of God who raised up Jesus from the dead, lives in you, he will make your dying bodies live again after you die, by means of this same Holy Spirit living within you." This last verse tells us plainly that the resurrection of Jesus' body as well as of our human bodies is by means of the Holy Spirit—spiritual not physical. The resurrection is by the Holy Spirit in our soul. We can assume that there never was a physical resurrection and there never will be. Anyone who informs himself about the God-Christ DNA creation process of all organic matter, including all human beings and including Jesus, will know that such resurrections are impossible.

Romans 8:16: "For his Holy Spirit speaks to us deep in our hearts...." 8:26: "And in the same way—by our faith [in our soul's content]—the Holy Spirit helps us with our daily problems and in our praying. For we don't even know what we should pray for, nor how to pray as we should; but the Holy Spirit prays for us [meditation] with such feeling that it cannot be expressed in words." These verses tell us how important it is for us to pray to the spirit within us, which is just waiting for us to give it a chance to express itself. We have quit praying to God-Christ out there somewhere; instead, we meditate upon the spirit within our own soul, using reason in meditation.

In 1 Corinthians 2:4, Paul says that "the Holy Spirit's power was in my words...." 2:10: "But we know about these things because God has sent his Spirit to tell us, and his Spirit searches out and shows us all of God's deepest secrets." 2:12: "And God has actually given us his Spirit...." In these verses are the unexplained but ethically credible concepts which we can now demonstrate in as yet a small degree as stages of the God-Christ DNA creationary process that is now called behavior genetics.

1 Corinthians 9:11: "We have planted good spiritual seed in your souls." These seeds of Bible times are now called genes.

In 1 Corinthians 12:1, Paul says: "And now, brothers, I want to write about the special abilities the Holy Spirit gives to each of you...." 12:4: "Now God [the first cause] gives us many kinds of special abilities [through God's creation process], but it is the same Holy Spirit who is the source of them all." 12:8: "To one person the Spirit gives the ability to give wise advice; someone else may be especially good at studying and teaching, and this is his gift from the same Spirit." Here Paul speaks to the mind and intelligence of the psyche that in our genetic creationary process was added to the spirituality of the soul. Most of the verses have told us about the religious aspects of the human culture evolution.

12:11: "It is the same and only Holy Spirit who gives all these gifts and powers, deciding which each one of us should have." The Holy Spirit within us has free will to make choices. We are free to choose to do evil and to sin or to do good deeds and feel good about them. But more important, our spirit of goodness has the *power* to make the right choices. That power comes from within us; we must therefore identify ourselves as to who we are through meditation.

12:13c: "But the Holy Spirit has fitted us all [Jews and Gentiles] together into one body. We have been baptized into Christ's body by the one Spirit and have all been given that same Holy Spirit." We were baptized into Christ's body by the one Spirit, not by anyone outside our spirit. The soul-spirit of the gene was baptized even into the human animal body of Jesus by that same gene of the genome.

1 Corinthians 14:1: "Let love be your greatest aim; nevertheless, ask also for the special abilities the Holy Spirit gives." 14:14: "...my spirit is praying...." This is short and to the point but most important. When you depend entirely on God's spirit of goodness, where does prayer fit in? In the concept of the soul, prayer is the communion of spirits. This can be

prayer within your own soul or communion of souls within the larger body of all human beings. This communion makes prayer more effective than it has ever been. The spirit of goodness in a group of soul-conscious individuals strengthens the NSB in their souls as they have communion with each other. Meditation each Sunday morning becomes an effective reality of all prayer.

2 Corinthians 3:6c: "The old way, trying to be saved by keeping the Ten Commandments, ends in death; in the new way, the Holy Spirit gives them life." This statement repeats the conversion (change) in religiosity from the Old Testament to the New Testament. We now have a second conversion when we put God-Christ's spirit, or NSB, resident in our own soul. With all these verses supporting such a concept, this sounds like a winner.

That all these scriptures do not indicate physical life after death is disappointing to many fundamentalist Christians. There can't be physical resurrection. (Reasons for such a statement are discussed elsewhere.) In the short run our afterlife is the influence for good that we have left on family and friends and the good deeds we have done. In the long run the genetic traits that each of us has left for the genetic training of future generations will live forever. The changes are infinitesimal, but they are there for sure and they operate in the genotype-phenotype environmental interaction mode.

This process, behavior genetics, about which books and findings are written, is slow. Science has created behavior patterns in the insect drosophila, which has a generation cycle of 10 days. Since the human generation cycle is around 25 years, it takes 1000 years for a change in the human that is done today in drosophila in less than a year.

2 Corinthians 3:17: "The Lord is the Spirit who gives them life, and where he is there is freedom."

Colossians 1:15-17 (see "Creation") says Christ is the exact likeness of the unseen God; therefore they must be made of the same stuff; in fact, they are as if the same, or they are in one as identified in John 1:1. Also, they are both unseen; therefore they cannot be material beings perceptible by the senses. As this unseen being, God-Christ is a spirit in our soul. God-Christ as the creator of everything has been active in different stages. Since the inorganic has no beginning, God-Christ goes back in time forever. Later in the Bible, Christ symbolizes the Jesus-spirit of love, mercy and forgiveness. His power that holds everything together is the *Lebenkraft* of the DNA molecule.

To create organic civilization, God-Christ started about three billion years ago, and to create humans and culture, more than three million years ago. The power that holds everything together is the power of creation (Colossians 1:16-17), not a power of strength or weapons. That power represents the cause of matter, motion, magnetism, centrifugal force, light, heat and all the laws by which these elements interact and function in the universe of the inorganic creation process. In organic creation this power is in the DNA molecule of plants, animals and humans. In culture creation it is DNA creating a psyche that contains soul, mind and intelligence.

Colossians 3:10: "...like Christ who created this new life within you." We have to look within us to find God's spirit of goodness to make life meaningful to us every day.

1 Thessalonians 1: 5b: "What we told you produced a powerful effect upon you, for the Holy Spirit gave you great and full assurance that what we said was true. " 1:6: "...you received our message with joy from the Holy Spirit in spite of the trials and sorrows it brought you." Paul assures us we will find God's NSB within our being. He also suggests there may be hard times when we make the right decisions within our soul. This is a matter of overcoming the evil desires of our animal genes with the Jesus-spirit within all of us through meditation.

2 Timothy 1:6: "This being so, I want to remind you to stir into flame the strength and boldness that is in you, that entered into you when I laid my hands upon you and blessed you. For the Holy Spirit, God's gift, does not want you to be afraid of people, but to be wise and strong, and to love them and enjoy being with them." When we are troubled by sins we have committed, the Holy Spirit in our soul needs to be stirred up into flames so that our spiritual strength and boldness will rid us of all such foolishness. Since Paul did not know about genes developing the soul in us, he called it the laying on of hands. This "laying on of hands" in developing the soul is the genetic process of three million years. I suggest that the million years of the creation of culture produced a Paul and all the Bible writers. How? Three million years ago the genetic chain started a "detour" by introducing genes that recreated animals into humans. They began to have characteristics of the psyche that contained soul, mind and

intelligence. When the spirit of goodness became strong in these souls, it called for identification. Then a Moses came along and devised a handle for this feeling of goodness and called it God. That is very likely how a heaven-God was created—a metaphor for the spirit of God the first cause.

Hebrews 9:14c: "For by the help of the eternal Holy Spirit, Christ willingly gave himself to God to die for our sins...." The Bible says that on the cross Christ gave up his spirit. It seems certain Jesus gave his spirit to every soul created since then. We have the eternal blessing to be able to pray to the spirit Jesus gave to us at the cross. However, to believe that blood and a cross saves you from all sin is unethical and immoral because then we absolve ourselves of a sense of duty by putting all our burdens on Christ to solve instead of praying to the Jesus-spirit of goodness in meditation. Since Jesus inserted his spirit into my soul, I am obligated to take responsibility to pray to his spirit in my soul. Blood and cross are not really important. I must reason.

1 John 1:5: "This is the message God has given us to pass on to you: that God is Light...." This is a spiritual concept.

1 John 3:4: "...for every sin is done against the will of God." 3:6b: "They sin because they have never really known him or become his." All this sinning requires us to find out who we are. The spirit has been inserted into our soul, so for the solution we have to dig into our soul to find it so that the Holy Spirit can serve us. 3:24b: "We know this is true because the Holy Spirit he has given us tells us so." The Holy Spirit is in us to serve us.

1 John 4:8: "But if a person isn't loving and kind, it shows that he doesn't know God—for God is love." God is love and love is God. This has been registered in all souls, and we had better find love to solve our problems. We can do this through meditation.

4:12: " For though we have never yet seen God, when we love each other God lives in us and his love within us grows ever stronger. And he has put his own Holy Spirit into our hearts [soul] as a proof to us that we are living with him and he with us." Clearly stated here is that God lives within us in spirit. In fact, John indicates that if it were not for the spirit, we would not know that God existed because he gave his spirit as proof.

Perceptions based on science and Scripture are:

1. We call the unknown cause of everything God-Christ.

2. The Jesus-spirit of goodness is love and mercy.

3. Presented in the New Testament, Jesus is the human-born role model of God's spirit (NSB).

4. Heaven is a concept of perfection.

5. There has never been resurrection of a body, only a spirit.

6. The God of the Old Testament never existed in a form but is a metaphor for the spirit.

In summary, these scriptures show us that God-Christ activities were activities of the spirit. They were without form. They also tell us that the presence of the Jesus-spirit of love, mercy, forgiveness and a simple lifestyle is real and active.

In our existence on this planet as a part of Nature we are forever controlled by a balance of the evil desires of our animal genes from our ancestors and the responses of the Jesus-spirit to overcome our evil ancestral genes that are always active. Our animal ancestors tolerated any crime, even murder, for their species to survive crimes perpetrated by their competitors. The body and the soul in the body are two opposing products living as one. The body is the product of the billion-year-old organic creation process. In the culture stage of this process our genes elevated us to the human level of existence; of necessity, body and soul live with each other but never in peace and tranquillity.

Bible writers felt this dualism; therefore they were forced to validate that dualism into form. Such a form created heaven and hell, God and Satan, and Christ and the devil, but Jesus modeled for us body and soul living together. The recognition of dualism within us occurred in Persia 10,000 years ago as later reported by Zoroaster, and it was taught by Socrates in 400 B.C. The biblical concept of Christ versus the devil survived partly due to Constantine, emperor of the Western world. He ruled that Christianity be the world religion. When the Roman Empire folded, the Catholic papacy ruled likewise. During those years of dictatorship, proponents of dualism have been few.

During the last 50 years the science of molecular biology has established a verifiable genetic creation process that changes the theology of the Bible to the human-born Jesus and his spirit in our souls. This spirit is our *Deus* (God). In order to use the Jesus-spirit within us to attack our problems, we have to realize that the evil within us is produced by our animal genes.

When religion and science can accept the human spirit as the vital force of life, on the same level in either discipline (accepting as true the metaphors of God, Christ and Allah), we have resolved the 3000-year-old controversy and have reached a solution to fill the gap—if science will accept the fact that only a mighty God can bear the incomprehensibles in Nature.

PRAYER—MEDITATING ON THE GOD-SPIRIT WITHIN

In DNA theology, prayer is meditation. Meditation is to ponder and reflect on the Jesus-spirit of love in our soul to receive help and strength. What does the Bible say about prayer (*The Living Bible*)?

Psalm 55:17: "I will pray morning, noon, and night, pleading aloud with God, and he will hear and answer." Here David tells the whole story of Bible worshipers; i.e., God is a deity in a form that can hear your words as you verbally pray for salvation.

In the New Testament, Matthew 5:44: "'...Love your *enemies!* Pray for those who *persecute* you!'" There are no telephone connections between me, God and the enemy; therefore this prayer is totally meditation. It is communication with the Jesus-spirit in our souls in our genes.

Matthew 6:6: "'But when you pray, go away by yourself, all alone, and shut the door behind you and pray to your Father...'" (in your soul). In either case, praying is not a process of words; it is a communication of spirits, a reflection which is meditation. Prayer in the gene theology of our soul demands to be meditation.

Matthew 26:41: "'Keep alert and pray. Otherwise temptation will overpower you. For the spirit indeed is willing, but how weak the body is!'" This scripture is a perfect metaphor of the dualism in human existence—the animal genes in us of evil with the goodness genes of the soul that must control our animal genes. Such an overcoming of the evil animal genes within us by the good genes also within us is therefore an internal process of meditation that Jesus refers to as overcoming temptation. Jesus is telling us that not God but the spirit of God's goodness makes him strong, and that not Satan but his own human body (the animal genes) makes him weak. We are half animal (body) and half Holy Spirit (*numen summum bonum*, or NSB). Jesus had to meditate three times while Peter slept.

Luke 11:28: "...'Yes, but even more blessed are all who hear the Word of God and put it into practice.'" Here Jesus responds to the deism of a woman who wants to worship the animal body plus the womb of Mary that produced the Jesus body.

11:13: "'...don't you realize that your heavenly Father [the first cause of all creation] will do at least as much, and give the Holy Spirit to those who ask for him?'" God did this a million years ago by infusing the spirit of goodness genetically into our animal body.

Romans 6:16: "Don't you realize that you can choose your own master? You can choose sin [animal genes] (with death) or obedience [the good in your soul] (with acquittal). The one to whom you offer yourself— he will take you and be your master and you will be his slave." Therefore the responsibility is ours alone as to who we are. Even if God ruled our life as the Bible says, this New Testament verse does not recognize a God ruling our life from a throne in heaven. Science knows that the God who controls our life and soul is the God gene of the DNA molecule. The biblical God of immortality and omnipotence is a perfect metaphor for the DNA molecule of science. The DNA is immortal and omnipotent.

1 Corinthians 14:14: "For if I pray in a language I don't understand, my spirit is praying but I don't know what I'm saying." Paul indicates that the words in a prayer are not credible in themselves. It is the spirit (the life in our soul) that does the praying (meditation).

I Timothy 2:1: "...Pray much for others; plead for God's mercy [metaphor for the spirit of God] upon them; give thanks for all he [the spirit] is going to do for them." In this verse Paul presents the God metaphor for the theology of the DNA molecule and its genes that expresses the basic concept of meditation, the true prayer in our life. Prayer is the communication of the God-spirit in the souls of all of us, one with another on this planet Earth.

James 5:16: "Admit your faults to one another and pray for each other so that you may be healed. The earnest prayer of a righteous man has great power and wonderful results." We can genetically enhance the divinity in our soul through meditation, one with another for all humans on this earth. New Testament scripture passages support the genetic concept of the importance of the Jesus-*spirit* of love, mercy, humility, forgiveness and a simple lifestyle that has come to our soul through the culture creation process of evolution through genotype-phenotype environmental interaction for more than a million years.

About 6000 years ago when cuneiform and hieroglyphic writing came into use, metamorphic gods were created in different cosmologies all over the world of antiquity, in which the God of Bible metaphors was just one story along with gods of Egypt, Babylonia, Assyria, Greece, and many others. Osiris, Zeus, Yahweh and later, Christ and Allah enthroned in heaven demanded worshipful prayers to a deity that in all cases was nothing more than imagination based on incarnation and eschatology, both of which are scientifically untenable and are based only in ignorance.

Besides the biblical aspects of the mechanics of prayer, politics now asks for an amendment to the U.S. Constitution that would allow verbal prayer in our public schools. The prayer of meditation has no such problem.

EASTERN RELIGION—
DEISM AS GOD IN SOUL

During the second millennium B.C., Indo-European people from the North cave country, which reached from France to the Caspian Sea, migrated east into India. They affected the theology of India with the Zoroastrian movement.

India was never burdened with the dictatorship of a God from above. Its religion has consistently emphasized the importance of the divine that works in the soul of every individual. Veda (ancient Hindu sacred writings) teaches that one reaches heaven by way of truth. Ritual is the spiritual communication with the divine world, and thereby the soul reaches divine advantage over the profane. Veda teaches that Atma, the individual soul, is identical with Brahman, the universal soul. "Thou art" means the content of the individual soul is identical with the supreme truth that leads to liberation—salvation from the evil desires within us inherited from our animal ancestors. In this process the external apparatus of the salvation of Brahman disintegrates to nothing; i.e., a person does not need to rely on an external power for salvation.

Veda teaches that existence (life) is a process that man suffers passively. Death is necessary for him to be born and die again and again. This Veda teaching relates exactly what is happening in the genetic chain of events. The soul which directs the body is passed on again and again— for example, by my and my wife Mariam's genes to my daughter Susan, who passes on those genetic directives to her progeny. These transitions can go on forever, but to make that happen, Mariam and I and Susan must die. We accept death with its suffering and endure passively according to what our gene has in store for us, as Veda tells. All this process is controlled by the God-gene that is the first cause of all creation. There needs to be no belief that a God out yonder somewhere is involved.

Veda also teaches that humankind can direct its own destiny. Such direction comes in two forms. Humans can establish heaven for themselves here on earth if they choose to pray to and activate the *numen summum bonum* (NSB), the spirit of supreme goodness that God in the gene potential has infused in every human being.

The second directive is for the destiny of our soul as it passes genetically into our offspring. In our behavior we can add to the quality of the genetic chains of our offspring—the process of genetic behavior enhancement. Today elaborate textbooks treat how qualities of behavior can be enhanced genetically by the environment, i.e., genotype-phenotype environmental interaction, or behavior genetics.

A positive aspect is that India teaches tolerance and nonviolence as active virtues. Hindus think of wisdom (DNA in our terms) rather than the spiritual as defining Hinduism. They say the ladder to heaven is truth. They consider that God and truth are the same being in our soul, directing our body. The body has the same mortality as that of all other animal bodies. In fact, the body is so mortal that its remains after death are either burned or dumped into the towers of silence (high round structures open to the sky) to be recycled by the vultures and the bones burned later.

When Mahatma Gandhi was hit by a bullet on January 30, 1948, he cried, like Jesus, "Oh God! Oh God!" Gandhi accepted the spirit or wisdom of Christ and Allah and Veda on equal terms. History may very well equate the spirit of Gandhi with the spirit of Jesus in the Bible.

Buddhism, Confucianism, Taoism and Shintoism have all made attempts at incarnation of the NSB that resides in the soul, into forms like the three monotheistic religions of Yahweh, Christ and Allah. Their incarnation forms soon returned to the reality of the spirit and wisdom in the soul as revealed in behavior patterns. They were not hooked to an incarnated God who ruled from above. Their deities were creeds of their spirits without form.

Buddhism has four noble truths for worshiping as its God:

1. All who live must suffer.
2. All suffering is due to desire, which can never be satisfied.
3. Suffering will end when all desires are suppressed.
4. The middle path of moderation that leads to the end of suffering is:

1. Right views, 2. Right resolves, 3. Right speech, 4. Right conduct, 5. Right occupation, 6. Right effort, 7. Right awareness, 8. Right meditation.

A significant item in Buddhism is emphasis on the suppression of desires to relieve suffering. The concept of genetic realism is that the NSB must overcome the animal desires that we carry in our genome in order for us to reach heaven here on earth.

Another significant item in Buddhism is to teach right meditation. Mary Taring, "daughter of Tibet" and a Buddhist, told me that Buddha was a teacher. He taught deep meditation on the reality of life; that was his "God." This meditation teaches compassion for all people. Meditation must enhance the intellect to produce better life in human affairs. Right meditation translates into our genetic road to heaven when we pray to the NSB that is God in our soul. Such meditation enhances the quality and quantity of that spirit in our soul's behavior.

The animal desires that we carry in our genome, according to Buddhism, are four: 1. Intoxication, 2. Sensuality, 3. Pride, 4. Ignorance and speculation. Hindrances to the divine, Buddhism teaches, are: 1. Fleshliness, 2. Crankiness, 3. Laziness, 4. Worry and hesitation.

Buddhism in essence repeats the Ten Commandments. Virtues are listed as: 1. Loving kindness or benevolence, 2. Compassion, 3. Joyous sympathy or gladness in others' well being, 4. Equanimity. These four qualities may be regarded in three ways: as virtues to be exemplified, as objects of meditation, as states of mind or being. Buddhism says that compassion succeeds when it makes cruelty subside and that it fails when it produces sorrow. Gladness succeeds when it makes aversion (boredom) subside, and it fails when it produces merriment.

Buddhism teaches that the soul at death is reborn in another body. At death that soul is relieved of body problems and enjoys transcendental bliss. All these concepts of the divine process are a present-day reality in the genetic culture creation process active today through the succession of generations.

Confucius teaches the Golden Rule: "Do not do to others what you would not want them to do to you." He says the soul animates the body; it is the life of humans from within. During life the soul moves in and out of the body. At death the soul leaves the body. Confucius says it is a fault to cling to a fault by one's own will. What a superior man seeks is in himself; what a small man seeks is in others. "Goody-goody people" are the thieves of virtue. When a man really wants true manhood, there it is right by him. A person who has a beautiful soul always has some beautiful things to say, but a person who says beautiful things does not necessarily have a beautiful soul. Confucius says the soul leads to heaven. In their religion, the Chinese worship the spirit of their ancestor's souls (that the DNA gene has given them), and they pray to the spirit that their gene passes on to their offspring. Their most important teaching is the interconnected prayers of souls of all human beings.

In conclusion: By and large, the Eastern religions of Buddhism, Hinduism and Confucianism do not need to concede anything to scientific facts. They are already in tune with scientific directives. To them, the NSB comes from within the human soul and no Christ from above is needed.

When I visited Dr. Albert Schweitzer in 1963, he told me that "God" can be found in every human being ever born on this earth if one digs deep enough into the soul. Gandhi said, "Truth is God."

THEOLOGY—THEOLOGIANS' CONCEPTS OF GOD

What do past theologians teach us about developing theology and the meaning of life for the 21st century?

We have discussed the contributions of Socrates, Plato and Aristotle to this subject as compared to the Old Testament of that period and have discussed Athanasius, who seemed to be a questionable character during the time of Emperor Constantine. He wrote the Apostles' Creed, with which Christians have worshiped for nearly 2000 years.

The next important theologian was Augustine, who was born November 13, 354 in Algeria. He was the product of Plato, who was teaching almost 1000 years before him. Augustine lived during the fourth century when Rome was crumbling along with the Greek theology that Rome had absorbed. He probably had the most influence on the theology of Catholic and Protestant churches. Even Calvin and Luther felt that they were referring back to Augustine when they left the Roman Catholic Church.

We will enumerate some of his teachings. He agreed with Athanasius that Jesus was the savior from sin, devil and hell. But he also preached a compromise with Arius. He said, "If you want to see God, look within your soul and you will find him." His principal argument is based upon the mind's possession of eternal and immutable truths. Augustine said: "Because there are such truths, there must be an eternal truth. This truth is God."

He says evil is not something real and positive but rather a privation of good. Hence it is caused by a deficiency rather than by an efficiency. Moral evil, or sin, is due to human free will, or choice, according to Augustine. Every sin is a turning away from eternal things and an acceptance of temporal things. "The likeness of God is imprinted in the soul," he said. "You seek God through his image in the soul." The individual thinker does not make the truth; he finds it, and he is able to do so because Christ, the revealing word of God, is the *magister interior*, the "inward teacher" who enables the thinker to see the truth for himself when he listens to him (truth).

Augustine infers that meditation is to open the psyche to the Jesus-spirit to solve all one's problems. He does not indicate that praying to a God (out there) will be of any help. What else does Augustine tell us? God with his goodness and truth can be found only in the soul and not out there somewhere. We can assume that God's goodness lives only in the souls of humankind. Also, sinfulness can, by free will, be forgiven in one's soul by Jesus, who lives there. The spirit of goodness of Christ and God has no other home. (Augustine had to abandon the soul concept to be accepted by the hierarchy of the Church as a bishop.)

Karl Barth, a Swiss theologian of a more recent time (1886-1968), believed in a Christ of personal saviourism, a religion of fear that was a holdover from biblical times. Believers in this religion have a strong mortal fear of the devil and hell, a fear that can be alleviated only by the grace of the savior—Christ. The Bible was the complete and only source to find God and who God is. A human was unable to reach the divine except by the grace of a personal God. Barth had no room for consideration of Nature and natural law. He called consideration of God as involved in the creation process, idolatry. He said man is born in sin because Adam ate the wrong fruit in the garden.

This concept of the divine is still the theology of many present members of Western Christianity. It is preached by virtually all modern evangelists. It is not only self-comforting; it also largely relieves believers of the burden of responsibility of "determining their own destiny." They place that burden on an imaginary God. This theology is also profitable money-wise. Western Christianity created a very absolute system with born-in-sin, the devil and hell. Therefore humans have to have the grace and forgiveness of Christ from heaven to keep them out of their concept of destruction by the devil and evil sin and hell. Some Catholics made money by collecting salvation buyouts with confession of sins. Modern evangelists collect huge sums of money for praying people out of hell and into heaven.

Other theologians such as Friedrich Nietzsche (1844-1900) say that all the facts we now know about the creation process make such a belief completely untenable technologically. The God of fear is out. The spirit of God in the human psyche—the soul—can open humans to God's presence within and help them reach divinity through meditation. A human does not need to pray to an image of God out there somewhere. He can agree with Augustine that the individual is by his own free will able to raise himself toward the divine. He will then find himself relieved of the fear and terror of his childhood God and Satan.

Paul Tillich (1886-1965) was a World War I chaplain in Germany in 1914. Later he taught in American universities. For him, spirit is a dimension of life. Tillich does not accept the personal savior of present popular Christianity. He recognizes the reality of God and considers himself between faith and reason. He called for a new Christianity to be expected and prepared for but not yet named. Tillich said the traditional concept of God is dead. It is obvious that he was not going into more detail in his theological convictions for fear of condemnation by his peers. (Tillich was the first non-Jewish theologian expelled by Hitler.)

Humans of today, who have genetically inherited the genes that have placed the contents of God's goodness in their souls, have the ability by their free will to attain divinity by putting that spirit of God to work. Everybody needs to discover who he is. Each person must ask himself: Have I made use of the spirit of goodness that God has planted in me? Complete salvation can come only by meditation and following Jesus.

Finally, Tillich says many Christians love their enemies so that they themselves will be sure to get to heaven—they relish the idea of watching enemies being tormented in hell. Nietzsche and Tillich agree that the prevailing God was a dead concept.

Alfred North Whitehead (1861-1947) was a British mathematician and theologian. His main tenet was abolition of all dualism. Like Aristotle he taught that soul and body belonged together in one being. Process and reality must unite. He saw religion as reaching its deepest level in humanity's solitude, i.e., as an attitude of the individual toward the universe rather than as a social phenomenon. He advised: Close the door behind you (the Bible) and meditate (pray).

Reinhold Niebuhr (1892-1971) was born in Missouri to a minister and his wife. He studied at Lutheran Seminary in St. Louis and at Yale University. (While at Yale, he taught Gordon Kaufman, who is now a theologian at Harvard University.) As a minister in an industrial Detroit area, Niebuhr was sensitive to the conflict between theology and science. He said science proved many Bible events to be nothing but fantasy. He wrote about the genius of religious myth and taught that Christianity has promoted old religious myths and symbols without rationalizing them. He taught that biblical myths should be taken seriously but not literally.

Niebuhr's gospel was called neo-orthodoxy. He reinterpreted the meaning of the ancient doctrine of creation, the fall and sin. He had a deep distrust of theological systems. He taught that a "divine forgiving and timeless love" beyond history gives meaning to human life. Niebuhr was both a naturalist struggling with the problems of existence with all the tools of human reason and a believer in the mystery upholding a superstructure of religious beliefs beyond the test of reason. Time alone will tell which will survive. Niebuhr saw more clearly the stand between science and the biblical. Therefore he was seeking a compromise by offering a mythology concept of at least some of the Bible stories.

In the Oct. 28, 1996 *Time*, I read a review of a public television Genesis Symposium hosted by Bill Moyers, in which many traditional theologians participated. Karen Armstrong of London, former nun and author of a best-selling book on how man created God, caused fireworks among the theologians when she presented evils of the Bible God as in the Flood genocide.

Mennonite theologians revitalized Tillich, Nietzsche, Niebuhr and even Augustine in a Gordon Kaufman Symposium Nov. 3-4, 1996, at Bethel College, North Newton, Kan. In a sermon preceding the symposium, Kaufman, a Harvard professor, quoted scriptures on human finiteness and the ultimate mystery of God. His theme is theology as imaginative construction.

The courage to write this book came from Zoroaster, Socrates, the historical Jesus, Mohammed, Aquinas, Joseph Smith, Gandhi, Schweitzer, Karen Armstrong, Kaufman, and, finally, Dr. Daryl Schmidt of Texas Christian University (another fellow Bethel College alumnus), whose recent seminar theme was "Get Jesus Out of the Bible" (i.e., look for the historically real Jesus).

The supporters of personal sainthood versus the Christ-in-a-heaven-up-above reached their conclusions on the basis of theophilosophical circumstances. I feel compelled to let science (knowledge—*Wissenschaft*) put the clincher on the fact that for more than a million years every human being has genetically received a soul that contains sainthood.

Humanity has to stop riding on ignorance!

CREDIBILITY—SCIENCE EXPOSES GOD MYTH

"Credible" means capable of being believable, worthy of confidence, reliable.

The Bible has been the guiding light for Christians for 2000 years. It has brought stability and meaning to our lives. We will always remember its importance in allaying the fear of the unknown, which is what religion is all about. Since Moses' time, we have cleared a great deal of the unknown. God-Christ, the first cause of the DNA creation process, infused the psyche into our animal body and brought enormous changes in our religious concepts.

In science we have demonstrated in the laboratory that gene engineering can completely change the behavior pattern of the drosophila (fruit fly). Such engineering by the genetic process is now done in human beings. By the same process of behavior genetics we now know that the soul that created the Old Testament God of anger, vengeance and killer of humanity was a metaphor for our animal genes, used through the imaginations of Moses and the other prophets. The intelligence in the psyche of the prophets that the God-DNA had infused in these humans over three million years was not willing to admit such metaphors, so another impossible concept was created—the concept of a messiah who was of a virgin birth, was crucified and was physically resurrected in three days. To evaluate the credibility of Old and New Testament concepts in a religiosity that has survived for more than 2000 years in Judeo-Christian cosmology, we refer to the Bible (quotes are from *The Living Bible*):

I John 4:12: "For though we have never yet seen God, when we love each other God lives in us and his love within us grows ever stronger." This verse infers that love is "his" alone and has to come down from "heaven" to lead us. To a thinking human, that is not credible. Love is a feeling (spirit), and a feeling cannot be stuffed in an envelope and mailed from "heaven."

4:13: "And he has put his own Holy Spirit into our hearts as a proof to us that we are living with him and he with us." He is not really concentrating on love but on the being that carries love living with us. As a metaphor that is all right, but finally we must tell ourselves that we in our souls are the only beings that can carry our love to each other. 4:14: "And furthermore, we have seen with our own eyes and now tell all the world that God sent his Son to be their Savior"—physically incredible in science.

Here are incredibilities and metaphors to consider:

1. Our hearts (4:13). In my assisting with chest surgery, I have held a pulsating heart in my hand and it never spoke to me.

2. Love has to be carried to us by a living form called God, a belief inferring that love resides with Christ in heaven above and has to be faxed to us.

3. John metaphorizes a process of a "physical" God sending his Son to be the savior for our evil animal genes. Did God send the Son by mail? Fundamentalists would say I am ridiculous, but this does show the incredibility of a literal following of the Bible.

4. Being "born in sin" by way of a snake and apple and Eve is impossible scientifically—and we know it is.

5. Virgin birth. This is scientifically possible only by artificial insemination—unlikely for Christ, Zeus, Osiris, and Sargon of antiquity.

6. Resurrection. In four billion years, dead cells are always dead, a well-established credibility..

We accept the fact that the account of the Old Testament God and his behavior as related to us by Moses and the prophets was a noble and honest attempt to put a handle to the God-spirit that was active in our soul. "In his image" was what they imagined the ultimate might look like. Unfortunately, they leaned too much on the cruelty of the gods of Babylon, Egypt, Mesopotamia and the Aegean area. Such similarities may account for most of God's behavior in the Old Testament, behavior that is incredible on all counts according to science.

Likewise, the New Testament revelation by the apostles is a beautiful attempt to present the God-spirit to us. In fact, the New Testament God-spirit is a complete turnabout from a God of anger and vengeance and killer of his human creation to a God in the form of Jesus, showing love,. mercy, forgiveness and a lifestyle of humility and simplicity. Jesus was a perfect God-spirit, still credible today.

Jesus surrendered the loving, merciful and forgiving spirit of his soul as the very last act of his living life on the cross. All four Gospels and even the fifth Gospel writer, Thomas (recently discovered), specifically state how Jesus on the cross passed the spirit of God in his soul to be added to the soul of everyone on this earth. However we have to pray for it, culture it and put it into action. This is entirely credible as meditation.

The credibility of the creation process of Jesus was hampered by the legacy of ancient culture—he had to be virgin-born, perform miracles, be crucified and have a physical resurrection in three days. This Jesus-life scenario was a copy of the lives of some gods and prominent people of that time and is entirely incredible in science.

One example is Pythagoras, a Greek philosopher. Every high-school student in the world knows him by his Pythagorean Theorum, which states that the sum of the squares of the base and altitude of a right-angle triangle is equal to the square of the hypotenuse. (To me as a student, it was most fascinating to prove.) In nearly 500 B.C. Pythagoras was considered partly divine by his followers in Greek philosophy, with some of the same trimmings that the Gospel writers attributed to Jesus. In science today Jesus is not a metaphor. Before I show why we have to question the credibility of God as related in the Bible, we must concede some very important aspects of God and Jesus. Despite all the mythology presented in the Bible, the Bible teaches us truths that are so valuable we can't ignore them. The spirit is credible in the Bible.

God is the first cause of the entire creation process. In Proverbs 8, Wisdom completely negates the seven-day creation story of Moses in Genesis. Science tells us Wisdom was the DNA molecule on this planet four billion years ago. DNA had the "blueprint" for all creation's evolutionary action at that time. Creation is scientifically credible.

In Colossians 1:15-17 the Apostle Paul speaks of Christ as creator and first cause of the universe and the culture phase of creation, and adds another dimension: "His power holds everything together." This is credible.

The power of Christ presented to us in Colossians 1 is incomprehensible, one of many incomprehensible mysteries that we attribute to God and can apply in all areas of the three-phase creation process for credibility. In the inorganic creation process, the power that Paul mentions maintains the equilibrium between the centrifugal force of the tectonic plates that carry all of us around the earth every day at 1000 miles per hour, and the gravity (centripetal force) that keeps our floating tectonic plates from flying out into space to kingdom come. That power is incomprehensible, but all incomprehensibles are credible to Christ-God. That power also applies to the organic creation process in the question of what started the DNA molecule function that is being agonized over at Scripps Laboratory, as we have related.

Finally, the power described by Paul becomes even more incomprehensible when applied to the "can-do" of the gene. That power is the essence of the gene's ability to produce and sustain life. That power is the supreme incomprehensible that we have called God. Several centuries ago Thomas Aquinas identified that God of time, space and inorganic evolution of tectonic-plate activity as the first cause of all creation. This concept adds to the credibility of genetics.

In contrast, the God-Jesus spirit of supreme goodness (*numen summum bonum*, or NSB) that the gene has planted in our soul is not incomprehensible. We feel its presence within us always if we search for it. We pray to that genetically-produced soul-spirit to enhance its strength and effectiveness in our behavior, through meditation.

The DNA molecule that gives us the gene of our soul is so small that it cannot be identified under a microscope. But with sophisticated equipment and knowledgeable expertise we begin to learn what the gene tells us. These genes have millions of directives including the gene characteristics of our animal ancestors dating back 3.5 billion years—a slowly evolving credibility. The genes reveal information and directives seemingly in two processes. The first is sequencing variations of pairs according to a predetermined combination. The second is the upside-downside variations of the gene's positions in the helix of the chromosome. This nucleotide activity has not only added soul potential but through genotype-phenotype environmental interaction enhances the quantity and quality of the psyche at an ever-increasing rate. Aristotle in the fourth century B.C. indicated this evolutionary enhancement of the psyche (related elsewhere).

Science is learning enormously about genetic activity. But the power that is the essence of the gene's ability to do what it does will very likely remain both credible and one of God's incomprehensible secrets. The power or smartness and ability of the millions of directives in the gene with which it does its work is incomprehensible. Scientists have identified the chromosome's genes under the electron microscope and recognize more every day how DNA operates. Though the first cause of the gene itself and its activity is incomprehensible, DNA action is credible.

Other incomprehensibles are: When did time begin? Where does space end in the universe? Finally, the most important question is about God-Christ. Nobody has ever seen or heard God, according to John 1:18. But for 4000 years God-Christ has had certain connotations that we choose to perpetuate as believable. The prime concept of God is *Almighty* and *Creator*, so we put all these "incomprehensibles" together under the name God-Christ. Science cannot handle them.

The second connotation of the word God-Christ is that it represents the NSB. After God-Christ as first cause had created for four billion years and started with genetic directives to create the psyche with our soul, it was then and only then that God's NSB started to grow in our soul. And it will continue to grow forever. This also is credible.

Other God connotations in the Bible are: immortality, omnipotence, omniscience, beneficence and divinity. They are all DNA-credible. The gene has been immortal for at least four billion years, as verified in science. The gene is omnipotent because it can create anything that God-Christ the first cause has on the agenda. The proof of such omnipotence is the millions of species that have been created. Nearly all species become extinct, to be replaced by new improved species, a credibility of archeology. The gene is omniscient because it knows in advance where it is going in the creation process. Proof of such omniscience is the introduction of the gene in our animal ancestry more than three million years ago. The gene was beneficent when it enhanced the human quality in us from Australopithecus to where we are today, at a soul level far above our animal ancestors. We can feel that quality as credible. The gene is divine because it gave us a soul that can host the spirit and activity of supreme goodness.

What a beautiful process that has given our animal body the quality of feeling, appreciation, sympathy and more! It has given us the Jesus-spirit of love, mercy, forgiveness and a simple lifestyle, all of which will save us from extinction and bring "thy kingdom come...on earth"—a quality we credit to genetics.

The existence of Christ as a human-born Jesus is well documented in the Bible. His life and service has no controversy with scientific knowledge. Scientifically Jesus had the right psychic soul genes in his genome, received from Joseph and Mary, so he could qualify as the messiah of the Old Testament prophets to represent the divinity of the Old Testament God to all people. This is very credible. In all his teaching Jesus never once described himself as the God that Athanasius proposed at the conference called by Constantine in 325 A.D. (See "Trinity" for details.) We therefore accept the teaching of Arius, who at that same conference taught that Jesus was a human-born representative of God among humanity on earth. He was crucified and surrendered his spirit to all humanity when he died on the cross. He is not a metaphor; he has total credibility.

Finally, a resurrected Christ sitting on a throne, ruling, intervening, and judging all humanity is, as such, not creditable and is totally unacceptable to scientific knowledge for reasons related elsewhere.

For those who believe in the literalness of the Bible, we offer some arguments for a change in thinking about its crredibility:

Item: Creating a woman out of the rib of Adam (Genesis 2:21-22). The law of the creation process of Christ and DNA molecule activity make such a process impossible. If he had the facilities, God could have transplanted a rib. Today God could create a human being by cloning as Dr. Hall did in a Petri dish at George Washington University in 1993. That very process was done by Wilmut in Scotland with mitosis cloning, as we explained elsewhere. But for God to make a woman out of a rib then was preposterous, not credible.

Item: In the story of Noah's Flood (Genesis 7 and 8), "the water covered all the high mountains under the whole heaven, standing twenty-two feet and more above the highest peaks" (7:19-20). In 8:1b,4,10,13, "He sent a wind to blow across the waters, and the floods began to disappear....150 days after it began, the boat came to rest upon the mountains of Ararat....Seven days later Noah released the dove again, and this time, towards evening, the bird returned to him with an olive leaf in her beak....Twenty-nine days after that, Noah opened the door to look, and the water was gone."

A thinking person acquainted with reality does not need any convincing that this story is a complete myth. To the ultra-conservative, we present some calculations. If the flood were as described, in order to cover

Mount Aconcagua in South America, the water in Newton, Kansas, would be more than four miles deep. We have several problems with that as nature created by God. For millions of years our rains have come from the ocean as evaporated moisture becomes super-saturated and is released as rain. Such rain has never covered all the level fields, let alone the mountains. Another problem is the evaporation rate. To evaporate with a little wind turned loose by God, a four-mile depth of water would take at least several years, if ever, to disappear instead of less than one year by God in the Noah story.

God in the Noah story has another problem. In the case of the dove bringing in an olive leaf, this fantasy will not hold water. After several months of four-miles-deep water pressure, all living trees would have been choked to death 10 times over. In fact, God says in 7:21a,22: "And all living things upon the earth perished....everything that breathed and lived upon dry land." It never occurred to God that in order for the dove to bring an olive leaf, God would have to send Noah out to plant an olive tree and then wait for that tree to grow a leaf.

We make here a statement that will be repeated often. In the case of the myths and fantasy events of the Bible, we humans are merely, and deservedly, acting out the God-spirit that the God-DNA molecule infused into our soul over a period of three million years. After all this time, we must accept our responsibility to make that God-spirit within us produce some results. We can no longer expect a fantasy God to help us—such an expectation is not credible.

To the ultra-Fundamentalist, we could give a scientific review of many Bible events—the extermination of Sodom and Gomorrah, the parting of the Red Sea, the serpent and the staff, the river of water changed to river of blood, the plagues in Egypt, two fish and five loaves, or walking on water—to prove the fantasy of worshiping a God and Christ sitting on the throne in heaven on the firmament that does not exist and never has existed. Such a God concept would also affect the other two monotheistic religions, Judaism and Islam, who also claim the God of Abraham. None are credible.

The final and clinching reason that the God of Abraham never existed is his demise over the last 3000 years. For more than 3000 years, he has not turned water into wine. Either he perceptually never existed, or he walked off the stage. In either case, he has ceased to function as credible.

However the concept of the God of first cause and the concept of the God-spirit of goodness that lives in our soul are very much alive and active today in the form of the DNA molecule and its gene and the Jesus-spirit in our soul. Jesus is not a metaphor in science today. Credibility is the deciding factor in the existence of a physical Christ and in the genetic evolution of the human spirit.

SCHWEITZER—
LIFE IS TO SERVE

The one person who shot into orbit my concept of *numen summum bonum* (NSB, or spirit of supreme goodness) was a fellow physician, Albert Schweitzer, of the Lamborene, Gabon, hospital in West Africa. In December 1963, as a doctor of medicine and surgery and a board member of the General Conference Mennonite Foreign Mission Board, I offered to make a world tour at my own expense to evaluate all the hospitals in foreign countries that the Conference operated. I was also to visit foreign medical schools that we supported. Visiting these institutions took me to Champa, Jagdeeshpur, Ludhiana and Velore in India, to Hualien in Taiwan, to Kimpesse and Kinchasa in West Africa, and to universities at Kampala in Uganda and at Nairobi in Kenya, both in East Africa. On my way from Paris to Kinchasa, I chose to stop on the way at Lamborene, Gabon, to absorb a bit of the spirit of the world-venerated Nobel laureate, Dr. Albert Schweitzer. The three-day visit with Dr. Schweitzer and his hospital confirmed my belief that there is more to life than what we read in the Bible. Dr. Schweitzer taught me that life is the fulfillment of love and the spirit of supreme goodness.

In response to my letter asking for my visit, Dr. Schweitzer wrote me to get off the airport bus at the bridge. Under the bridge would be two lepers in a boat with a note on paper for identification. The bridge scenario proved superfluous. When I stepped into a DC-7 in Paris, only one other white person was boarding. I asked this vivacious, blue-eyed blonde teenage girl if I could be her seatmate on that all-night flight to Libreville in Gabon. As we conversed in German, to my total surprise she told me she was the granddaughter of Dr. Albert Schweitzer and was spending Christmas with her grandfather.

When we arrived in a boat hollowed out from a 30-foot-long tree trunk, I was completely ignored. But after hugs and kisses for the granddaughter by

Dr. Schmidt (right) with Dr. Albert Schweitzer
at his Lambarene hospital in West Africa
in December 1963.

the doctor and his staff, Dr. Schweitzer escorted me to his office, a shack on stilts. Here he grabbed one of several kerosene lanterns hanging from the ceiling and showed me to the room where I spent two nights.

In the large staff dining room he still played the old piano for the table grace. At mealtime he asked me to sit across the table so that he could look at me while we visited. While I ate meat and potatoes, he took a pocketknife out of his righthand pants pocket and dried fruit out of the lefthand pocket and had snippets of fruit for his meal. He wanted to let me know he had quit eating the flesh of his ancestors.

The real Schweitzer was not a traditional missionary doctor. He was a practitioner of the lifestyle of the historical human Jesus. He had no need for worshiping the deism of an incarnated metaphor of the Holy Spirit detailed in the Bible. In his writing of religion he does not mention God in heaven, nor heaven, nor the resurrected Christ, nor born-in-sin, nor Satan, nor hell, nor the apocalypse in Revelation in the New Testament. In 1906 he wrote a thesis on *Quest for the Historical Jesus*. The title of the thesis for his doctorate in 1913 was *The Psychiatric Study of Jesus*. When he applied to be recognized by the Paris Mission Board as a missionary, he had to promise not to do any preaching because of his lack of theological orthodoxy. He worked without pay from the mission board, earning his way through lectures and organ concerts in Europe.

Because of his German (Alsatian) background, beginning in 1917 he had spent some years as a French prisoner of war during World War I. Later on he spent many years serving people in Africa. Like Mahatma Ghandi he read the Sermon on the Mount (Matthew 5-7 in the New Testament) for its beautiful illustrations of the spirit of life. The incomprehensibles related in this book are what Dr. Schweitzer called the mysteries of life and of God.

From the three-day consultation and from the writings he gave me, I will give a few of his religious concepts. Schweitzer said that *all life is one. Science reveals the common ancestry of plants, animals and humans*. He indicated that God-Christ, the first cause of all creation, initiated a system of life. *This system of the evolution of life is a mystery* (in science it is an incomprehensible). Schweitzer said that *creation is evolution*. In modern science that evolutionary creation process comes in three phases: inorganic, organic, and culture (detailed elsewhere).

He also said that *life is a mystery*. We follow Dr. Schweitzer with the incomprehensibles (mystery) of the gene that creates a soul able to host the *numen summum bonum*. The mystery refers to an unknown God who empowers creationary evolution but is incarnated in our Bible as a real physical God. Since we humans are half animal, that animation of the spirit is still necessary because our animal genes are not yet adequately controlled by the genes of the pysche to accept a spirit guide that does not have a handle on it.

Schweitzer said that his *life philosophy is a search for truth, and this search can be taken only in spiritual freedom and devotion to reason.* The inference here is that the dogma of literal interpretation of the Bible is out. He chooses not to be hampered in his search for truth by the metaphors incarnated in the Bible as God, Christ, hell, heaven and apocalypse.

Dr. Schweitzer said to me that *reason and emotion must be reconciled to each other.* In this writing I show that such reconciliation calls for concessions on the part of science and Christianity. He said that *in equating the spirits of the Bible, of the Koran, of Zoroaster, of Buddha, of Confucius, of Hinduism and Taoism, feeling is always paramount. In all of them, emotions hold their ground against reason.*

He asked *why we need to be condemned to live in the dualism of emotional and rational truths.* Schweitzer said that *reason must discover the true and profound nature of the good, the only truth capable of satisfying man's spirit and love.* The Bible corroborates the truth of this and of his belief in the life-spirit of love.

This Nobel Peace Prize winner said that *every human being who has the courage to allow his mind to probe deeply into the nature of truth will discover in himself the idea of that love, which is supreme knowledge that will direct his way through life.* Science tells us how the gene has infused that loving behavior in our animal bodies.

Finally, Dr. Schweitzer told me that *the purpose of life is to serve and to show compassion. It is only then that we become human beings.*

With humility and with all respect to him, I ask his spirit to allow us, in this writing, to continue this concept of his that the culture evolution of spirit enhancement is continuing in the form of behavior control by the genetic process.

We review briefly the creation of a God in various religions as incarnated metaphors of the spirit that has resided in the soul of every human being on earth for more than a million years.

CHANGE—SCIENCE CHANGES CONCEPTS OF GOD

The development of humans took place in less than 5000 years according to narratives in the Old and New Testaments of the Bible. Scientific findings say that the organic creation process started four billion years ago. Obviously since the ratio of difference is as one to one million, one of these two concepts is false.

How important is the veracity of either of these two time estimates of creation variables? For fundamentalist Christians, scientific facts do not matter to their belief. The average Western churchgoer attends a worship service every Sunday for a sermon, some singing and prayer, and that settles everything. To the scientist who is a realist, the veracity of the creation variable presented here needs to be fixed.

Another variable that needs changing is the concept of who God is. In general over the centuries, the connotations of God have been the Creator of everything, the Almighty to be feared, the Giver of all good things and the One who responds actively when we pray to him for help. God is respected as the One who needs to be worshiped.

The first 17 books of the Bible present the God of the second millennium B.C. as the creator of everything *ex nihilo* (out of nothing) according to a teleological mode of cosmology. He was also depicted as a God of anger and vengeance and as a cruel exterminator of people who were enemies of his chosen people. The Old-Testament-God myth was modeled after the cruel-god myths of Babylon, Mesopotamia, Greece (Zeus) and Egypt.

In accounts of the first millennium B.C., the Old Testament presents a much more benign God. Also, the creation story changed. In Proverbs 8, "Miss" Wisdom (the legendary wisdom of King Solomon personified) says she worked side by side with God in ages past before the earth was formed.

This statement negates the earlier delineation of God. Also, the prophets tried to change other Old-Testament-God behaviors. Their only solution to changing this God was a messiah who would change everything.

At the beginning of the first century A.D., Jesus started what is now Christianity. For 2000 years we have been praying to God and to Christ to help us with our problems. During the last 100 years we have come to the end of the road with unsolved problems everywhere. Overpopulation has brought pollution, killings and starvation to the planet. Sex addiction has caused overpopulation, rape, abortions and murders. Our extravagant lifestyle pollutes our beautiful planet into a cesspool.

Joseph Smith (1805-44) of near Palmyra, New York, noticed the "deterioration" of Christ's sainthood and therefore in 1830 founded Latter-day Saints with the publication of its first pamphlet. It has been said that the sainthood of Christ had deteriorated so much that Smith had to seek a more true sainthood in the souls of himself and his followers for an effective religion that would elevate the quality of life on this planet. Although he came to such conclusions, he had no knowledge of how God, as the first cause of the gene of the culture creation process, created that sainthood in every human being. We can now have scientific documentation proving the existence of that process.

I can assume that the power of Fundamentalism assassinated Joseph Smith at the age of 39 in a manner similar to the crucifixion of Jesus 2000 years ago by people who worshiped the God of the Old Testament—in both cases, to stop a movement. Brigham Young, the succeeding Mormon prophet, chose—in fear—to hide in the mountains of Utah to survive Christian persecution 150 years ago.

That is history, and the salient point is that today the Mormons are showing us how to reorient the concept of who God is and who we are, to create heaven on earth now if we choose to do so. Joseph Smith taught that human sainthood cannot be achieved through praying by demeaning oneself to a deteriorating concept of Christ on a throne above the firmament but is attained by meditation: thought and planning with the sainthood in one's soul. The result of Mormon teaching is that statistically the Mormons have created a life behavior that seems far better than any previous cosmology has taught. Mormons have fewer murders, and they have near perfection in social service.

Although we have prayed to God and to Christ to help us solve our problems, not once has either come down from heaven to give us some help. Where are Christ and God sitting on the throne? Do they have any power on their own? Our prayers to them out there somewhere have brought us to a dead end. Very competent writers, philosophers and theologians are sure that God and Christ are on the way out. This is not so!

God and Christ are well and working, but we have to change our concept of where to find them. They are active in the souls of all human beings.

Since the God-Jesus spirit lives in our souls only, we have to direct our prayers into our soul. We must find the God-spirit in our soul. The responsibility is all ours. Our prayers directed to a God on a throne in heaven on the firmament will fail because a God in heaven on the firmament does not exist. This concept of God never did exist except in the imagination of the ancient prophets. We must find the Jesus-spirit in our soul through meditation. Jesus showed us how to do so. Jesus was human and real; Christ-God is a metaphor of the Jesus spirit.

In the culture phase of the creation process, the God-Christ-DNA molecule created in us the psyche containing the soul, mind and intelligence. A scientific interpretation is that God-Christ as first cause of the creation process genetically infused soul-forming genes into the mammals of the then-existing animal kingdom about three million years ago. Today genes can be infused into the drosophila (fruit fly) through genetic engineering, and geneticists have actually created human beings through cloning.

To change our mindset, we need to understand how the Old-Testament-God concept was created by us humans, and we must match the theologian with the scientist—a match that Aristotle tried to bring about before 300 B.C. Today we have enough specificity in the field of genetics so that we can identify the God of first cause and the God-spirit of goodness and delete the ancient God of Abraham. For the geneticist, that change is evident. For the ultra-Fundamentalist, the change will take some doing.

The change is not a matter of elimination of God or Christ. The God-Christ concept has been and will be with us forever because the DNA molecule of God-Christ, the first cause of all creation, put it there during the last million years. The change is a matter of reorientation.

The Bible narrative presents us with many "in his image" metaphors of who God is, as we have related. One such metaphor is Moses' God, who created everything on the basis of incarnation, teleology and *ex nihi-lo*. Another is the Old-Testament God who spends most of his time and energy killing and exterminating all of the human beings he created whom he calls his enemies—and his enemies include nearly all humans except the offspring of Abraham.

Another God image is found in Proverbs 8, in which "Miss" Wisdom works side by side with God to draw a "blueprint" (*The Living Bible*) to create the universe long before the earth was formed. Still another metaphor comes from John and Paul, who wrote that Christ and God were the same being. He was the resurrected Jesus in heaven, who said he was the only way to heaven; no one could be "saved" except through him.

In addition, there is the God of Jesus, who preached "Love your enemies." Then follows the God of apocalypse, called Christ the Resurrected One. The writer of the book of Revelation said Christ will come down from heaven, declare the end of the world and order the resurrection of all the dead from their graves to be judged to heaven or hell. All these God-concepts were metaphors that science changed to the incomprehensible God of the first cause and all other creation incomprehensibles, and left Jesus to us.

While the Old Testament of the Bible was being written, the Greek Academy of Plato taught another concept, that God is in the soul. The Academy of Athens survived nearly 1000 years until Emperor Justinian realized its Greek theology threatened the God of Christianity. In the sixth century A.D. he forced the Academy out of existence. In spite of that act the Academy of Plato was the introduction of all our universities and institutions of higher learning.

Among all these metaphors are ideas of God that science can accept as true and real. To the God-Christolgy connotations of immortality, omnipotence and omniscience, science will relegate the incomprehensibles in nature including all first causes of creation that science will never completely comprehend. The formula that completely delineates the first cause of creation scientifically in three phases (inorganic, organic, culture) has to rest as the secret that only God carries within himself as the incomprehensible mystery of science and God.

The Bible concept of God's divinity is a metaphor for the DNA gene's insertion of the psyche—soul, mind, intelligence—into our ancestors to make us humans. The influence of this gene is a fact scientifically verifiable with knowledge we possess today. The Bible presents this indwelling spirit as Jesus; this spirit is real and not a metaphor. In reorienting the concept of God and Jesus, we are not losing any of the Bible metaphors of the NSB (*numen summum bonum*, or spirit of supreme goodness), and we make it possible for science and the Bible to talk to each other.

Finally, if a culture of the NSB is to survive and save us from extinction we need to change our concept and have a reorientation of God and Jesus in our Christian institutions, seminaries and churches. We have no other mechanism that can implement such reorientation. (I have written more about that elsewhere.)

The conclusion is simple:

1. God possesses the incomprehensibles in nature, including the DNA culture creation process of the psyche.

2. Jesus is the human-born "deity-spirit" of love, mercy, humility, forgiveness and a simple lifestyle. If we live in that spirit, it will "save" us and our beautiful planet and serve us with heaven on earth.

Jesus is real and true. God and Christ are metaphors of the Jesus soul as it operates in human affairs. The Mormons (and Unitarians) started a change, and we can do no less. Science forces traditional concepts of heaven-Gods to make bigger changes more definite.

EPILOGUE

To repeat the preface, this book is not well written because I am not a writer, This book does not attempt to inform anybody of any details in science or religion. They are not important to this dissertation. This book is entirely consumed by the process of reasoning as to who we are and who God is.

The reasoning process presents many parameters in the field of religion and in the field of science. The parameters are constants whose values determine the operation or characteristics of a system.

The validity of my religious parameters are based mostly on quotes from the Bibie, Koran and many theologians.

The validity of my scientific parameters are the result of my lifelong exposure to mathematics, chemistry, organic chemistry, biochemistry, physics, biology, comparative anatomy, human anatomy, human cell (microscopic) anatomy, bacteriology and physiology. Since Crick and Watson's discovery of DNA in 1953, I have studied genetics and recently have read many textbooks that teach how human genetic engineering can direct and control our behavior and beliefs today. The gene against crime is coming.

The many parameters in religion and science are matched against each other for a diagnosis of who we are and who God is.

My courage to write this is a result of the history of 20,000 years of the belief in the divinity or the soul by our ancestors (at Avignon), a belief reported in the sixth century B.C. by Zoroaster, about 400 B.C. by Socrates, and then by the historical Jesus, Mohammed, Thomas Aquinas, Joseph Smith, Ghandi, Schweitzer, and now Dr. Gordon Kaufman of Harvard University and Dr. Daryl Schmidt of Texas Christian University.

The diagnosis has God-Christ as creator of all incomprehensibles in

Nature. Jesus is the embodiment of the God-spirit in our souls. We are the progeny of all animal evil genes in our soul.

Now our daily meditation has to determine how much of our evil animal desires we will act out or how much we will act out the Jesus-spirit that God gave us through evolution to enjoy in our brief lifetime and pass on to our offspring forever. The Jesus-spirit is love, mercy, humility, forgiveness and a simple lifestyle.

The windup of 1997 presents a few items relevant to the context of my book.

The final bulletin of this year's Kansas University School of Medicine relates the circumstances of the professor of pediatrics who is also the staff ethicist, who has been diagnosed with terminal cancer. He reaffirmed that his mortality be the "light of death" in order to increase the value of his life with more love and compassion for the moments left to him. He will not let the search for the afterlife of the present culture cheat him out of these last moments of divinity.

The *New York Times* December 6, 1997 magazine presents a God decentralized. If the *Times* had consulted scientific knowledge it would read "the heaven God is out."

Time magazine of the week of December 22, 1997 relates the resurrection of the spirit of Numen Summun Bonum in the soul of Princess Diana, worldwide in all human souls. Here also is itemized the cloning of "Dolly" (a human equivalent) and writes a new chapter about the knowledge of the gene.